ANNOTATED TEACHER'S

SADLIER

Vocabulary Workshop®

TOOLS FOR COMPREHENSION

Level Blue

Jerome Shostak

Consultants

Joseph Czarnecki, Ph.D.
Former Faculty Associate,
School of Education
Johns Hopkins University
Baltimore, MD

Christine Gialamas
Reading Specialist
Chicago Public Schools
Chicago, IL

Cover Series Design: Silver Linings Studios; **Cover pencil:** Shutterstock.com/VikaSuh.
Photo Credits: Alamy Stock Photo/Big Cheese Photo LLC: T47. Getty Images/Fat Camera: T7; Westend61: T16.
Shutterstock.com/Plan-B: *sunburst*; Theus: *sky and clouds background*; VikaSuh: T1.

Lexile Trademark and Copyright Statement: METAMETRICS®, the METAMETRICS® logo and tagline, LEXILE®, LEXILE®
FRAMEWORK, LEXILE ANALYZER®, LEXILE ANALYZER® EDITOR ASSISTANT™, LEXILE TITLES DATABASE™, LEXILE CAREER
DATABASE™, LEXILE GROWTH PLANNER™, the LEXILE® logo, POWERV™, QUANTILE®, QUANTILE® FRAMEWORK, QUANTILE
GROWTH PLANNER™, MATH@HOME® and the QUANTILE® logo are trademarks of MetaMetrics, Inc., and are registered in the
United States and abroad. The trademarks and names of other companies and products mentioned herein are the property of
their respective owners. Copyright © 2017 MetaMetrics, Inc. All rights reserved.

For digital resources, go to SadlierConnect.com and enter the Teacher Access Code: VWS214BD5E.

CONTENTS

Vocabulary Workshop

TOOLS FOR COMPREHENSION

In Level Blue of **Vocabulary Workshop, Tools for Comprehension** students are introduced to 216 carefully selected, high-utility words, many of which are drawn from academic vocabulary word lists relevant to students' reading. Mastery of these words promotes word consciousness and, together with practice in vocabulary strategies, leads to improved reading and writing skills and improved performance on standardized tests.

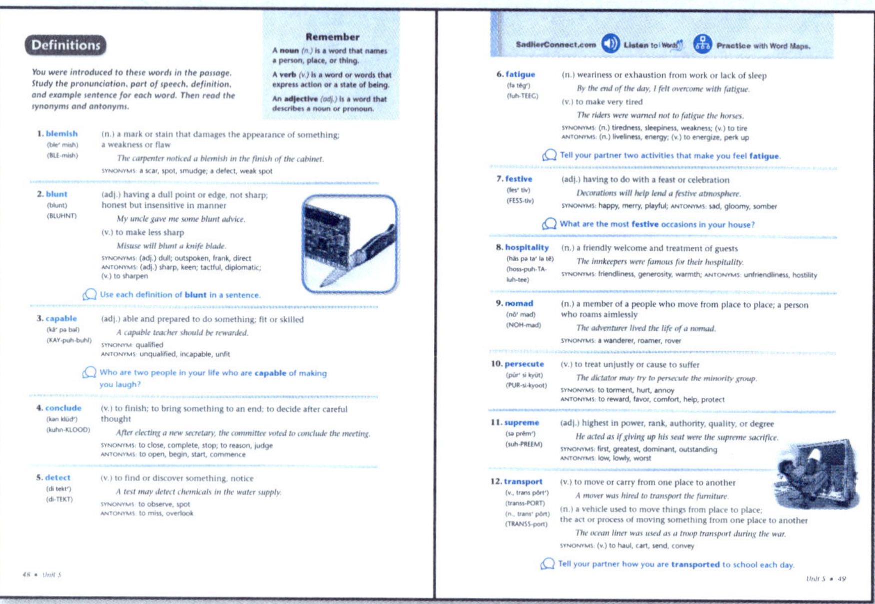

Level Blue presents 216 vocabulary words organized into eighteen Units. Each Unit provides both contextual learning and direct instruction on twelve vocabulary words. Suggested activities are included to promote collaboration and deeper understanding.

Introducing the Words and **Words in Context**—two reading passages related in theme or topic—begin and conclude each Unit. Students are introduced to Unit words in context. Content-rich and engaging texts prompt student interest and provide examples of proper usage. A connection to grade-level grammar instruction is embedded in the Words in Context passage.

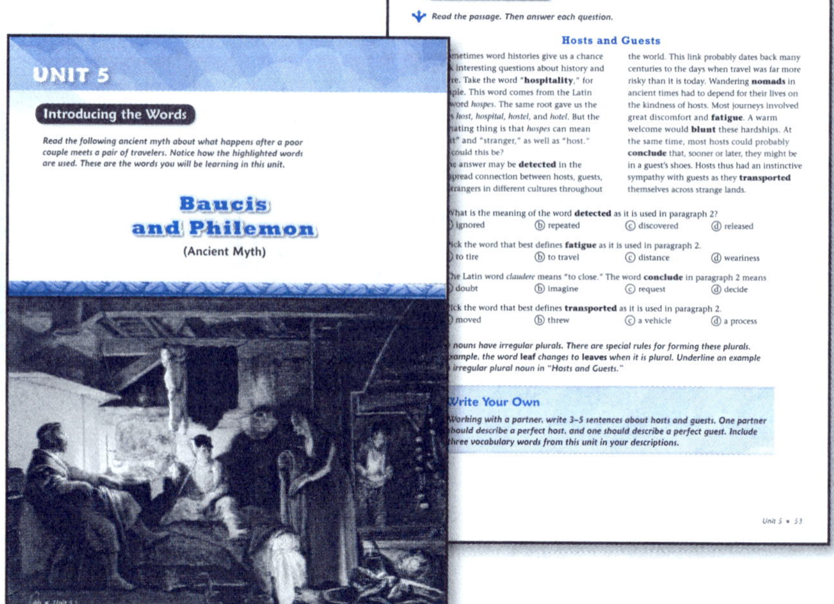

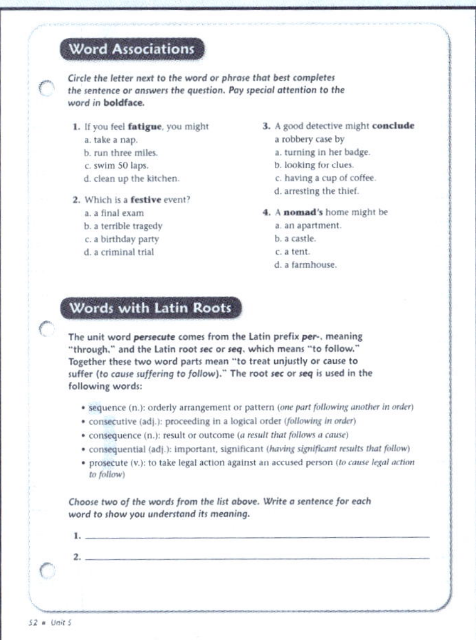

Instruction in classical roots will help students unlock the meanings of English words derived from Latin and Greek roots. Each Unit presents a **Words with Latin/ Greek Roots** activity for instruction and application.

Practice in standardized-test formats helps students prepare for state exams. Modeled on the reading sections of these tests, **Vocabulary for Comprehension** has students read a passage and answer questions associated with the passage, including questions that ask students to support answers with details from the text. A writing prompt is also included for students to demonstrate understanding and proper usage of Unit words.

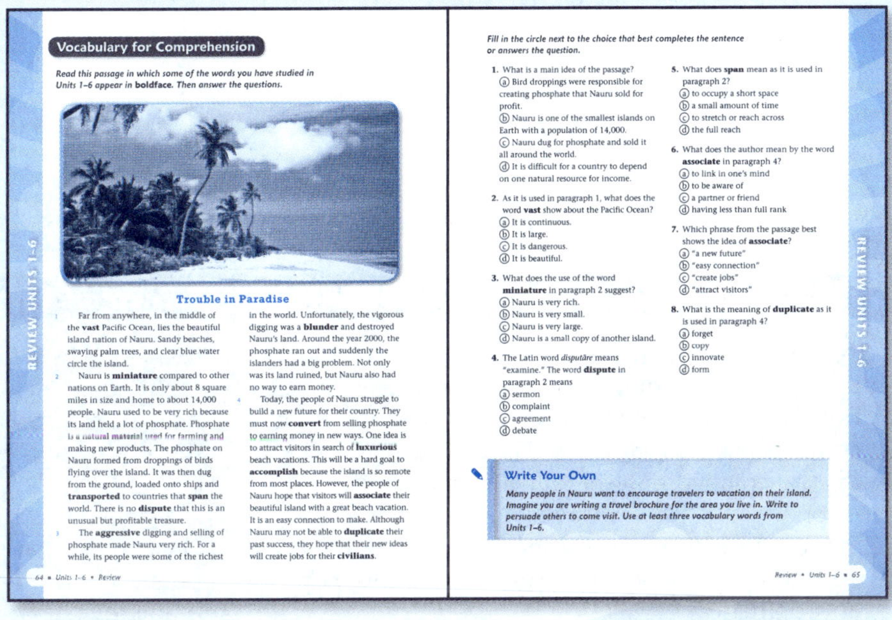

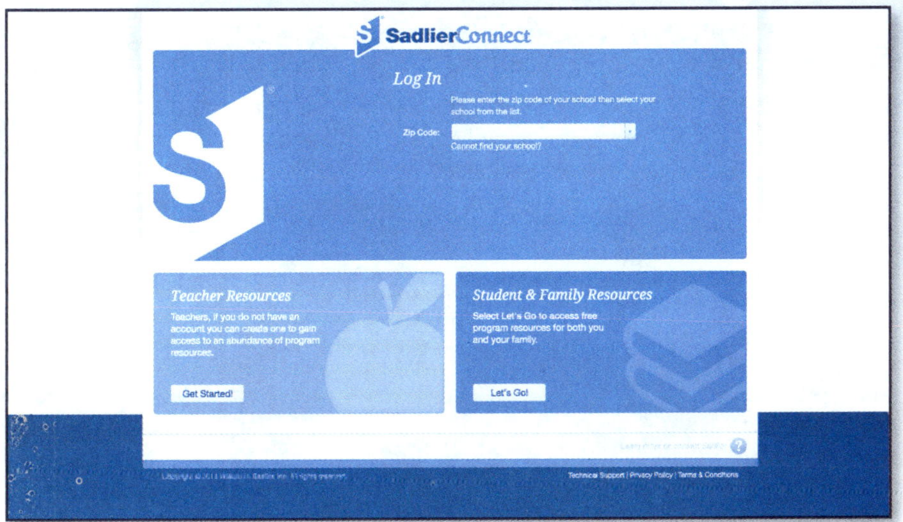

A variety of digital resources and enrichment activities, including **iWords** audio program, are available to students and teachers at **SadlierConnect.com**. Digital resources include differentiated reading passages, interactive activities, quizzes, and audio for taught words and reading passages—ideal support for English language learners and striving readers.

A RESEARCH-BASED PROGRAM

Vocabulary Workshop is designed to promote language acquisition with an instructional approach that is supported by research and best practices as prescribed by vocabulary scholars. Research shows that vocabulary plays a critical role in learning to read and comprehend text (Biemiller, 2003; Stahl & Stahl, 2004). It also shows that a student's vocabulary is one of the best predictors in how well that student will understand text and be able to communicate in writing (Stahl & Nagy, 2006).

Research Shows: | Vocabulary Workshop

The Value of Direct Instruction

Researchers agree that although extensive reading is important to vocabulary growth, direct instruction is more effective and more efficient than incidental learning in achieving deeper, richer levels of lasting vocabulary understanding (McKeown & Beck, 1988). Stahl and Fairbanks (1986) recommend using a definitional and contextual approach to direct instruction, and Nagy (1988) recommends including integration, repetition, and meaningful use. Beck and McKeown (2004) suggest that for direct instruction to be most effective, it should focus on useful words that students are most likely to encounter.

Level Blue provides direct instruction for 216 carefully selected words. These words are introduced in Units that give concise definitions and examples of usage and then provide exercise sets in which students see and use the words in a variety of contexts. To promote retention, students must interact with each word five times over the course of a Unit.

The Value of Contextual Learning of Vocabulary

Research has shown that for vocabulary instruction to be effective, it must not only provide definitions, but also demonstrate how words are used in natural contexts (Nagy, 1988). Many researchers also agree that much of vocabulary growth occurs indirectly through language exposure (Cunningham & Stanovich, 1998). Vocabulary development is enhanced when students are exposed to print-rich environments.

Level Blue introduces the twelve taught words of each Unit in the natural context of a reading passage before students learn the dictionary meanings of the words. All Units conclude with Words in Context, a second reading passage that provides further examples of selected Unit words in context. In the Reviews, students read additional passages with taught words in context, focusing on words with multiple meanings. Here, the words are from the previous Units. Students answer questions that assess word meaning and general comprehension.

The Value of Providing Multiple Exposures to Words

If students are truly to gain ownership of new words, vocabulary instruction must provide multiple and varied encounters with those words (Daniels, 1996; Leung, 1992; Senechal, 1997; Stahl & Fairbanks, 1986). Research (National Reading Panel, 2000) also suggests other practices that should inform the way vocabulary is taught in the classroom; these include using multiple methods of instruction and actively engaging students in word learning. Any word that is introduced should continue to be provided in a variety of contexts to reinforce and enrich students' understanding (Beck & McKeown, 2004).

Level Blue presents a variety of contexts that represent as fully as possible each word's semantic range and application. Level Blue also provides activities in which students are active participants. They are encouraged to collaborate with partners about word meanings, share ideas, and engage with words in writing and speaking activities.

According to *Put Reading First* (Armbruster, Lehr, & Osborn, 2001), children need to develop strategies that include using word parts to figure out the meanings of words in text and also using context clues. According to Aranoff (1994), word structure helps to determine the meaning of an unfamiliar word that is derived from the same stem as a familiar word. Many researchers promote teaching strategies that enable students to access the words they will encounter in school texts, including teaching morphemic and contextual cues in tandem (Baumann, Kame'enui, & Ash, 2003).

Level Blue teaches word-learning strategies such as analyzing word parts (affixes and roots) and consulting references. Level Blue also provides instruction on words with Latin or Greek roots, homographs, and multiple-meaning words that can help students to build their vocabularies.

According to Beck, McKeown, and Kucan (2002), instruction that offers rich information about words and their uses enhances students' language comprehension and production. Effective instruction should integrate instructed words with other knowledge, including how words relate to one another and how words relate to real-world and personal experiences (Nagy, 1988).

Level Blue provides students with opportunities to interact with word meanings on a deeper level in Shades of Meaning. Each Shades of Meaning page focuses on a specific strategy, including analyzing idioms, adages, proverbs, and figurative language. Students will explore the nuances between word meanings, enabling them to recognize the importance of word choice.

Vocabulary Workshop implements best practices in the areas of vocabulary development and vocabulary skills. The program provides both contextual learning and direct instruction of specific vocabulary words, and it explicitly teaches vocabulary building strategies. Its blend of print and digital resources helps to enrich and support instruction for all learners. Level Blue is part of a comprehensive elementary-through-high-school series. **Vocabulary Workshop** features:

- **Contextual learning.** Units begin and end with reading passages that represent a variety of genres.

- **Systematic, direct instruction.** Each Unit features direct instruction essential to help students learn words that are not part of students' everyday experiences.

- **Multiple exposures.** Each core word appears at least five times per Unit, so students encounter words repeatedly in different and multiple contexts.

- **Writing exercises.** Activities, such as Write Your Own, ask students to demonstrate their understanding of the words.

- **Vocabulary building strategies.** Units include instruction on words with Latin or Greek roots. Word Study lessons teach students how to implement specific strategies, such as using context clues.

- **Word relationships and meanings.** Shades of Meaning lessons teach students about the nuances of word meanings.

- **Review of words.** Vocabulary for Comprehension, Classifying, and Completing the Idea provide additional opportunities for students to demonstrate understanding of taught words.

WORD LIST

At the heart of **Vocabulary Workshop** Level Blue are the 216 core Unit words. The core Unit words:

- appear in a wide variety of texts, both academic and trade publications.

- appear in written and verbal interactions with mature language users.

- pertain to a broad spectrum of content areas.

- apply to standardized tests.

The list of core Unit words for Level Blue has been developed from many sources, including spelling and vocabulary lists; current content-area textbooks, glossaries, and ancillary materials (especially for general, nontechnical terms); and classic and contemporary fiction and nonfiction. University-level scholars and classroom teachers also played an integral role in generating this list by contributing to and approving the selection of the words.

GRADE-LEVEL PLACEMENT

The chart suggests grade placement for each level of **Vocabulary Workshop**. These placements reflect teacher experience and recommendations but should not be taken too literally. Teachers should determine appropriate placement based on knowledge of their students' abilities, background knowledge, and reading levels. Diagnostic materials, available for each level at **SadlierConnect.com**, can also help in determining appropriate placement.

Grade-Level Placement	
Level	**Grade**
Red	1
Purple	2
Green	3
Orange	4
Blue	5

PROGRAM COMPONENTS

Vocabulary Workshop Level Blue combines print and digital resources and components to motivate students and enrich their vocabularies. This integrated approach delivers multiple exposures to each Unit word in support of vocabulary building. For information about digital components for each level of **Vocabulary Workshop**, see pages T16–T17 for **Interactive Edition** and pages T18–T19 for **Online Assessment**.

Print materials for each level include:

- Student Edition
- Annotated Teacher's Edition
- Unit Test Booklet with Teacher Answer Key (optional purchase)

Student Edition/Annotated Teacher's Edition

Introducing the Words
(Reading Passages)

- Reading passages introduce the twelve Unit words in a variety of genres.

- Audio versions of the Unit reading passages are available at **SadlierConnect.com**.

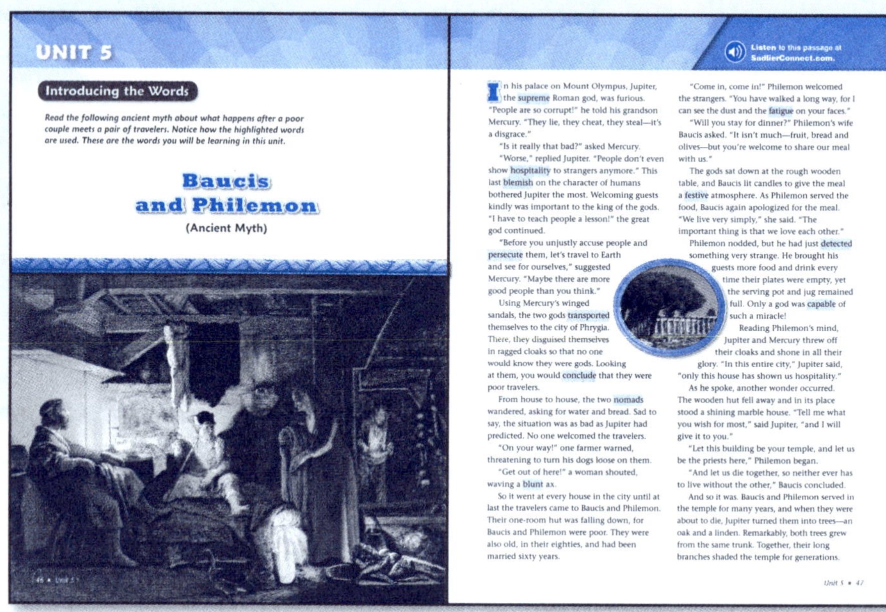

Definitions

- Phonetic pronunciations, word meanings, and example sentences are featured.

- Grade-appropriate synonyms and antonyms expand vocabulary.

- Collaborative activities provide additional opportunities for students to interact with the words and enrich understanding.

- iWords audio program, available at **SadlierConnect.com**, supports all learners.

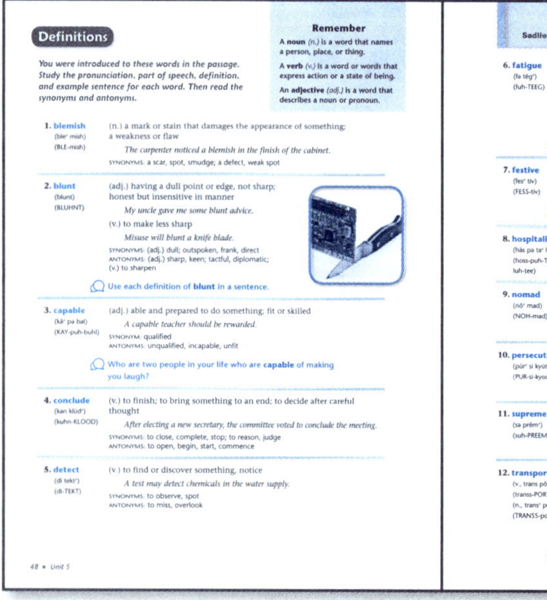

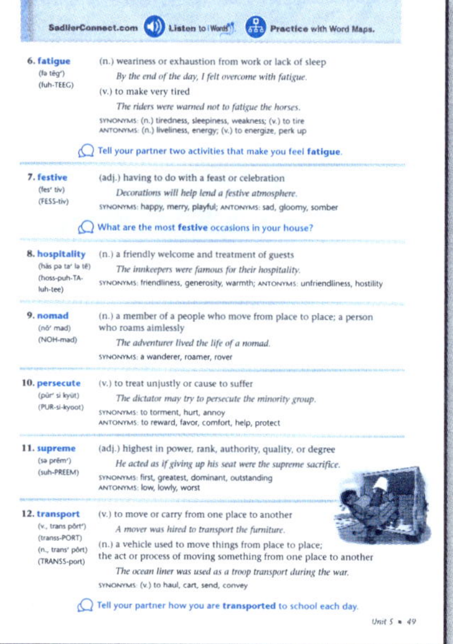

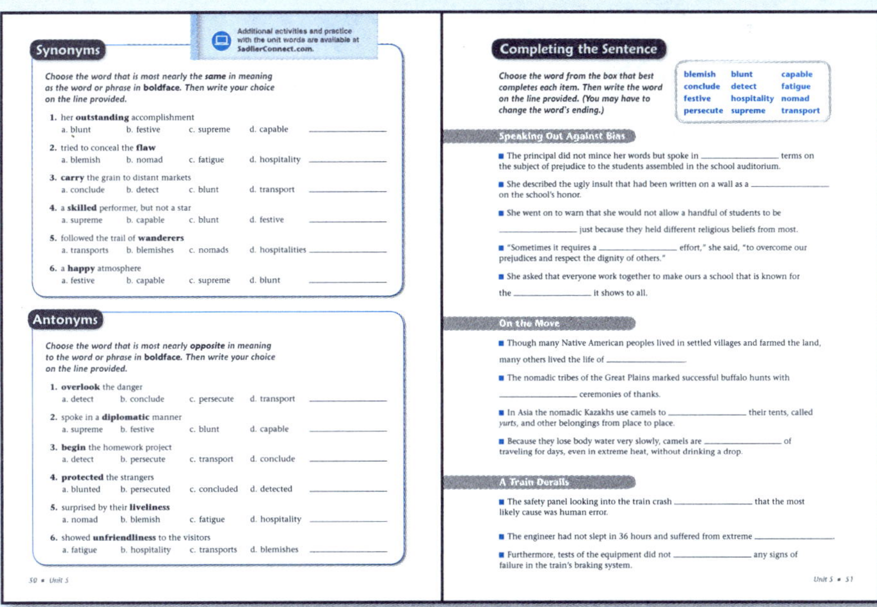

Synonyms/Antonyms

- Promotes analysis of word relationships.

Completing the Sentence

- Uses context clues to determine word meanings.

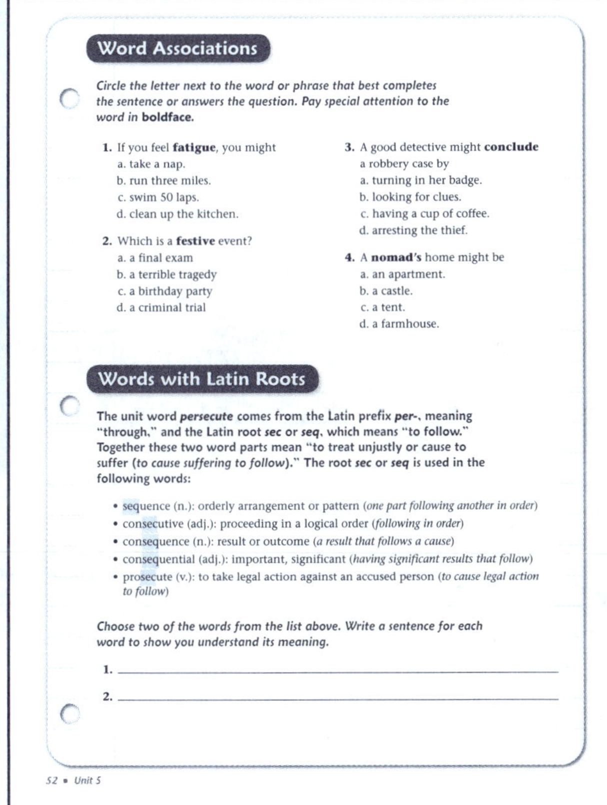

Word Associations

- Promotes interaction with words and word relationships.

Words with Latin/Greek Roots

- Provides instruction and application of a Latin or Greek root.

Words in Context

- A second reading passage, containing selected multiple-meaning words from the Unit, monitors students' ability to use context within a reading passage to determine word meaning. A connection to grade-level grammar instruction is also included in the reading passage.

 Words That Are Often Confused

Words that look similar and have similar pronunciations but that have different meanings often cause confusion. For example, the word *persecute* (page 49) is often confused with the word *prosecute*. Read this sentence: *The king who had* **persecuted** *the peasants was* **prosecuted** *for his crimes.* Here, *persecuted* means "caused to suffer" and *prosecuted* means "to bring legal action against."

Look at the chart to find other examples of words that are often confused.

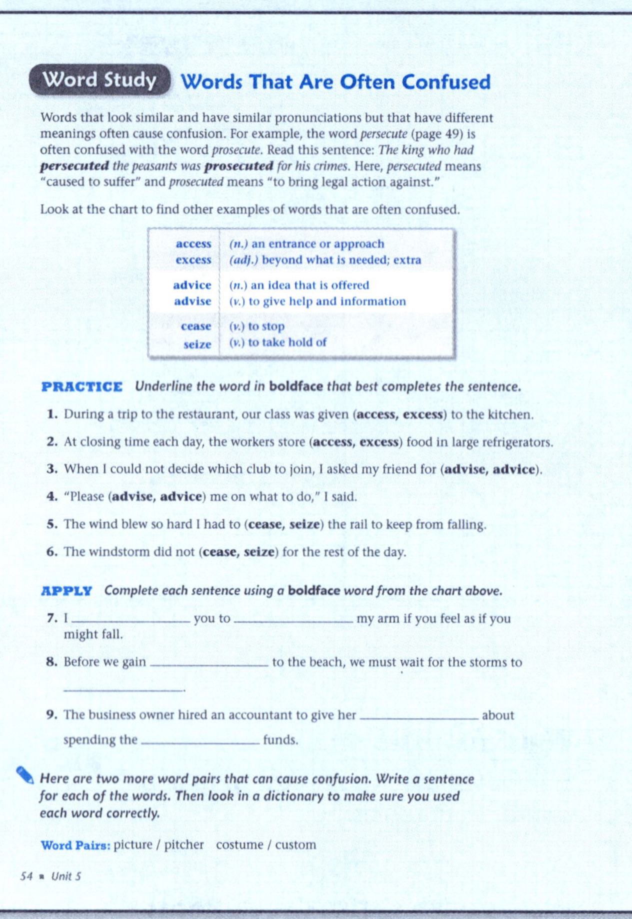

access	(n.) an entrance or approach
excess	(adj.) beyond what is needed; extra
advice	(n.) an idea that is offered
advise	(v.) to give help and information
cease	(v.) to stop
seize	(v.) to take hold of

PRACTICE *Underline the word in* **boldface** *that best completes the sentence.*

1. During a trip to the restaurant, our class was given (**access, excess**) to the kitchen.

2. At closing time each day, the workers store (**access, excess**) food in large refrigerators.

3. When I could not decide which club to join, I asked my friend for (**advise, advice**).

4. "Please (**advise, advice**) me on what to do," I said.

5. The wind blew so hard I had to (**cease, seize**) the rail to keep from falling.

6. The windstorm did not (**cease, seize**) for the rest of the day.

APPLY *Complete each sentence using a* **boldface** *word from the chart above.*

7. I _______________ you to _______________ my arm if you feel as if you might fall.

8. Before we gain _______________ to the beach, we must wait for the storms to

   _______________.

9. The business owner hired an accountant to give her _______________ about

   spending the _______________ funds.

Here are two more word pairs that can cause confusion. Write a sentence for each of the words. Then look in a dictionary to make sure you used each word correctly.

Word Pairs: picture / pitcher   costume / custom

Word Study

- Presents word study topics such as homographs and multiple-meaning words to expand students' vocabularies.

- Provides speaking and writing activities to apply word study skills.

- Additional Word Study topics are available at **SadlierConnect.com**.

Shades of Meaning

- Promotes understanding of literal and nonliteral meanings of words.

- Develops skills in analyzing figurative language, word relationships, and nuances in word meanings.

 Words That Name Travelers

In the passage "Baucis and Philemon" on pages 46–47, you read this sentence: *From house to house, the two* **nomads** *wandered, asking for water and bread.* In the passage, Jupiter and Mercury are the *nomads*. They are travelers wandering the city of Phrygia and looking for someone to show them hospitality.

Here are some other words that name travelers. Notice that one difference among the travelers is their purpose for traveling.

nomad	A **nomad** roams from place to place.
commuter	A **commuter** travels a long distance between home and work.
tourist	A **tourist** travels to visit a place for pleasure.
pilgrim	A **pilgrim** journeys to a sacred place, usually for religious reasons.

PRACTICE *Write the word from the chart that best names the person making each statement.*

1. I traveled a great distance to visit a holy shrine. _______________

2. I take the train to work every day. _______________

3. I never live in one place for a long time. _______________

4. I went to the Grand Canyon to see the sights. _______________

5. Each year, I travel with my family to visit the origins of my religion. _______________

6. The job requires me to be in Boston every month. _______________

APPLY *Answer each question to show the meaning of the word in* **boldface.** *Be sure to use the* **boldfaced** *word in your answer.*

7. Who is a **commuter** you know? Why is that person a commuter?

   ____

8. What might a **tourist** do in your area?

   ____

9. What are some examples of places a **pilgrim** might travel to?

   ____

10. What reasons might a person have for being a **nomad**?

   ____

The Reviews in **Vocabulary Workshop** Level Blue are designed to provide additional exposure to taught words and to allow students to apply and expand their word knowledge. Each sequence of three Units is followed by a Review in the form of Vocabulary for Comprehension pages, which contain words from those three Units. Each sequence of six Units is followed by a Review in the form of Vocabulary for Comprehension, Classifying, and Completing the Idea pages, which contain words from those six Units.

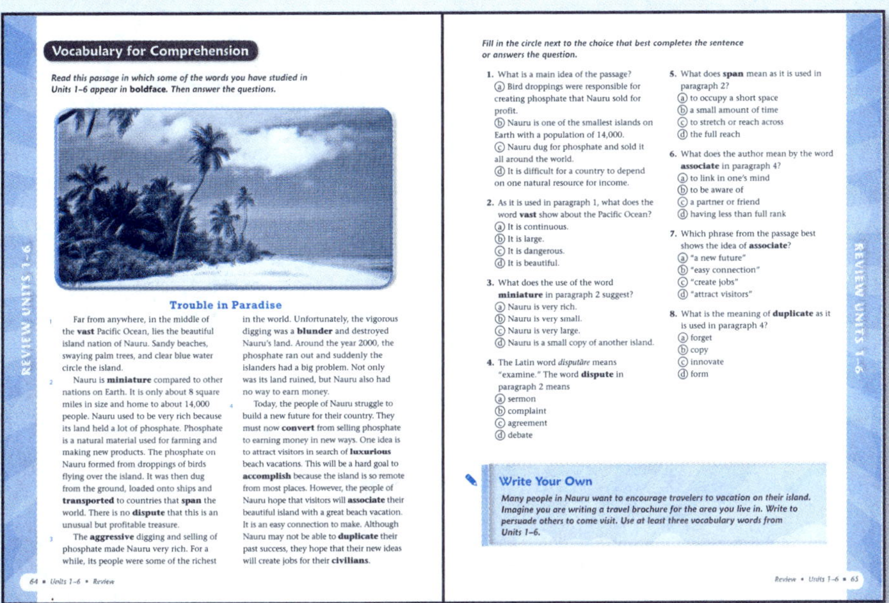

Vocabulary for Comprehension

- Reviews words from previous Units in the context of a reading passage.

- Presents items similar to those on standardized tests in order to assess students' comprehension and understanding of word meaning.

- Includes a writing prompt for students to demonstrate understanding and proper usage of Unit words.

Classifying

- Challenges students to identify a missing word from words that are alike in some way.

- Provides an opportunity for students to explain the relationship among words in a group.

Completing the Idea

- Uses sentence stems that contain the Unit words.

- Provides an opportunity for students to make connections between vocabulary and real-life experiences.

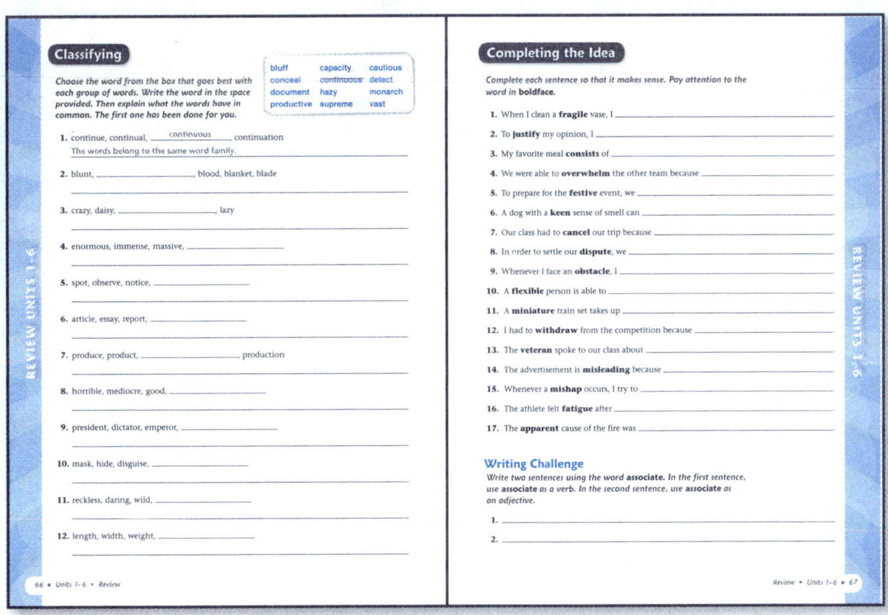

Annotated Teacher's Edition

The Annotated Teacher's Edition contains tools to promote successful vocabulary instruction. Because each Unit has a similar structure, the Teaching Notes on pages T25–T33 can be used for any given Unit. More comprehensive Teaching Notes for Word Study and Shades of Meaning can be found on pages T34–T43.

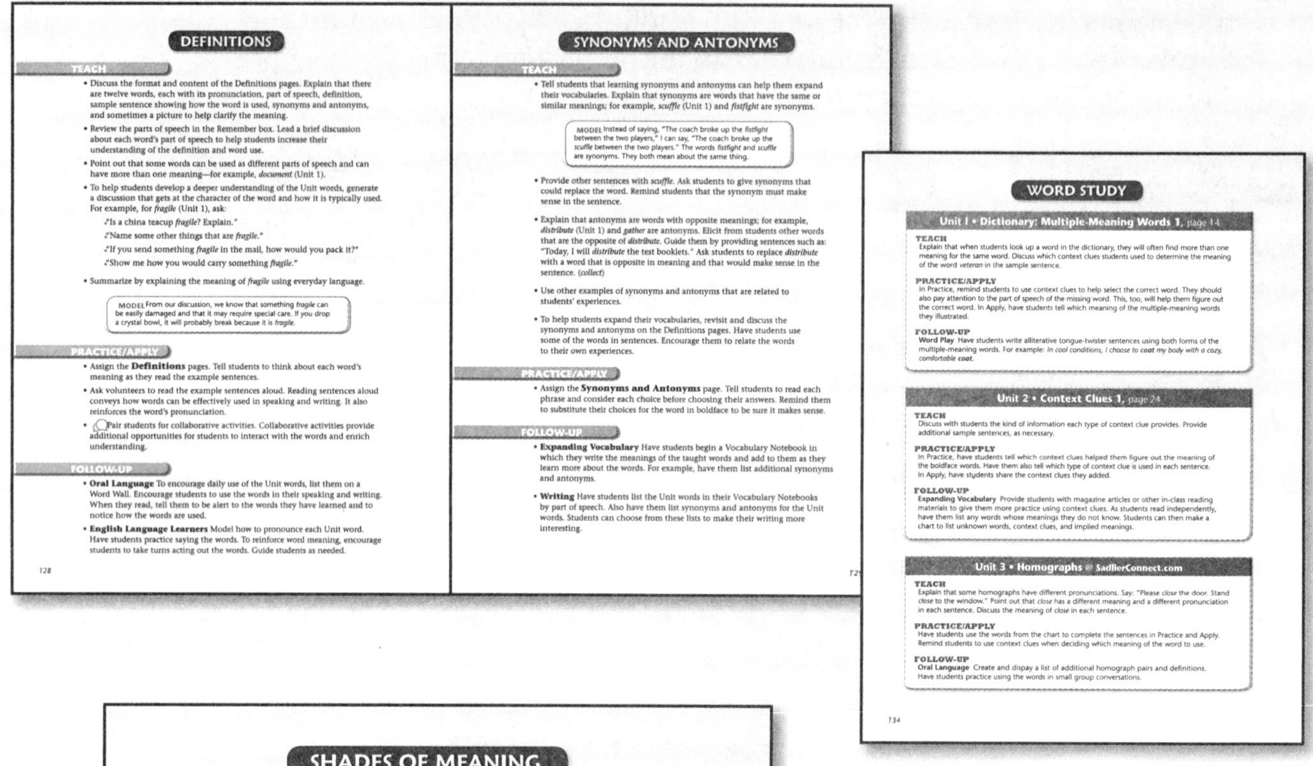

Teaching Notes

- Consistent instructional routines with teacher modeling.
- Follow-up activity choices to support and extend learning.

Unit Test Booklet with Teacher Answer Key (optional purchase)

The Unit Test Booklet contains eighteen Unit tests, to be administered after the completion of a Unit. The Unit tests assess student knowledge of the twelve vocabulary words taught in each Unit. The Unit Test Booklet also contains six cumulative tests. The cumulative tests serve as a continuous assessment of students' retention of previously taught words. Cumulative Test 6, meant to be administered at the completion of the program, is designed to determine the students' degree of mastery in Level Blue's word list.

Unit Test Booklet

- Eighteen Unit tests assess the twelve vocabulary words taught in each Unit.
- Six cumulative tests provide continuous assessment of previously taught words.

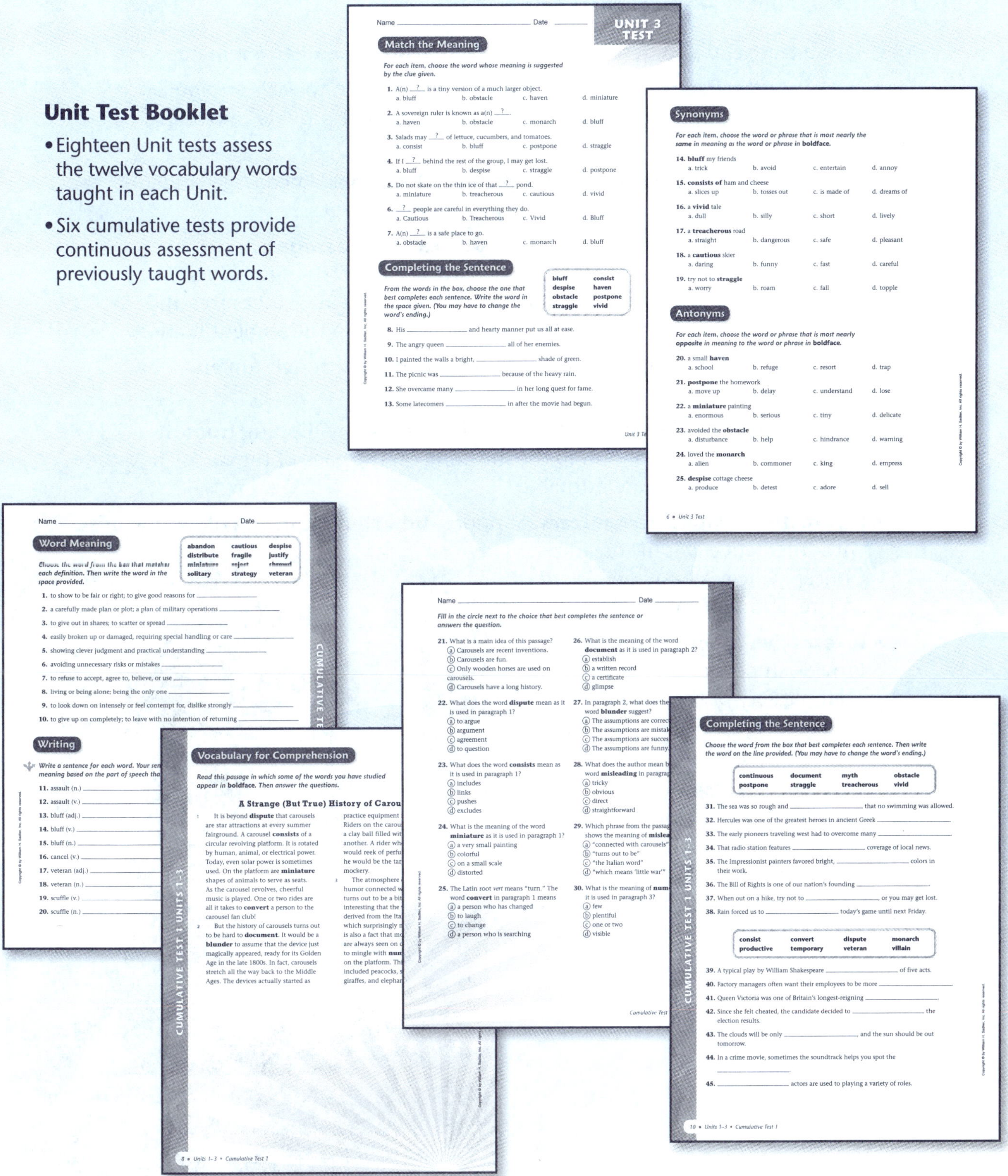

DIGITAL RESOURCES

Digital Resources for **Vocabulary Workshop** Level Blue are available to students and teachers at **SadlierConnect.com**. Students and families may use these digital resources without a username and password. Teachers may access answer keys and additional digital resources by creating an account under Teacher Resources at **SadlierConnect.com**. See the bottom of the copyright page (the back of the title page) in your Annotated Teacher's Edition for an access code needed to register for a teacher account at **SadlierConnect.com**.

Student and teacher digital resources available at **SadlierConnect.com** include:

- **iWords Audio Program.** Encourage students to listen to each vocabulary word, its definition, and an illustrative sentence that provides modeling and context.

- **Audio of Introducing the Words Reading Passages.** Encourage students to track print as they listen to the Unit reading passages.

- **Differentiated Introducing the Words Reading Passages.** Provide support for English language learners and striving readers. The differentiated Unit reading passages have a lower Lexile® measures and are shorter in length than the Unit reading passages in the Student Edition.

- **Interactive Activities.** Review the Unit vocabulary through fun and engagement.

- **Interactive Flash Cards.** Reinforce word meanings by flipping from the word on the front of the card to the meaning on the back of the card. The interactive flash cards are printable.

- **Interactive Graphic Organizers.** Support and extend learning of Unit words with interactive graphic organizers: Concept Circle, Word Map, Word Square, and Word Web.

- **Interactive Practice Quizzes.** Provide students with feedback on their mastery of the Unit words. Interactive practice quizzes are automatically scored.

- **Practice Quiz Worksheets.** Review Unit words in multiple-choice and passage-based, critical reading formats. Worksheets can also be used as reteaching tools for all learners.

iWords Audio Program

The **Vocabulary Workshop** Level Blue iWords Audio Program provides students with pronunciations, definitions, parts of speech, and examples of usage for all taught vocabulary words.

The iWords Audio Program is especially useful for English language learners. Students hear the recommended pronunciation of each Unit word and are given an opportunity to pronounce each Unit word themselves. Pronunciations are followed by parts of speech, brief definitions, and examples of the word used in complete sentences.

Interactive Edition (optional purchase)

Vocabulary Workshop Interactive Edition provides all of the program's print components, including the program's ancillary component (Unit Test Booklet), in a fully interactive online format. **Vocabulary Workshop Interactive Edition** includes exercises that build academic vocabulary knowledge by using contextual and definitional information and ample practice of Unit words in multiple contexts, including responding to text-based questions. Audio versions of differentiated reading passages are also available for children to track print as they listen.

Vocabulary Workshop Interactive Edition also provides personalized student learning by allowing teachers to build custom assessments that meet the varying needs of students. Teachers have the ability to adjust instruction and track student progress based on data reports.

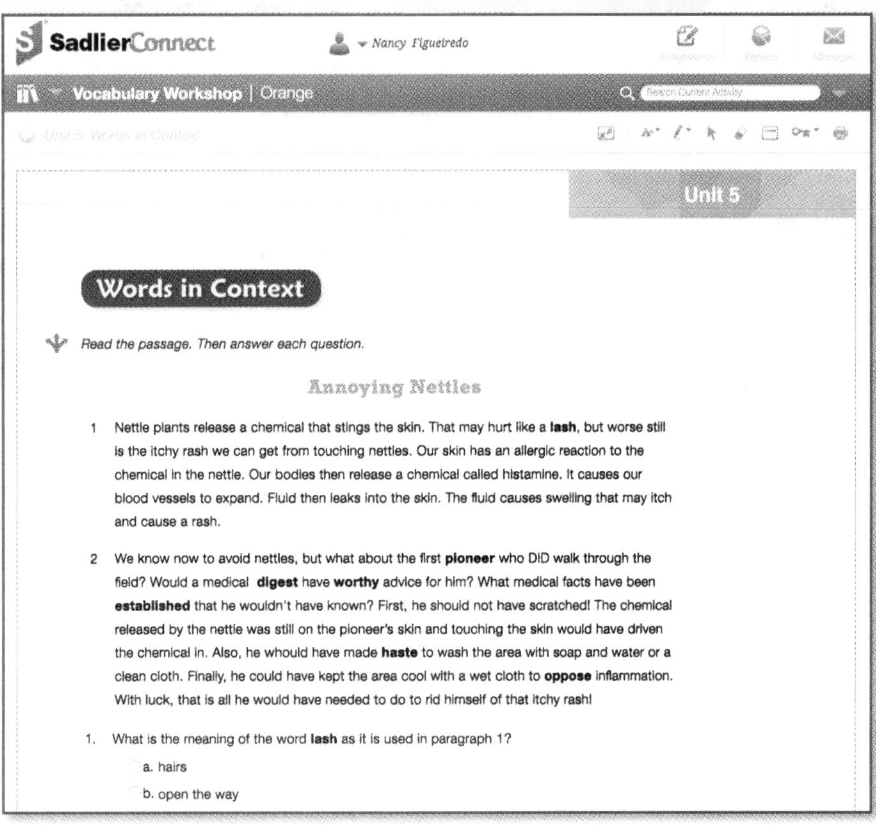

ASSESSMENT OPTIONS

Vocabulary Workshop Level Blue has a comprehensive assessment plan. Diagnostic, formative, and summative assessment options—in print and digital formats—are available to measure students' vocabulary development. Teachers may choose from among these assessments to monitor and track students' vocabulary mastery throughout the school year.

Vocabulary Workshop, Tools for Comprehension Comprehensive Assessment Plan				
Assessment	**Type of Assessment**	**What Is Assessed**	**Where Found**	**When to Administer**
Beginning-of-Year Diagnostic Test	Diagnostic	Sampling of vocabulary words from Level Blue	• Digital Resources	At the start of the school year
Beginning-of-Year Pre-Test	Diagnostic	Sampling of vocabulary words from Level Blue	• Online Assessments	At the start of the school year
Unit Practice Tests	Formative	Unit Vocabulary Words	• Online Assessments	At the end of each Unit
Unit Tests	Summative	Unit Vocabulary Words	• Unit Test Booklet • Online Assessments • Digital Resources	At the end of each Unit
Reviews	Formative	Select words from the review Units	• Online Assessments	After every 3 Units
Cumulative Tests (Units 1–3, 1–6, 1–9, 1–12, 1–15, 1–18)	Summative	Select words from the cumulative Units	• Unit Test Booklet • Online Assessments	After each cumulative grouping of Units
Mid-Year Test	Summative	Select words from Units 1–9	• Online Assessments • Digital Resources	After Unit 9
Final Mastery Test	Summative	Select words from Units 1–18	• Online Assessments	At the completion of the program
Post-Test	Summative	Select words from Level Blue	• Online Assessments	At the completion of the program

Assessments in the Student Edition

Each Student Edition includes six Review sections, one after every three Units. The Reviews reinforce the application of word knowledge of the vocabulary words introduced in the previous Units. Vocabulary for Comprehension, featured in each review, presents questions that assess word meaning and comprehension. These questions are similar in format to those on standardized state exams.

Unit Test Booklet with Teacher Answer Key (optional purchase)

The Unit Test Booklets contain eighteen Unit tests, to be administered after the completion of a Unit. The Unit tests assess student knowledge of the twelve vocabulary words taught in each Unit. Exercises in the Unit tests include: Match the Meaning, Completing the Sentence, Synonyms, and Antonyms. The Unit Test Booklets also contain six cumulative tests, which serve as a continuous assessment of students' retention of previously taught words. Exercises in the cumulative tests include: Word Meaning, Writing, and Vocabulary for Comprehension.

Assessments at SadlierConnect.com

- **Beginning-of-Year Diagnostic Test.** This interactive diagnostic assessment contains a sampling of the level's 216 taught words and is meant to be administered at the start of the school year to assess students' prior knowledge of that grade level's words.

- **Unit Quiz.** The Unit Quiz assesses students' knowledge within a given Unit. These interactive quizzes are administered at the end of each Unit. Teachers can send students to the appropriate follow-up for additional exposure to the Unit words: Practice Worksheets, Interactive Activities, iWords Audio Program, and Interactive Graphic Organizers, all available at **SadlierConnect.com**.

Vocabulary Workshop Online Assessments (optional purchase)

Vocabulary Workshop Level Blue Online Assessment is a secure, web-based assessment program that includes all program assessments in an interactive format, plus Pre- and Post-Tests to measure annual vocabulary acquisition and growth.

Vocabulary Workshop Level Blue Online Assessment features auto-scoring formative and summative assessments in an interactive format. The Build an Assessment feature personalizes student learning with the option of customizing assignments. The program also offers flexible administration of assessments to individual students, small groups, or an entire class, either online or in print for a more traditional test-taking environment. **Vocabulary Workshop** Level Blue Online Assessment is equipped with tools to monitor student progress and to adjust instruction using real-time, standards-based data and a variety of class and student reports to help drive instruction.

- **Beginning-of-Year Pre-Test**
- **Unit Tests**
- **Practice Unit Tests**
- **Cumulative Tests**
- **Final Mastery Test**
- **End-of-Year Post-Test**

ADDRESSING DIFFERENT LEARNERS

Depending on the needs of their students, teachers may differentiate and/or scaffold instruction to accommodate individual or small-group learning differences. Students who are on or above grade level often already have a basic understanding of many of the vocabulary words. The goal for these students should not just be to recognize the words, but rather to incorporate them into their personal lexicon for writing and speaking.

Differentiating Daily Instruction for Striving and ELL Students

- Begin with audio. Beginning each Unit by playing the audio of Introducing the Words and the iWords of each word being spoken, defined, and used in example sentences can help all learners—especially striving and ELL students—understand how vocabulary words are used in multiple contexts. Differentiated passages at lower Lexile® measures are available in printable format as part of Digital Resources and in printable and audio format in the Interactive Edition at **SadlierConnect.com**.

- Encourage students to repeatedly listen to iWords to deepen their understanding of word pronunciations and meanings. Show examples of correct use in varied contexts. Providing students with opportunities to encounter words repeatedly and in more than one context helps students place these words in their long-term memories and improves word consciousness.

- Provide opportunities for oral practice. Engaging students in actively using the new vocabulary in classroom discussions and conversations allows them to enrich their understanding of the words' meanings and to make connections between words while building their vocabularies.

- Utilize graphic organizers. Concept Circle, Word Map, Word Square, and Word Web are available at **SadlierConnect.com** in interactive and static formats. Using graphic organizers is especially important for striving readers and ELL students, as they help learners visualize their words and come to a richer recognition of word meanings.

- Work together. Pair striving and/or ELL students together to complete the Unit's exercises. They should work at a similar pace and clarify word meaning through discussions over answers.

- Encourage practice and multiple exposures to Unit words. There are a variety of exercises available at **SadlierConnect.com** to help students gauge for themselves their level of understanding. What's the Word?, Match It!, and other interactive activities help make word retention fun.

Differentiating Assessment for Striving Readers and ELL Students

■ Modify assessments. Reducing the number of incorrect answer choices in test items makes the assessment more accessible and does not harm the psychometric properties of the test.

■ Create an alternative test. Have students demonstrate their knowledge of words through the real-world medium of their choice. Success should be determined based on correct usage with context and/or an explanation to show understanding.

■ Recognize context clues. Consider giving partial credit to students who can underline the context clues correctly in the Completing the Sentence, Words in Context, and/or Vocabulary for Comprehension exercises when used as assessments.

Differentiating Exercises and Assignments for Above Grade-Level Students

■ Use words in conversations. During discussions of current events or literature, teachers can encourage students to use vocabulary words when making claims and expressing ideas.

■ Categorize vocabulary. Have students not only learn word meanings but also categorize words as they relate to general labels, such as "travel words" or "food words."

■ Get to the root of it. The Words with Latin/Greek Roots activity in each Unit helps students move beyond individual word meaning to understanding the roots of words and etymological concepts and to build their own vocabularies.

Differentiating Assessment for Above Grade-Level Students

■ Assign a written test. Require students to use several of the vocabulary words in their response to a writing prompt. Alternatively, have students write on topics of their choice.

■ Practice for standardized tests. The Vocabulary for Comprehension exercises in the Review sections provide other ways to assess students not only on their vocabulary knowledge but also on literary analysis questions crucial to success on standardized tests.

Grade 5	Level Blue
Determine or clarify the meaning of unknown and multiple-meaning words and phrases based on *grade 5 reading and content,* choosing flexibly from a range of strategies. Use context as a clue to the meaning of a word or phrase.	Introducing the Words, pp. 6–7, 16–17, 26–27, 36–37, 46–47, 56–57, 68–69, 78–79, 88–89, 98–99, 108–109, 118–119, 130–131, 140–141, 150–151, 160–161, 170–171, 180–181 Definitions, pp. 8–9, 18–19, 28–29, 38–39, 48–49, 58–59, 70–71, 80–81, 90–91, 100–101, 110–111, 120–121, 132–133, 142–143, 152–153, 162–163, 172–173, 182–183 Synonyms and Antonyms, pp. 10, 20, 30, 40, 50, 60, 72, 82, 92, 102, 112, 122, 134, 144, 154, 164, 174, 184 Completing the Sentence, pp. 11, 21, 31, 41, 51, 61, 73, 83, 93, 103, 113, 123, 135, 145, 155, 165, 175, 185 Words in Context, pp. 13, 23, 33, 43, 53, 63, 75, 85, 95, 105, 115, 125, 137, 147, 157, 167, 177, 187 Vocabulary for Comprehension, pp. 34–35, 64–65, 96–97, 126–127, 158–159, 188–189 Completing the Idea, pp. 67, 129, 191 Word Study, pp. 24, 86
Use common, grade-appropriate Greek and Latin affixes and roots as clues to the meaning of a word.	Words with Latin/Greek Roots, pp. 12, 22, 32, 42, 52, 62, 74, 84, 94, 104, 114, 124, 136, 146, 156, 166, 176, 186 Word Study, pp. 76, 106, 138, 168, 178, **SadlierConnect.com**
Use reference materials, both print and digital, to find the pronunciation and determine or clarify the precise meaning of key words and phrases.	Definitions, pp. 8–9, 18–19, 28–29, 38–39, 48–49, 58–59, 70–71, 80–81, 90–91, 100–101, 110–111, 120–121, 132–133, 142–143, 152–153, 162–163, 172–173, 182–183 Word Study, pp. 14, 86, 148
Apply understanding of figurative language, word relationships, and nuances in word meanings. Understand figurative language, including similes and metaphors, in context.	Shades of Meaning, pp. 15, 77
Explain the meaning of common idioms, adages, and proverbs.	Shades of Meaning, pp. 25, 107, 149, 179
Demonstrate understanding of words by relating them to their opposites (antonyms) and to words with similar but not identical meanings (synonyms).	Word Study, pp. 24, 44, 86, **SadlierConnect.com** Synonyms and Antonyms, pp. 10, 20, 30, 40, 50, 60, 72, 82, 92, 102, 112, 122, 134, 144, 154, 164, 174, 184
Use grade-appropriate general academic and domain-specific words and phrases, including those that signal contrast, addition, and other logical relationships.	Vocabulary for Comprehension, pp. 34–35, 64–65, 96–97, 126–127, 158–159, 188–189 Introducing the Words. See *Introducing the Words* at the top of this column.

PLANNING AND PACING GUIDE

The **Vocabulary Workshop** program is designed to be used with any Reading and Language Arts program. Its simple format allows for great flexibility. This chart shows how Level Blue might be taught and assessed over an academic year.

Weeks	Student Book	Resources to Enrich, Support, and Assess
1–2	**Unit 1**, pp. 6–15	**†Online Beginning-of-Year Diagnostic Assessment**
3–4	**Unit 2**, pp. 16–25	**Follow-Up Activities**, pp. T24–T48
5–6	**Unit 3**, pp. 26–33 **Review**, pp. 34–35	**†Digital Resources** (audio, visual, interactive) Units 1–3 ***Flash Cards** ***Test Booklet** Units 1–3 Tests, pp. 1–6 Units 1–3 Cumulative Test, pp. 7–10 ***Online Assessment**
7–8	**Unit 4**, pp. 36–45	**Follow-Up Activities**, pp. T24–T48
9–10	**Unit 5**, pp. 46–55	**†Digital Resources** (audio, visual, interactive) Units 4–6 ***Flash Cards**
11–12	**Unit 6**, pp. 56–63 **Review**, pp. 64–67	***Test Booklet** Units 4–6 Tests, pp. 11–16 Units 1–6 Cumulative Test, pp. 17–20 ***Online Assessment**
13–14	**Unit 7**, pp. 68–77	**Follow-Up Activities**, pp. T24–T48
15–16	**Unit 8**, pp. 78–87	**†Digital Resources** (audio, visual, interactive) Units 7–9 ***Flash Cards**
17–18	**Unit 9**, pp. 88–95 **Review**, pp. 96–97	***Test Booklet** Units 7–9 Tests, pp. 21–26 Units 1–9 Cumulative Test, pp. 27–30 ***Online Assessment**
19–20	**Unit 10**, pp. 98–107	**Follow-Up Activities**, pp. T24–T48
21–22	**Unit 11**, pp. 108–117	**†Digital Resources** (audio, visual, interactive) Units 10–12 ***Flash Cards**
23–24	**Unit 12**, pp. 118–125 **Review**, pp. 126–129	***Test Booklet** Units 10–12 Tests, pp. 31–36 Units 1–12 Cumulative Test, pp. 37–40 ***Online Assessment**
25–26	**Unit 13**, pp. 130–139	**Follow-Up Activities**, pp. T24–T48
27–28	**Unit 14**, pp. 140–149	**†Digital Resources** (audio, visual, interactive) Units 13–15 ***Flash Cards**
29–30	**Unit 15**, pp. 150–157 **Review**, pp. 158–159	***Test Booklet** Units 13–15 Tests, pp. 41–46 Units 1–15 Cumulative Test, pp. 47–50 ***Online Assessment**
31–32	**Unit 16**, pp. 160–169	**Follow-Up Activities**, pp. T24–T48
33–34	**Unit 17**, pp. 170–179	**†Digital Resources** (audio, visual, interactive) Units 16–18 **†Online Final Mastery Test** Unit 18
35–36	**Unit 18**, pp. 180–187 **Review**, pp. 188–191	***Flash Cards** ***Test Booklet** Units 16–18 Tests, pp. 51–56 Units 1–15 Cumulative Test, pp. 57–60 ***Online Assessment**

*Optional purchase   †SadlierConnect.com

Vocabulary Workshop Level Blue can be combined with the grade-level appropriate titles listed below to form a literature-based approach to vocabulary study. Seeing the words encountered in such classic and contemporary literature can reinforce students' appreciation of the value of possessing a strong vocabulary.

Author	Title	Type
Avi	*The True Confessions of Charlotte Doyle*	Historical/Adventure
Babbit, Natalie	*The Search for Delicious*	Fantasy/Dictionary Definitions
Banks, Lynne Reid	*The Indian in the Cupboard*	Fantasy/Adventure
Brink, Carol Ryrie	*Caddie Woodlawn*	Historical/Prairie
Brittain, Bill	*The Wish Giver*	Mystery/Suspense
Burnford, Shirley	*The Incredible Journey*	Animal/Adventure
Byars, Betsy	*Summer of the Swans*	Realistic/Family
Clement, Andrew	*Frindle*	Realistic/History of Language
Conrad, Pam	*Our House*	Short Stories/Humor/Levittown
Curtis, Christopher Paul	*The Watsons Go to Birmingham–1963*	Historical/African American
Dorris, Michael	*Morning Girl*	Historical/Native American
Fitzgerald, John D.	*The Great Brain*	Realistic/Humor
Fitzhugh, Louise	*Harriet the Spy*	Realistic/Humor
George, Jean Craighead	*My Side of the Mountain*	Adventure/Survival
Giblin, James Cross	*Many Rides of Paul Revere*	Nonfiction/Historical/Revolutionary War
Gipson, Frederick	*Old Yeller*	Animal/Realistic
Gray, Lulu	*Falcon's Egg*	Fantasy/Family
Hale, Shannon	*Princess Academy*	Fantasy/Friendship
Hiassen, Carl	*Hoot*	Humor/Animal/Environmental
Jackson, Donna	*ER Vets: Life in an Animal Emergency Room*	Nonfiction/Animals/Medicine
Kelly, Jacqueline	*The Evolution of Calpurnia Tate*	Realistic/Family/Science
King-Smith, Dick	*School Mouse*	Animal/Books & Reading
Konigsburg, E.L.	*The View from Saturday*	Realistic/Language Contest
Lofting, Hugh	*The Story of Doctor Doolittle*	Animal/Fantasy/Adventure
Lord, Betty Bao	*In the Year of the Boar and Jackie Robinson*	Historical/Chinese American
Lowry, Lois	*Number the Stars*	Historical/WWII
MacLachlan, Patricia	*Sarah, Plain and Tall* *The Facts and Fictions of Minna Pratt*	Historical/Prairie Realistic/Musicians
Martin, Ann M.	*A Corner of the Universe*	Realistic/Family/Disabilities
Merrill, Jean	*The Pushcart War*	Realistic/Humor
Mohr, Nicholasa	*Felita*	Realistic/Hispanic
Murphy, Jim	*An American Plague: The True and Terrifying Story of the Yellow Fever Epidemic*	Nonfiction/Historical
Naylor, Phyllis Reynolds	*Shiloh*	Realistic/Animal
North, Sterling	*Rascal*	Autobiography/Animal/Humor
Norton, Mary	*The Borrowers*	Fantasy/Family
Schmidt, Gary	*The Wednesday Wars*	Realistic/Historical/1960s
Snyder, Zilpha Keatley	*Cat Running*	Historical/Great Depression/Dust Bowl
Steig, William	*Dominic*	Animal/Humor/Fantasy
Tate, Eleanor	*Thank You, Dr. Martin Luther King, Jr.!*	Historical/Realistic
Taylor, Sidney	*All-of-a-Kind Family*	Historical Fiction/NYC/Jewish
Woodson, Jacqueline	*Last Summer with Maizon*	African American/Friendship/Realistic

TEACHING NOTES FOR THE UNIT

Each Unit of **Vocabulary Workshop** has a unique structure designed to give maximum coverage to each of the key words within the space available. Units of the Student Book include the following lessons.

Unit Overview

Introducing the Words (Unit Reading Passages)	In **Introducing the Words**, students read a reading passage that incorporates all the words they will be learning in the Unit. Different genres and themes are presented in the reading passages.
Definitions	In **Definitions**, students are introduced to the twelve vocabulary words in the Unit. After learning about the definitions and various elements associated with each word, students complete collaborative activities to work with the Unit words.
Synonyms and Antonyms	In **Synonyms**, students select the taught word that is the synonym for the highlighted word in an illustrative phrase. In **Antonyms**, students choose the antonym for the highlighted word.
Completing the Sentence	In **Completing the Sentence**, students use context clues to choose the word that meaningfully completes each sentence. The sentences are connected by a theme.
Word Associations	In **Word Associations**, students demonstrate understanding by applying word knowledge in a way that calls for a measure of inference, reasoning, perception, and imagination.
Words with Latin/Greek Roots	In **Words with Latin/Greek Roots**, students study the root of a Unit word and apply its meaning to other words.
Words in Context	In **Words in Context**, students read a passage that is related in topic or theme to the introductory reading passage and contains multiple-meaning words. Then students answer comprehension questions in formats found on standardized tests.
Word Study	In **Word Study**, students build vocabulary by applying strategies, such as using context clues and analyzing word parts, including roots and affixes.
Shades of Meaning	In **Shades of Meaning**, students deepen their understanding of word meanings by examining relationships between related words and by analyzing nuances of meaning.

Because each Unit has a similar structure, the teaching notes on pages T26–T33 can be used for any given Unit. More comprehensive teaching notes for Word Study and Shades of Meaning can be found on pages T34–T43.

INTRODUCING THE WORDS

Each Introducing the Words reading passage presents the twelve words students will learn in the Unit. When reading a passage, students will want to pay close attention to the context of these highlighted Unit words. This will both improve their comprehension of the passage and help them begin to figure out the word meanings.

PREPARING TO READ

- **Access Prior Knowledge** Ask students prompting questions to help them access their prior knowledge about the theme or topic of the passage. In a class discussion, expand on the topic to help students build background knowledge. See page T27.

- **Presenting the Words** Introduce the twelve Unit words to students. Read aloud each word, emphasizing correct pronunciation. Have students repeat each word after you. Provide students with a brief explanation of each word that will prepare them for their encounter with the word within the passage.

DURING READING

As students read the passage, point out its key elements, and ask questions to encourage critical thinking.

- With students, read the brief introduction. Discuss the genre of the passage, and encourage students to name other stories and books they have read in the genre. Discuss any photographs or illustrations, pointing out how students can use the information in these visuals to help them better appreciate the passage.

- Depending on the needs of individual students, assign the passage as independent reading, allow them to read it together as a Read Aloud, or have them listen to the audio version of the passage, available at **SadlierConnect.com**, while reading.

- Guide the class's focus and comprehension by having students answer key questions about the passage.

- Remind students to pay attention to context clues that can help them figure out the meanings of the words and develop a better understanding of the passage.

AFTER READING

Invite students to summarize the passage. Then review the answers to the questions that were asked while they were reading. Encourage students to ask any questions they may have about the passage or the meanings of the words.

- Return to each of the highlighted words in the passage. Discuss context clues and the meanings of the words as they relate to the passage.

- Remind students that they will be learning more about the words throughout the Unit. Point out that the more connections students make to the words, the easier it will be to remember the words and interact with them in other contexts.

Background Information

As students prepare to read each passage, provide background information about the theme or topic they will encounter. Although some themes will be familiar to students, others will be new and pique their curiosity. Encourage students to make connections to any prior knowledge and to further explore these topics.

• **Why Bear Sleeps So Much** Unit 1 pp. 6–7, **880L**: Russian animal folktales are often origin stories. The bear is a common character in Russian folklore as it is an animal that traditionally represents Russia. Misha, the bear cub, was the mascot for the 1980 Moscow Olympics.

• **Sybil Ludington's Ride** Unit 2 pp. 16–17, **960L**: The Revolutionary War (1775 to 1783) began as a war between Great Britain and the original 13 colonies. With battles occurring right in their backyards, many young Americans played a role in defending the country.

• **The Flight of the Monarch** Unit 3 pp. 26–27, **920L**: Many environmentalists are concerned about the monarchs that summer east of the Rocky Mountains. This group of butterflies is decreasing in size each year. Excessive rainfall in Mexican wintering grounds as well as fewer milkweed plants in their summer home may be causing the problem.

• **Wagon Train Diary** Unit 4 pp. 36–37, **810L**: The California Gold Rush began on January 24, 1848, when gold was discovered in Coloma, California. Families from across the United States trekked to California to find gold. Many gold seekers were called forty-niners after the year of their arrival.

• **Baucis and Philemon** Unit 5 pp. 46–47, **740L**: Much of mythology explains the relationships and roles of the gods and goddesses. The king of the Roman gods, Jupiter, is the equivalent of Zeus from Greek mythology.

• **The Surprising Life of Emily Dickinson** Unit 6 pp. 56–57, **910L**: Emily Dickinson is considered one of the greatest American poets, even though she never received this recognition during her lifetime. Her rich and beautiful poetry has intrigued and inspired countless people.

• **Eugenie Clark: Swimming with Sharks** Unit 7 pp. 68–69, **950L**: Ichthyologists are scientists who study fish to learn about their behavior, feeding habits, and interactions with other fish. These scientists educate others and work to protect fish and their living environments.

• **What Happened to Pennsylvania Station?** Unit 8 pp. 78–79, **810L**: Pennsylvania Station is a major train station that has undergone changes since its original construction. Today, Madison Square Garden, the country's busiest arena, is located on top of the station.

• **The Competitive Edge** Unit 9 pp. 88–89, **660L**: For many athletes, competition is often just as much a mental game as it is a physical one. In order to win, athletes need to have a desire to win, confidence in their abilities, and focused attention when it matters most.

• **Ireland's Great Famine** Unit 10 pp. 98–99, **920L**: An estimated one million Irish arrived in America during the famine years. They faced great hardships in the form of poverty and discrimination as American cities were overwhelmed by the mass influx of people.

• **National Ski Patrol to the Rescue** Unit 11 pp. 108–109, **880L**: The National Ski Patrol (NSP) is composed of more than 27,000 members serving over 600 patrols. Upon joining, members receive training in emergency care, search and rescue, mountaineering, avalanche control, and other skills.

• **A Message for Norrod** Unit 12 pp. 118–119, **830L**: Although sci-fi stories may include strange creatures or aliens, these characters often experience problems similar to those humans deal with.

• **Crispus Attucks Changes History** Unit 13 pp. 130–131, **980L**: Attucks was buried at Granary Burying Ground in Boston. It is the final resting place for all five victims of the Boston Massacre as well as three signers of the Declaration of Independence.

• **A Giant Hoax** Unit 14 pp. 140–141, **900L**: To get the materials to make the Cardiff Giant, Hull hired men in Iowa to carve out a block of gypsum, a white mineral. He told them it was for a monument to Abraham Lincoln.

• **Pecos Bill Ends a Drought** Unit 15 pp. 150–151, **880L**: Pecos Bill has a female tall-tale match— a wife named Slue-Foot Sue, who rode a giant catfish down the Rio Grande.

• **Why Did the Woolly Mammoths Disappear?** Unit 16 pp. 160–161, **930L**: In 2007, a nearly perfectly preserved baby mammoth was found in Siberia, providing scientists with new insight into the lives of mammoths.

• **The Hunger Strike** Unit 17 pp. 170–171, **870L**: Aesop is a storyteller who was born about the year 620 BCE in ancient Greece. His fables, including "The Fox and the Grapes" and "The Tortoise and the Hare," are world-famous and enduring.

• **Sequoyah, Advocate of His People** Unit 18 pp. 180–181, **940L**: The first person to learn the written language of Cherokee was Sequoyah's daughter Ayokeh. She helped him legitimize the writing system, turning the skeptical Cherokee into supporters of his writing system.

DEFINITIONS

- Discuss the format and content of the Definitions pages. Explain that there are twelve words, each with its pronunciation, part of speech, definition, sample sentence showing how the word is used, synonyms and antonyms, and sometimes a picture to help clarify the meaning.

- Review the parts of speech in the Remember box. Lead a brief discussion about each word's part of speech to help students increase their understanding of the definition and word use.

- Point out that some words can be used as different parts of speech and can have more than one meaning—for example, *document* (Unit 1).

- To help students develop a deeper understanding of the Unit words, generate a discussion that gets at the character of the word and how it is typically used. For example, for *fragile* (Unit 1), ask:

  - "Is a china teacup *fragile*? Explain."

  - "Name some other things that are *fragile*."

  - "If you send something *fragile* in the mail, how would you pack it?"

  - "Show me how you would carry something *fragile*."

- Summarize by explaining the meaning of *fragile* using everyday language.

> **MODEL** From our discussion, we know that something *fragile* can be easily damaged and that it may require special care. If you drop a crystal bowl, it will probably break because it is *fragile*.

PRACTICE/APPLY

- Assign the **Definitions** pages. Tell students to think about each word's meaning as they read the example sentences.

- Ask volunteers to read the example sentences aloud. Reading sentences aloud conveys how words can be effectively used in speaking and writing. It also reinforces the word's pronunciation.

- Pair students for collaborative activities. Collaborative activities provide additional opportunities for students to interact with the words and enrich understanding.

FOLLOW-UP

- **Oral Language** To encourage daily use of the Unit words, list them on a Word Wall. Encourage students to use the words in their speaking and writing. When they read, tell them to be alert to the words they have learned and to notice how the words are used.

- **English Language Learners** Model how to pronounce each Unit word. Have students practice saying the words. To reinforce word meaning, encourage students to take turns acting out the words. Guide students as needed.

SYNONYMS AND ANTONYMS

- Tell students that learning synonyms and antonyms can help them expand their vocabularies. Explain that synonyms are words that have the same or similar meanings; for example, *scuffle* (Unit 1) and *fistfight* are synonyms.

> **MODEL** Instead of saying, "The coach broke up the *fistfight* between the two players," I can say, "The coach broke up the *scuffle* between the two players." The words *fistfight* and *scuffle* are synonyms. They both mean about the same thing.

- Provide other sentences with *scuffle*. Ask students to give synonyms that could replace the word. Remind students that the synonym must make sense in the sentence.

- Explain that antonyms are words with opposite meanings; for example, *distribute* (Unit 1) and *gather* are antonyms. Elicit from students other words that are the opposite of *distribute*. Guide them by providing sentences such as: "Today, I will *distribute* the test booklets." Ask students to replace *distribute* with a word that is opposite in meaning and that would make sense in the sentence. (*collect*)

- Use other examples of synonyms and antonyms that are related to students' experiences.

- To help students expand their vocabularies, revisit and discuss the synonyms and antonyms on the Definitions pages. Have students use some of the words in sentences. Encourage them to relate the words to their own experiences.

PRACTICE/APPLY

- Assign the **Synonyms and Antonyms** page. Tell students to read each phrase and consider each choice before choosing their answers. Remind them to substitute their choices for the word in boldface to be sure it makes sense.

FOLLOW-UP

- **Expanding Vocabulary** Have students begin a Vocabulary Notebook in which they write the meanings of the taught words and add to them as they learn more about the words. For example, have them list additional synonyms and antonyms.

- **Writing** Have students list the Unit words in their Vocabulary Notebooks by part of speech. Also have them list synonyms and antonyms for the Unit words. Students can choose from these lists to make their writing more interesting.

COMPLETING THE SENTENCE

- Remind students that some words have more than one meaning. Explain that when a multiple-meaning word is used in a sentence, they can figure out the intended meaning by using the context clues. Point out, however, that first they need to be familiar with the various meanings. Provide cloze sentences with enough context for students to figure out which Unit word correctly completes a sentence.

- Explain that context clues in sentences can be before or after an unfamiliar word. The context clue is sometimes a single word located within the same sentence.

- Write the following on the board:
An all-sports channel on cable TV usually provides _______ coverage of events, such as the Olympic Games.

> **MODEL** To figure out the Unit word that fits in the sentence, I look for clues in the sentence. The words *all-sports channel* and the *Olympic Games* make me think that *continuous* (Unit 1) is the correct word. I know that an all-sports channel broadcasts nothing but sports. I also know that the Olympic Games take place over many days. When I read the sentence with the word *continuous*, it makes sense.

- Briefly discuss the topics on the **Completing the Sentence** page. Explain that each sentence can be completed using one of the Unit words in the box at the top of the page. Each word can be used only once. Point out that as required by the sentence, the missing word may be the plural form of a noun or any tense or form (participle, for example) of a verb.

- Have students tell the context clues they used to complete the sentences.

- **Synonyms** Challenge student pairs to complete the student page again, this time reading aloud the sentences and using synonyms in place of Unit words.

- **Unit Assessment** See pages T18 and T19 to select appropriate practice and assessment tools, including Interactive Practice Quizzes and Practice Quiz Worksheets (available at **SadlierConnect.com**) and Unit Tests in the Test Booklet (optional purchase).

WORD ASSOCIATIONS

- Help students continue to build on the meanings of the Unit words. Ask questions that require them to associate Unit words with known words. For example, ask the following questions using the Unit 1 words *solitary*, *fragile*, and *continuous*:

    - "Which word would you use to describe a person who lives alone, *fragile* or *solitary*? Explain."

    - "Would you expect a highway to be *continuous* or *fragile*? Explain."

- In another activity, show how you might connect a Unit word with something else. For example:

myth	birth certificate
blunder	unicorn
document	clumsy move

> **MODEL** I know that a *myth* is something that is imaginary. A *unicorn* is a creature that does not exist. So *myth* goes with *unicorn*.

- Ask students to relate *blunder* and *document* to the remaining phrases, and then explain the relationships.

PRACTICE/APPLY

- The exercises in the Word Associations feature are comprised of sentence completions and questions, each containing a highlighted Unit word.

- Assign the **Word Associations** activity. When students finish, have them explain their choices.

FOLLOW-UP

- **Unit Assessment** See pages T18–T19 to select appropriate practice and assessment tools, including Interactive Practice Quizzes and Practice Quiz Worksheets (available at **SadlierConnect.com**) and Unit Tests in the Test Booklet (optional purchase).

WORDS WITH LATIN/GREEK ROOTS

- Tell students that learning about Latin/Greek roots can help them unlock the meanings of English words derived from Latin and Greek roots. Explain that the Unit 1 word *reject* comes from the Latin root *ject*.

> **MODEL** The Unit word *reject*, meaning "refuse to accept, agree to, or use," comes from the Latin prefix *re-* meaning "back," and the Latin root *ject*, which means "to throw." Together, the two word parts mean "to throw back or refuse." Write *reject* on the board and underline the Latin prefix *re-* and the Latin root *ject*.

- Provide sentences with *reject* that contain context clues. Example: The committee will meet to approve or *reject* theme suggestions for the party. Ask students to suggest additional sentences that use the word contextually.

PRACTICE/APPLY

- Assign the **Words with Latin/Greek Roots** activity. Tell student to read each word containing the root and its definition.

FOLLOW-UP

- **Expanding Vocabulary** Have students begin a Words with Latin/Greek Roots section in their Vocabulary Notebooks in which they write the Latin/Greek root and its meaning that is introduced in each Unit. Include the Unit word that contains the root.

- **Writing** Have students include another word with the Latin/Greek root and write a contextual sentence to reflect the meaning of the root.

WORDS IN CONTEXT

TEACH

- Tell students that the Words in Context page contains a short reading passage related in topic or theme to the Introducing the Words reading passage that began the Unit.

- Remind students to pay close attention to the context of the Unit words in the passage. This will help students improve their comprehension of the passage and help them to determine word meaning.

- Point out the grammar skill that is included in the reading passage.

PRACTICE/APPLY

- Assign the **Words in Context** page. Tell students that they will use their word knowledge and reading skills by reading a passage and answering questions based on the passage. Point out that the passage and questions are similar to those on standardized tests. Tell students to read carefully and to be sure to base their answer choices on what they read.

- Remind students to go back into the reading passage to identify the grammar skill that is embedded in the passage.

- Students will also have the opportunity to apply the context of the Unit words with a partner by completing the Write Your Own activity.

FOLLOW-UP

- **Expanding Vocabulary** Encourage students to use the interactive Graphic Organizers, available at **SadlierConnect.com**, to make connections to the Unit words.

- **Writing** Challenge students to write their own summary of the Introducing the Words or Words in Context reading passage, using five Unit words.

Unit 1 • Dictionary: Multiple-Meaning Words 1, page 14

TEACH
Explain that when students look up a word in the dictionary, they will often find more than one meaning for the same word. Discuss which context clues students used to determine the meaning of the word *veteran* in the sample sentence.

PRACTICE/APPLY
In Practice, remind students to use context clues to help select the correct word. They should also pay attention to the part of speech of the missing word. This, too, will help them figure out the correct word. In Apply, have students tell which meaning of the multiple-meaning words they illustrated.

FOLLOW-UP
Word Play Have students write alliterative tongue-twister sentences using both forms of the multiple-meaning words. For example: *In cool conditions, I choose to **coat** my body with a cozy, comfortable **coat**.*

Unit 2 • Context Clues 1, page 24

TEACH
Discuss with students the kind of information each type of context clue provides. Provide additional sample sentences, as necessary.

PRACTICE/APPLY
In Practice, have students tell which context clues helped them figure out the meaning of the boldface words. Have them also tell which type of context clue is used in each sentence. In Apply, have students share the context clues they added.

FOLLOW-UP
Expanding Vocabulary Provide students with magazine articles or other in-class reading materials to give them more practice using context clues. As students read independently, have them list any words whose meanings they do not know. Students can then make a chart to list unknown words, context clues, and implied meanings.

Unit 3 • Homographs @ SadlierConnect.com

TEACH
Explain that some homographs have different pronunciations. Say: "Please *close* the door. Stand *close* to the window." Point out that *close* has a different meaning and a different pronunciation in each sentence. Discuss the meaning of *close* in each sentence.

PRACTICE/APPLY
Have students use the words from the chart to complete the sentences in Practice and Apply. Remind students to use context clues when deciding which meaning of the word to use.

FOLLOW-UP
Oral Language Create and dispay a list of additional homograph pairs and definitions. Have students practice using the words in small group conversations.

WORD STUDY

Unit 4 • Analogies, page 44

TEACH

Explain that to complete an analogy, students must first figure out the relationship between the first two words. Model the process with this example: "*Ice* is to *cold* as *fire* is to _______." Provide additional modeling as necessary for the different types of analogies presented.

PRACTICE/APPLY

In Practice and Apply, have students share their answers and suggest other pairs of words that could complete each analogy.

FOLLOW-UP

Informal Assessment Have students create an original analogy for each type of analogy listed in the chart.

Unit 5 • Words Often Confused, page 54

TEACH

Write this sentence on the board: "After a day in the dessert, I was hungry for a cold desert." Ask students: "What is wrong with this sentence?" Point out how knowing the difference between commonly confused words can help students when reading and writing.

PRACTICE/APPLY

In Practice and Apply, instruct students to complete each sentence using the correct word. For each sentence, have students explain the meaning of the sentence if the wrong word were used.

FOLLOW-UP

Word Play Tell students that many people use tricks, or mnemonic devices, to remember the difference between commonly confused words. For example, a trick often used for *desert* and *dessert* Is: "*Desert* has one s and a *desert* Is a place you may only want to visit for one day. *Dessert* has two s's and many people like to eat two helpings of *dessert*." Have students work with a partner to create other tricks.

Unit 6 • Suffixes *-ance, -age, -hood* @ SadlierConnect.com

TEACH

Remind students that base words are complete words to which prefixes and suffixes can be added. Discuss the meanings of the four suffixes and the given examples. Ask students to brainstorm other words that contain these suffixes, and then have them figure out the meanings of these words.

PRACTICE/APPLY

In Practice, encourage students to use a dictionary, in a book or online, to check their answers. In Apply, remind students to look for context clues to help them complete the sentences.

FOLLOW-UP

Oral Language Make a Word Wall using words that contain the suffixes learned. Ask students to look for the suffixes as they are reading. When students discover new words that contain any of the suffixes, have them add the words and their meanings to the Word Wall.

WORD STUDY

Unit 7 • Prefixes *pre-, in-, im-, ir-, il-,* page 76

TEACH

Explain to students that knowing the meanings of a few common prefixes, such as the ones on page 76, can help them uncover the meanings of many words. For example, have students brainstorm additional words with the five prefixes to make the point.

PRACTICE/APPLY

In Practice, encourage students to use a dictionary, in a book or online, to check their answers. In Apply, remind students to look for context clues to help them complete each sentence with the correct word. They may also use a dictionary, either in a book or online, to check their answers.

FOLLOW-UP

Expanding Vocabulary Have students create a Word Web (available online at **SadlierConnect.com**). Have students write one of the prefixes in the center circle of the web and then list words that contain the prefix in the surrounding circles.

Unit 8 • Using a Thesaurus, page 86

TEACH

Explain to students that a thesaurus is a book of synonyms. Remind students that synonyms have similar but slightly different meanings. When replacing a word with a synonym, students must choose a word that fits the sentence. Point out that not every word has a synonym, and these words would not be in a thesaurus.

PRACTICE/APPLY

In Practice, have students share their synonyms. Discuss the differences between the words. In Apply, discuss why certain synonyms "work" in a sentence and why some are poor replacements.

FOLLOW-UP

Informal Assessment Have students create a Concept Circle (available online at **SadlierConnect.com**) that contain two synonyms and one unrelated word. Have students identify the unrelated word and replace it with a third synonym.

Unit 9 • Context Clues 2 @ SadlierConnect.com

TEACH

Write the three sample sentences on the board, underlining each signal word. Model how to use a signal word to recognize the type of context clue used and to figure out the meaning of the unfamiliar word. Say: "In the first sentence, the word *because* shows cause and effect. Flexible bones allow a mouse to squeeze through cracks, so *flexible* likely means 'able to be bent.'" Use probing questions to discuss the other two sample sentences.

PRACTICE/APPLY

In Practice, have students give their definitions of the boldface words. Then, for each sentence, have students tell which context clues and which signal words were clues to the word's meaning. Have students share the sentences they completed in Apply.

FOLLOW-UP

Writing Instruct students to choose three Unit words. Then have students write one sentence for each word, using a different type of context clue within each sentence.

WORD STUDY

Unit 10 • Roots *port, mit,* page 106

TEACH

Model how knowing the meaning of the root *port* can help you figure out the meaning of *portable* in this sentence: "A cell phone is a *portable* type of phone." Continue similarly with the word *emit*. Then relate the meanings of each root and each chart word.

PRACTICE/APPLY

Begin by asking students to brainstorm examples of each word in the chart. Remind students to use context clues when completing the Practice sentences. Have students explain how their responses to the Apply sentences relate to the meanings of each root.

FOLLOW-UP

Oral Language Have student pairs ask and answer questions using words with the lesson's roots, such as "Why might a dog *emit* a growl?"/"It *emits* a growl when scared."

Unit 11 • Homophones, page 116

TEACH

Introduce the topic by writing this sentence on the board: "I carried my *plain*, black suitcase onto the *plane* with me." Ask: "How are the words *plain* and *plane* alike and different? What happens if you switch the two words?" Then discuss the chart words.

PRACTICE/APPLY

Remind students to use context clues for the Practice sentences. After each student shares an Apply sentence, ask the class: "Which homophone was used?"

FOLLOW-UP

Informal Assessment Create several sentences in which homophones are used correctly or incorrectly—for example, "Our school *principle* is retiring." Have students write *right* or *wrong* after each sentence to indicate whether the correct homophone was used.

Unit 12 • Prefixes *re-, in-, im-* @ SadlierConnect.com

TEACH

Have students recall the prefixes they learned on page 76. Explain that some prefixes, such as *in-* and *im-*, can mean both "not" and also "in" or "into." Discuss the example words, and provide example sentences for each word on the page.

PRACTICE/APPLY

Ask students for an example of each new word. Remind them to use context clues to help them choose the answer for each Apply sentence. After they complete the sentences, ask students to relate the prefix of each inserted word to the context of the sentence.

FOLLOW-UP

Writing Have students continue the Practice chart by listing words with prefixes *re-, in-,* and *im-*. Allow students to use a dictionary. Point out that students should only include words in which *in-* or *im-* mean "in" or "into."

WORD STUDY

Unit 13 • Suffixes *-ion, -tion, -sion, -ous, -ic,* page 138

TEACH

Have students recall the relationship between a suffix and a base word. Write the lesson's suffixes on the board, and discuss their meanings and the given examples. Ask prompting questions, such as "What kind of competition would you like to enter?"

PRACTICE/APPLY

Encourage students to use a dictionary, print or digital, to check their answers for the Practice exercises. Discuss the new words, asking students to use each new word in a sentence. Remind students to use context clues when completing the Apply sentences.

FOLLOW-UP

Expanding Vocabulary After students add new words to the chart, have them choose one new word for each suffix. Have students complete a Graphic Organizer Word Square (available online at **SadlierConnect.com**) for each new word they choose.

Unit 14 • Dictionary: Multiple-Meaning Words 2, page 148

TEACH

Remind students that a print or online dictionary will often list multiple meanings for a word, such as the lesson word *negative*. Model using the sample sentence on the page for *negative* to demonstrate the use of context clues to determine meaning.

PRACTICE/APPLY

Explain that students will use one of the three multiple-meaning words on the page to complete each sentence in Practice and Apply. Remind students that they can determine word meaning by paying attention to both part of speech and context clues in sentences.

FOLLOW-UP

Expanding Vocabulary Have students draw pictures to illustrate the multiple meanings of the words in the chart on the page. Students can also write captions.

Unit 15 • Roots *spect, photo, tele* @ SadlierConnect.com

TEACH

Ask students to recall what they know about roots. Write the lesson's three roots on the board. Encourage students to name words with these roots. Model how knowing the meaning of the root *tele* can help you figure out the meaning of *telescope* in this sentence: "The scientist aims the *telescope* toward the surface of the moon." As you discuss the words in the chart, relate the meaning of the root to the meaning of each word.

PRACTICE/APPLY

Before assigning the exercises, ask students to brainstorm examples of each word in the chart. Remind students to use context clues when completing the Practice sentences. Ask how their responses to the Apply sentences relate to the meaning of the roots.

FOLLOW-UP

Oral Language Have students use words with the roots *spect, photo,* and *tele* to ask each other questions about their own experiences, such as, "What is the best spectacle you have ever seen?" or "What is something you have photocopied?"

WORD STUDY

Unit 16 • Suffixes *-ity, -ty, -ence, -al,* page 168

TEACH

Have students recall suffixes. Write the lesson's suffixes on the board. Discuss their meanings and the given examples. Ask prompting questions to further students' understanding, such as "What is something *accidental* that could happen in a diner?"

PRACTICE/APPLY

Encourage students to use a dictionary, print or digital, to check their answers. Further the discussion by asking for examples of each new word. Ask students to supply meanings for the words in the chart and then to check their answers in a dictionary.

FOLLOW-UP

Writing Have students use any words with the suffixes *-ity, -ty, -ence,* and *-al* to write news headlines. Provide examples such as, "Sales of personal computers have reached an all-time high."

Unit 17 • Prefixes *de-, post-, trans-, sub-,* page 178

TEACH

Write the word *depress* on the board and underline the prefix *de-*. Model how knowing the meaning of *de-* can help figure out the meaning of *depress* in the sentence, "When the button gets stuck, you have to depress it more forcefully."

PRACTICE/APPLY

Further the discussion of new words by asking students for examples of each new word. Remind students to use context clues. After students complete the sentences, ask how the prefix of each inserted word relates to the context of the sentence.

FOLLOW-UP

Intormal Assessment Tell students to write four words that contain a prefix on the front of separate note cards. On the reverse side, students can write any things they associate with the word. For example, for *subzero,* they might list *freezing, winter, wool coat,* and *Antarctica.*

Unit 18 • Roots *dict, tract* @ SadlierConnect.com

TEACH

Ask: "What do you know about roots?" Write the roots *dict* and *tract* on the board. Now ask: "What words contain these roots?" Model how the meaning of the root *dict* can help you figure out the meaning of *contradict* in this sentence: "These two theories *contradict* each other." Then relate the meaning of the root to the meaning of each word in the chart.

PRACTICE/APPLY

Before assigning the activities, ask students to brainstorm examples of each word in the chart. Remind students to use context clues when completing the Practice sentences. Ask how their responses to the Apply sentences relate to the meaning of the roots.

FOLLOW-UP

Word Play Have students work in small groups. One at a time, students can give a clue, and the rest of the group can guess the word that matches the clue. For example, a student may give this clue: "If you guess how a movie will end, you do this: _______." (*predict*)

SHADES OF MEANING

Unit 1 • Similes, page 15

TEACH

Write the example sentence: "Fortunately, at that moment, Eagle flew in like a bolt of lightning." Ask: "What is being compared?" As students respond, underline *flew* and *bolt of lightning*. Discuss similes. Model how to figure out the meaning: "A bolt of lightning can strike quickly, so that must mean that Eagle flew in very quickly."

PRACTICE/APPLY

Have students share phrases in the sentences that helped them complete the similes. Ask students to explain each simile's meaning and how their responses fit those meanings.

FOLLOW-UP

Expanding Vocabulary Allow students to use resources to find three additional examples of similes. Ask students to draw a picture of each simile and then label it.

Unit 2 • Adages and Proverbs 1, page 25

TEACH

Discuss Sybil's journey, emphasizing her determination to complete her mission. Ask: "What is the meaning of *a will to succeed*? How did Sybil show a will to succeed?" Write on the board, "Where there's a will, there's a way." Guide students to an understanding of the saying—that is, you can accomplish anything if you want it enough and work hard.

PRACTICE/APPLY

After students finish the exercises, discuss the meaning of each proverb. Ask: "How does the meaning of each proverb fit the example sentence?"

FOLLOW-UP

Writing Ask students to choose a proverb from the page to apply to their own life. Have them write a paragraph explaining the relation to their life.

Unit 4 • Words That Describe Behavior, page 45

TEACH

Discuss the word *aggressive* as used in the passage—that is, the narrator wants the oxen to move at a more aggressive pace. Then write on the board, "How I wish the oxen were more aggressive!" Ask: "How is this sentence different from the one in the passage?" Discuss how this new sentence relates to the behavior of the oxen, not to their pace. Point out that words like *aggressive* can be used to describe behavior.

PRACTICE/APPLY

Ask students to explain how each word fits the behavior described in Practice. After they complete Apply, have them describe how somebody might react to each behavior.

FOLLOW-UP

Informal Assessment Provide Graphic Organizer Concept Circles (available at **SadlierConnect.com**) that contain three adjectives—two that can be used to describe behavior and one that cannot (for example, *courteous, passive, foggy*). Have students identify the misplaced adjective and replace it with a third adjective that can be used to describe behavior.

SHADES OF MEANING

Unit 5 • Words That Name Travelers, page 55

TEACH
Read aloud the words in the box and their definitions. Then pose questions that hint at each traveler's reason, or purpose, for traveling. Ask: "Have you ever been a tourist in another city? How might a commuter get to school or work?"

PRACTICE/APPLY
Have students explain which type of traveler fits each sentence in Practice. In Apply, have them share their answers to the questions.

FOLLOW-UP
Expanding Vocabulary Have students complete a Word Square for each word in the chart. The Word Square (available at **SadlierConnect.com**) can be used as an interactive tool or a printable tool. Students should indicate the type of traveler in the center circle and add words related to that type of traveler in the surrounding circles. For example, for *commuter*, students might include the words *train*, *business*, *suit*, and *briefcase*.

Unit 7 • Metaphors, page 77

TEACH
Discuss the difference between metaphors and similes. On the board, write: "Life is a journey," and "Life is like a journey." Have students tell which statement is a metaphor and which is a simile and then give the meaning of each.

PRACTICE/APPLY
In Practice and Apply, have students share key phrases in the sentences that helped them define the metaphors. For each example, encourage students to suggest other possible metaphors that could replace the one in boldface without changing the meaning of the sentence.

FOLLOW-UP
Writing Have students complete metaphors about themselves, such as: My mind is _______. My body is _______. My spirit is _______. I am _______.

Unit 8 • Words That Describe People, page 87

TEACH
Ask students to consider this question: "If someone asked you to describe a friend, what would you say?" Some students might describe appearance, using a word like *tall*; students describing personality might use the word *friendly*. Discuss other words in the chart that describe personality.

PRACTICE/APPLY
Have students explain which type of personality fits each sentence in Practice. In Apply, have them share their answers to the questions.

FOLLOW-UP
Oral Language List the four words in the chart on a Word Wall with the heading *Words That Describe People*. Have students add synonyms and antonyms of the words to the Wall.

SHADES OF MEANING

Unit 10 • Idioms 1, page 107

TEACH

Explain that to understand the meaning of an idiom, students have to think beyond the literal, or actual, meanings of the words. Elaborate on the idiom *either feast or famine*. Say: "A *feast* is an abundance of food and a *famine* is a severe shortage of food. 'Business is *either feast or famine*' means 'business goes from one extreme to the other.'"

PRACTICE/APPLY

After students finish the Practice and Apply, discuss the meaning of each idiom with students. Have students explain how each idiom fits the example sentence.

FOLLOW-UP

Expanding Vocabulary Have students look in magazines and other books for additional examples of idioms. For each idiom students find, have students list the idiom, the surrounding sentence, and the meaning of the idiom.

Unit 11 • Word Choice *request, plea, demand, interrogation,* page 117

TEACH

Explain that writers choose words carefully to get across specific thoughts. On the board, write the example sentence: "As they race closer, they call in an urgent plea for help." Ask: "How would the meaning of the sentence change if the writer had used the word *request* instead? The word *demand*? If the writer said the skiers had conducted an *interrogation*?"

PRACTICE/APPLY

After students complete the Practice and Apply, have them discuss the context clues in each sentence that indicated which word to choose.

FOLLOW-UP

Oral Language Explain to students that the differences between a *request*, a *plea*, a *demand*, and an *interrogation* can also be seen in conversation based on differences in facial expressions, body language, and tone of voice. Provide students with scenarios, and have them act the scenarios out to demonstrate their understanding of the words.

Unit 13 • Word Choice *acquire, receive, purchase, borrow,* page 139

TEACH

Remind students what they have learned about the importance of word choice. Then write the words *acquire, receive, purchase,* and *borrow* on the board. Ask: "How are the words similar? How are they different?" Now read these two sentences: "I *received* this vase as a gift. I *borrowed* this vase." Ask students: "What is the difference between these two ideas?"

PRACTICE/APPLY

After students complete the Practice and Apply, have them discuss the context clues in each sentence that indicated which word to choose.

FOLLOW-UP

Writing Have students use all four words from the lesson to write short paragraphs about a real or fictional event.

SHADES OF MEANING

Unit 14 • Adages and Proverbs 2, page 149

TEACH

Write on the board, "All that glitters is not gold." Help students understand the meaning of the proverb by asking: "What if someone showed you a large, shiny rock that looked just like gold. Would you assume that it was real gold just because it looked like gold?" Discuss how some things may look like something else, but are not genuine, or real. Then discuss how the proverb relates to the passage "A Giant Hoax."

PRACTICE/APPLY

After students finish the exercises, discuss the meaning of each proverb. Have students explain how each proverb fits the Apply sentence.

FOLLOW-UP

Writing Ask students to choose two proverbs from the lesson to apply to their own life. Have them write a paragraph that explains the relation to their life.

Unit 16 • Words That Describe Size, page 169

TEACH

Write the words *mammoth*, *miniature*, *microscopic*, and *vast* on the board. Ask, "What do these words have in common?" Discuss the differences in their meaning. Encourage students to name other words that describe size.

PRACTICE/APPLY

After students complete the sentences, have them discuss the context clues in each Practice sentence that indicated which size word to choose. Have students share their answers to the Apply exercises with the class.

FOLLOW-UP

Informal Assessment Have students complete a Word Square for each word in the chart. The Graphic Organizer Word Square (available at **SadlierConnect.com**) can be used as an interactive tool or a printable tool.

Unit 17 • Idioms 2, page 179

TEACH

Ask students to recall what they know about idioms. Explain that some idioms refer to body parts. Write the example, "When I took two helpings of potatoes, *my eyes were bigger than my stomach.*" Remind students that the meaning of an idiom is different from the literal meaning of the words in the saying. Discuss what the idiom actually means.

PRACTICE/APPLY

After students complete the exercises, discuss the meaning of each idiom. Have students explain how each idiom fits the sentence.

FOLLOW-UP

Word Play Have students write an idiom on the front of a note card and any thoughts, feelings, and things they associate with the idiom on the reverse side. For example, for *butterflies in my stomach*, they might list *anxious*, *singing a solo*, *sweaty palms*. Have volunteers read their clues aloud and the class guess the idiom.

TEACHING NOTES FOR THE REVIEW

Each sequence of three Units of **Vocabulary Workshop** is followed by a review in the form of Vocabulary for Comprehension, which contains words from those three Units. Each sequence of six Units additionally includes Classifying and Completing the Idea as part of the review. These pages review words from the previous six Units. The Reviews are designed to provide additional exposure to the taught words and to allow students to apply and expand their word knowledge.

Overview of the Review

Vocabulary for Comprehension	In **Vocabulary for Comprehension**, students read a passage that incorporates several of the taught words from the three Units. After reading, students answer questions based on the passage. Each **Vocabulary for Comprehension** concludes with **Write Your Own**. This writing prompt gives students the opportunity to demonstrate understanding of taught words as part of their writing vocabularies. The prompt may ask students to interact with the reading and vocabulary in a variety of ways, including expanding on the theme of the passage, expressing feelings about the subject, and relating the passage to personal experience.
Classifying	In **Classifying**, students look for a relationship among a group of words and choose the word that may be considered a member of the group. Students then explain the relationship.
Completing the Idea	In **Completing the Idea**, students apply their knowledge of word meanings by completing a writing activity. They relate their prior knowledge or a personal experience to a sentence starter that contains a taught word and then complete the thought. Each **Completing the Idea** concludes with a **Writing Challenge**. This writing exercise provides students with the opportunity to demonstrate an understanding of multiple-meaning words. For each **Writing Challenge**, students write sentences that provide context clues for different meanings and parts of speech of a given taught word.

All six Reviews include Vocabulary for Comprehension. Because of their similar structure, the teaching notes on pages T45–T46 can be applied to all Reviews. Teaching notes on pages T47–T48 can be applied to Classifying and Completing the Idea pages.

VOCABULARY FOR COMPREHENSION

- Tell students that to understand what they are reading, they must know the meanings of key words or be able to figure out the meanings. They must also use comprehension skills to help them grasp the meaning of the passage.

- Present the paragraph and questions below.

   On April 14, 1912, the *Titanic*, a magnificent ocean liner, hit an iceberg about 400 miles off Newfoundland, Canada. Nobody knew at first how bad the damage was. People were very calm. But soon it was clear that the ship was doomed. In less than three hours, the *Titanic* split into two pieces and sank into the deep, cold sea.

   1. What is the main idea of the paragraph?
   2. What details tell about the main idea?
   3. What is the meaning of *doomed*?
   4. What do you think happened to the people on board the ship?

- Discuss the reading skills below. Model how to use them to answer the questions.

- **Identify Main Idea/Details** The main idea of a passage is what the passage is about. It is the most important point that the author makes about a topic or subject. The main idea is often stated at the beginning of the passage. The rest of the passage usually gives details that help explain or support the main idea.

> **MODEL** To answer the first two questions about the *Titanic*, I use the information in the paragraph. The main idea tells me what the paragraph is about. From reading the paragraph, I know that it is mainly about the sinking of the *Titanic*. The details tell me when the *Titanic* sank (in April, 1912), where it sank (about 400 miles off Newfoundland, Canada), and why it sank (it hit an iceberg).

- **Vocabulary in Context** Sometimes, using context clues can help a reader figure out the meaning of a word. The clues can be in the surrounding sentences, or they can be other words in the sentence.

> **MODEL** To figure out the meaning of *doomed*, I look at the other words in the sentence and at the sentences that come before it. In the sentence with *doomed*, the word *but* tells me that the situation was not hopeful. This, together with the other clues, makes me think that *doomed* means "certain to fail or be destroyed."

- **Make Inferences** Authors do not always state directly everything that happens. Instead, they provide details that allow readers to figure out things for themselves. Making inferences is combining clues or details in the passage with prior knowledge to make logical decisions about events and actions.

> **MODEL** To answer the last question, I put together everything that I know happened. I know that the *Titanic* hit an iceberg, and I know that the ship was doomed. The last sentence tells me that the *Titanic* split in two and sank. All this makes me think that the people on board drowned.

Using the paragraph, model how to monitor comprehension. Show how you would stop and reread to understand important details or what you might do to clarify confusing parts.

> **MODEL** The *Titanic* hit an iceberg about 400 miles off the coast of Newfoundland. It's hard to imagine what a distance of 400 miles is like. To help me better understand the situation, I will ask the librarian for a map of the North Atlantic that shows Newfoundland. Then I will ask for help in pinpointing a distance that is about 400 miles off the coast of Newfoundland.

PRACTICE/APPLY

- Assign the **Vocabulary for Comprehension** pages. Tell students that they will use their word knowledge and reading skills by reading a passage and answering questions based on the passage. Point out that the passage and questions are similar to those on standardized tests. Tell students to read carefully and to be sure to base their answer choices on what they read. Point out that there may be answer choices that make sense but that are not based on the passage.

- In **Write Your Own**, students have the opportunity to write on a topic related to the passage. The writing may expand on the passage, or it may tell how students feel about what they read. Remind students to use some of the taught words in their writing.

FOLLOW-UP

- **Oral Language** Create a Word Wall of interesting words. Have students contribute new words encountered in their reading, in conversations, on TV, and in their daily experiences. Before you add a word, encourage students to tell where they found it and describe the situation in which it was used.

CLASSIFYING

- Explain that words can be classified, or grouped together, according to the way in which they are alike. For example, *shoes*, *socks*, and *slippers* are all things that are worn on the feet. *Bushes*, *trees*, and *flowers* are all things that are planted. Tell students that classifying words can help them see the connection between words. It can help them build their vocabularies.

- Write the following words on the board: *limber*, *elastic*, and *adaptable*. Discuss which word, *fragile*, *reliable*, or *flexible*, belongs with the group of words.

> **MODEL** To figure out the answer, I look to see what the words *limber*, *elastic*, and *adaptable* have in common. I see that they all describe something that can bend without breaking or is able to change or take in new ideas. Of the three choices, *flexible* goes best with the group.

PRACTICE/APPLY

- Assign the **Classifying** page. Have students familiarize themselves with the words in the word box before completing the page.

FOLLOW-UP

- **Word Play** Have students make up questions such as the following for a partner to answer. Partners should be prepared to explain their answers.

  - Which words might you use to talk about a vacation, *solitary*, *luxurious*, *linger*, or *transport*?

  - Which words might you use to describe doing homework, *calculate*, *document*, *postpone*, or *strive*?

TEACH

- To help make the taught words a permanent part of students' vocabularies, give students many opportunities to use and think about the words. Have students discuss and answer questions such as the following:
  - Can a villain be both *treacherous* and *cautious*? Explain.
  - When might it be necessary to *bluff*? Explain.

- Tell students that any answer they can adequately support is acceptable. Model how you might answer the first question. Encourage students to offer other answers.

> **MODEL** A *villain* is someone who is wicked or evil. Such a person might betray another and so could be described as *treacherous*. A *villain* might also avoid taking risks in carrying out his or her plans and so might be described as *cautious*.

- Remind students that some words have more than one meaning. Explain that when a multiple-meaning word is used in a sentence, they can figure out the intended meaning by using the context clues. Point out, however, that first they need to be familiar with the various meanings.

PRACTICE/APPLY

- Assign the **Completing the Idea** page. Point out that the taught words in the sentence stems are in boldface. Tell students to think about the definition of each taught word and how to complete the idea meaningfully before they begin to write. Remind them that there is more than one correct way to complete an idea.

- In **Writing Challenge**, students are provided with a multiple-meaning word from the reviewed Units. They must provide a sentence for two different meanings of the word. Remind students to use the parts of speech indicated in the directions. For example, one sentence should use the Unit word as a verb and the other as an adjective.

FOLLOW-UP

- **Expanding Vocabulary** Have students keep track of unfamiliar words that they encounter in their reading. For each word, have them consult a dictionary, print or digital, and use prior knowledge to explain its meaning. Have them also include examples, nonexamples, synonyms, and antonyms, if appropriate.

- **ELL** Dictate sentences that include the taught words so students can hear them in context. Ask students to touch each word in the sentence with their pencils as you repeat it. You might also tell students how many words are in the sentence and allow them time to count. Provide at least three opportunities for students to hear a sentence before moving on to the next one.

SADLIER

Vocabulary Workshop®

TOOLS FOR COMPREHENSION

Level Blue

Jerome Shostak

Consultants

Joseph Czarnecki, Ph.D.
Former Faculty Associate,
School of Education
Johns Hopkins University
Baltimore, MD

Christine Gialamas
Reading Specialist
Chicago Public Schools
Chicago, IL

Cover Series Design: Silver Linings Studios;
Cover pencil: Shutterstock.com/VikaSuh.

Photo Credits: Alamy Stock Photo/First Light/Peter Reali: 27 *left*; Jim M. McDonald: 48; Nigel Cattlin: 99 *left*; North Wind Picture Archives: 181 *inset*; Pictorial Press Ltd: 130 *inset*; Ted Foxx: 132; Louise A. Heusinkveld: 98–99; image100 Sports H: 88; Mary Evans Picture Library: 56; moodboard: 111; NorthernExposure: 108 *inset*; SOCCER/Balan Madhavan: 58. Animals Animals/Patti Murray: 26–27 *background*. Bridgeman Images/Bibliotheque des Arts Decoratifs, Paris, France/Archives Charmet/Troop of mammoths in the Ice Age (colour litho) by Wilhelm Kuhnert (1865-1923) (after): 160–161; © Staatliche Kunstsammlungen Dresden/Jupiter and Mercury in the House of Philemon and Baucis (oil on copper) by Adam Elsheimer (1578-1610) Gemaeldegalerie Alte Meister, Dresden, Germany: 46. Corbis/Naturbild/Kentaroo Tryman: 121. Dreamstime.com/Catalin Petolea: 140–141 *background*; Martin Allinger: 183; Vassiliy Mikhailin: 29; Patrick Poendl: 173. Everett Collection, Inc.: 19. Getty Images/AFP/Brendan Smialowski: 9; AFP/Therence Koh: 142; DEA Picture Library: 163; Realistic Reflections: 70; Riser/Bob Elsdale: 152; Michael Rosenfeld: 133; Bettmann: 36–37, 57, 79 *bottom*, 79 *top*, 80, 140 *top*, 158 *inset*; Corbis Historical: 172, 188; Corbis/VCG/Danny

Lehman: 27 *right*; Library of Congress: 78, 130–131 *background*; Museum of the City of New York: 96 *inset*; National Geographic Image Collection/Walter Meayers Edwards: 126; Nativestock.com/Marilyn Angel Wynn: 181 *background*; Panoramic Images: 161. The Granger Collection LTD: 37 *top*, 98 *inset*, 99 *right*, 34. iStockphoto.com/luoman: 96 *background*; Pierre-Yves Babelon: 59; thinair28: 28; tintin75: 158 *background*; ventdusud: 39. Library of Congress, Prints & Photographs Division/LC-USZC4-2566: 180. National Geographic Stock/David Doubilet: 69. New York State Historical Association/The Farmer's Museum: 140 *bottom*, 141 *inset*. North Wind Picture Archives: 16–17 *background*. Photographers Direct/Darlene Bordwell: 17 *inset*. Punchstock/Panoramic Images: 153; Comstock Images: 108–109. Shutterstock.com: 64; akva: 131; Alperium: 118–119 *background*; iKandy: 143; Liem Bahneman: 90; Michael Pettigrew: 38; Mohamed Farouk Badawi: 47; Plan-B: *sunburst*; Theus: *sky and clouds background*; tonobalaguerf: 118 *inset*; VikaSuh: 1; Ivonne Wierink: 89. Smithsonian/National Postal Museum: 16 *inset*. SuperStock/Image Source: 100. University of Maryland/John Consoli: 68.

Illustration Credits: Monica Armino: 170–171. Jared Beckstand: 8, 49, 120, 162. David Neale: 6–7. Tim Raglin: 150–151. Chris Vallo: 18, 71, 81, 91, 101, 110, 182.

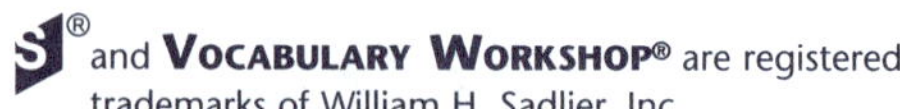

and **VOCABULARY WORKSHOP** are registered trademarks of William H. Sadlier, Inc.

Printed in the United States of America.
ISBN: 978-1-4217-1645-9
2 3 4 5 6 7 8 9 BRR 25 24 23 22 21

NOTE TO THE STUDENT

Most of the vocabulary words in **Level Blue** will be new to you. Some words you may recognize. Others you may not know at all. The words have been chosen because they are words you will come across often. You will see them in schoolbooks and on tests. You will see them in books and magazines, as well as on the Internet. You will also hear them spoken by teachers and others in a variety of professions.

In each of the 18 units, you will read a passage that contains the 12 unit words. You will see and hear how the words are used in the passage. Then you will learn more about them, including their definitions, pronunciations, parts of speech, and how they are used in sentences. You will also find synonyms and antonyms for the words. As you complete the pages in the unit, not only will you practice using the words, but you will also show what you know about them.

Vocabulary Workshop also helps you build vocabulary beyond the unit words. In **Word Study**, you will learn how to use word parts (prefixes, suffixes, roots) to figure out the meanings of unfamiliar words. In **Shades of Meaning**, you will learn the meanings of some idioms, proverbs, similes, and metaphors.

When you finish this book, your vocabulary will have grown. All the words you have learned will be part of your personal vocabulary, helping you to become a better reader, writer, and speaker.

Digital Resources

Don't forget to look at the digital resources that extend and enrich the instruction and practice provided by **Level Blue**. Access to these free resources and more is available at **SadlierConnect.com**.

CONTENTS

Introducing the Words

Read the following Russian folktale about some clever forest animals. Notice how the highlighted words are used. These are the words you will be learning in this unit.

Why Bear Sleeps So Much

(Russian Folktale)

A differentiated version of this passage is available at SadlierConnect.com.

Long ago, when the world was as fresh and new as a daffodil in springtime, the animals faced a serious problem. Troublesome Bear was ruining everything in their forest.

The songbirds were all terrified whenever Bear passed through the woods in his usual clumsy way. He would blunder into branches, smashing the birds' fragile nests and eggs. Bear also crushed the hives of the bees and stole their honey, so the bees had a continuous argument with him. Bear squashed the tunnel-like homes of the gophers and the rabbits with his big feet, and in general caused so many disturbances that the animals couldn't relax. As angry as they were, however, the animals didn't really want to get into a scuffle with Bear. He was much too big and strong!

Desperate, the animals called a meeting to decide on a course of action. "Why don't we just ask Bear to be more considerate?" suggested Deer timidly.

Squirrel was quick to reject Deer's idea. "That won't work," Squirrel insisted, "because Bear never listens to anyone. I think he just enjoys walking all over us!"

"Throw Bear in jail," Rat shouted. "Force him to live a solitary life in a jail cell and he won't be able to injure and torment us ever again."

The animals nodded in approval at this idea until Mouse pointed out an obvious problem. "We don't have a jail," Mouse squeaked, "and if we did, someone would have to feed Bear in his cell." The very thought of feeding Bear made all the animals shake in fear.

Other animals offered more ideas. Skunk suggested that Porcupine distribute some of his extra sharp quills in Bear's bed. Porcupine suggested that Skunk send some smelly spray into Bear's den. Neither animal was brave enough to try the other's plan, however, and the ideas probably wouldn't have worked anyway. Indeed, it looked as if there were no solution to the problem, and the animals were about to cancel the rest of their meeting.

Fortunately, at that moment, Eagle flew in like a bolt of lightning. The animals cheered because Eagle was a veteran problem solver. Whenever there was trouble in the forest, Eagle found a way to put an end to it. This time, Eagle clutched a document in his sharp claws. "As we all know," Eagle thundered, "Bear can't hurt anyone or destroy anything when he's asleep. This statement," he said, waving the document, "requires Bear to sleep from October to April every year. I hope you will all sign it!"

What a great idea! The animals read the document and added their names to it. True, it didn't get rid of Bear permanently, but it gave them temporary relief. At the very least, the animals could look forward to peace and quiet for six months of every year.

The myth doesn't say how the animals gave their signed document to Bear or what his reaction was to it. Who knows? Maybe he liked the animals' suggestion, for one thing is certain: Bear has been sleeping away half the year ever since!

Definitions

You were introduced to these words in the passage. Study the pronunciation, part of speech, definition, and example sentence for each word. Then read the synonyms and antonyms.

1. blunder
(blun′ dər)
(BLUHN-dur)

(v.) to make a foolish or careless mistake; to move clumsily and carelessly

> *I saw the hiker blunder through the woods.*

(n.) a serious or thoughtless mistake

> *I was terribly embarrassed by my blunder.*

SYNONYMS: (v.) to err, foul up, bungle, goof; (n.) an error, blooper
ANTONYMS: (v.) to triumph, succeed; (n.) a success, hit

 **Use each definition of blunder in a sentence.**

2. cancel
(kan′ səl)
(KAN-suhl)

(v.) to call off or do away with; to cross out with lines or other marks to show that something cannot be used again

> *Maybe the principal will cancel classes if it continues to snow.*

SYNONYMS: to stop, discontinue, drop, repeal, revoke
ANTONYMS: to renew, continue, extend, maintain

3. continuous
(kən tin′ yü əs)
(kuhn-TIN-yoo-uhss)

(adj.) going on without a stop or break

> *Continuous TV coverage began shortly after news of the disaster broke.*

SYNONYMS: ongoing, endless, ceaseless, unbroken, constant, perpetual
ANTONYMS: broken, discontinuous, interrupted

4. distribute
(di stri′ byüt)
(di-STRI-byoot)

(v.) to give out in shares; to scatter or spread

> *Our class will distribute leaflets announcing the school's fund-raising drive.*

SYNONYMS: to divide, share, deal, issue
ANTONYMS: to gather, collect, hold

 **Distribute supplies from your desk to the people around you.**

5. document
(dä′ kyə mənt)
(DAH-kyuh-muhnt)

(n.) a written or printed record that gives information or proof

> *The librarian found the old document inside a book.*

(v.) to give written or printed proof; to support with evidence

> *Writers often document their sources.*

SYNONYMS: (n.) a certificate, deed; (v.) to prove, establish

 **As time allows, have partners complete graphic organizers for select words, available at SadlierConnect.com.**

6. fragile
(fra′ jəl)
(FRA-juhl)

(adj.) easily broken or damaged, requiring special handling or care

The fragile antique was damaged during transit.

SYNONYMS: weak, frail, breakable, delicate, brittle, flimsy
ANTONYMS: sturdy, hardy, strong, rugged, tough

💬 **What are three fragile objects around the classroom?**

7. myth
(mith)
(MITH)

(n.) an old story that explains why something is or how it came to be; something imaginary

The play is based on an ancient Greek myth.

SYNONYMS: a legend, fable, tale, fantasy, fairy tale; ANTONYM: a fact

💬 **Make up a myth to explain why the sun rises each morning.**

8. reject
(ri jekt′)
(ri-JEKT)

(v.) to refuse to accept, agree to, believe, or use

Why did you reject the offer?

SYNONYMS: to deny, discard, junk, scrap, decline, dismiss
ANTONYMS: to take, accept, receive, welcome

9. scuffle
(skə′ fəl)
(SKUH-fuhl)

(v.) to fight or struggle closely with

A witness saw the two men scuffle in an alley.

(n.) fight or struggle

Police officers were called in to break up the scuffle.

SYNONYMS: (v.) to tussle, roughhouse, battle, brawl; (n.) a fistfight, clash

10. solitary
(sä′ lə ter ē)
(SAH-luh-ter-ee)

(adj.) living or being alone; being the only one

The old man led a solitary life.

SYNONYMS: single, sole, lone; ANTONYMS: sociable; several, many, numerous

11. temporary
(tem′ pə rer ē)
(TEM-puh-rer-ee)

(adj.) lasting or used for a limited time

A blow to the head can cause a temporary loss of memory.

SYNONYMS: short-term, passing, brief, momentary
ANTONYMS: lasting, long-lived, permanent

12. veteran
(ve′ tə rən)
(VE-tuh-ruhn)

(n.) a former member of the armed forces; an experienced person

The army veterans listened attentively.

(adj.) having much experience in some job or field

The actress will play a veteran reporter.

SYNONYMS: (adj.) expert, professional, experienced, skilled, accomplished
ANTONYMS: (n.) a beginner, newcomer, novice, rookie

Synonyms

*Choose the word that is most nearly the **same** in meaning as the word or phrase in **boldface**. Then write your choice on the line provided.*

1. a **constant** flow of traffic
   a. fragile   b. temporary   c. continuous   d. veteran   _continuous_

2. tried to hide the **blooper**
   a. document   b. myth   c. blunder   d. scuffle   _blunder_

3. not a **single** cent
   a. temporary   b. fragile   c. solitary   d. veteran   _solitary_

4. witnessed the **fight**
   a. myth   b. blunder   c. document   d. scuffle   _scuffle_

5. very important **records**
   a. veterans   b. documents   c. myths   d. blunders   _documents_

6. a collection of ancient **stories**
   a. documents   b. myths   c. veterans   d. blunders   _myths_

Antonyms

*Choose the word that is most nearly **opposite** in meaning to the word or phrase in **boldface**. Then write your choice on the line provided.*

1. **renew** my subscription
   a. cancel   b. blunder   c. scuffle   d. distribute   _cancel_

2. **accept** the marriage proposal
   a. scuffle   b. reject   c. blunder   d. distribute   _reject_

3. a **novice** mountain climber
   a. temporary   b. fragile   c. continuous   d. veteran   _veteran_

4. **collect** the homework sheets
   a. reject   b. document   c. distribute   d. cancel   _distribute_

5. a **sturdy** device
   a. temporary   b. solitary   c. veteran   d. fragile   _fragile_

6. a **permanent** filling
   a. veteran   b. continuous   c. temporary   d. solitary   _temporary_

Choose the word from the box that best completes each item. Then write the word on the line provided. (You may have to change the word's ending.)

blunder	**cancel**	**continuous**
distribute	**document**	**fragile**
myth	**reject**	**scuffle**
solitary	**temporary**	**veteran**

A Visit to a Museum

■ Our class visited the museum on the last day of a(n) __________**temporary**__________ exhibit of ancient Greek vases.

■ Because the vases were so old and __________**fragile**__________, we weren't allowed to touch them.

■ Security guards kept visitors a few feet from the display cases, so there was no chance that someone could __________**blunder**__________ into them.

■ The guide told us that the pictures painted on some of the vases were not of real people but of characters from legends and __________**myths**__________.

■ One picture showed a(n) __________**solitary**__________ warrior fighting off a band of attackers.

A Famous Declaration

■ In refusing to accept English rule, the writers of the Declaration of Independence __________**rejected**__________ the claim that Parliament had power over the American colonies.

■ Those who supported the cause of American independence quickly printed and __________**distributed**__________ copies of the Declaration throughout the thirteen colonies.

■ The original __________**document**__________ is now on view at the National Archives building.

On the Soccer Field

■ Two days of __________**continuous**__________ rain had turned the soccer field into a sea of mud and threatened to spoil the opening game of the season.

■ Before the game began, a __________**scuffle**__________ broke out in the stands when a few home-team fans came to blows with those rooting for the visiting team.

■ The referee threatened to __________**cancel**__________ the game and send all of the fans home if order was not restored.

■ Only when a handful of popular __________**veterans**__________ from both teams asked the fans to behave themselves did they finally settle down and let the game get under way.

*Circle the letter next to the word or phrase that best completes the
sentence or answers the question. Pay special attention to the word
in **boldface**.*

1. Someone who has **blundered** would
   a. feel embarrassed.
   b. be confident.
   c. feel proud.
   d. be rewarded.

2. A **solitary** tree would probably
   a. have needles.
   b. be chopped down.
   c. change color in the fall.
   d. stand alone.

3. When a teacher **distributes** a test
   a. he or she grades it.
   b. he or she loses it.
   c. he or she passes it out.
   d. he or she collects it.

4. Which is a creature of **myth**?
   a. a rabbit
   b. a giraffe
   c. a duck
   d. a dragon

Words with Latin Roots

The unit word *reject*, meaning "refuse to accept, agree to, or use,"
comes from the Latin prefix *re-*, meaning "back," and the Latin root
ject, which means "to throw." Together, the two word parts mean "to
throw back or refuse." The root *ject* is used in the following words:

- eject (v.): to expel (*to throw out*)
- object (v.): to disagree (*to throw a feeling or opinion up against*)
- subject (v.): to force or compel (*to throw someone or something down*)
- dejected (adj.): sad or mournful (*thrown down or under*)
- projectile (n.): an object designed to be shot forward (*something thrown forward*)

*Choose two of the words from the list. Write a sentence for each word
to show you understand its meaning.*

1. Accept answers that show an understanding of the vocabulary.

2. ____

Words in Context

Read the passage. Then answer each question.

Hibernation Lessons

1   Animals cope with the cold, hard times of winter in many ways. Some simply go to sleep. This solution to the **temporary** problems of winter is called hibernation. When chipmunks, woodchucks, and bats hibernate, their body temperature drops greatly. Bears and raccoons also hibernate, but they spend the winter in a somewhat lighter state of sleep.

2   Hibernation has been studied by many scientists and is accepted as a fact of nature, not a **myth**. However, researchers today continue to **scuffle** with a hibernation-related mystery. It involves the kidneys. These are organs that keep the blood clean and healthy.

3   During its long, **solitary** slumber, a black bear's kidney function sinks to very low levels. In the spring, however, the animal regains full kidney function. Could black bears hold the key to curing kidney disease? Some scientific **veterans** who **document** kidney function in bears believe that animal hibernation may hold important lessons for human medicine. Such scientists are careful to avoid overly high expectations and **blunders**, though. They point out that curing kidney disease may take many years of research.

1. What does the word **scuffle** mean as it is used in paragraph 2?
    (a) engage   (b) organize   (c) agree   **(d) struggle**

2. What is the meaning of the word **solitary** as it is used in paragraph 3?
    (a) lone   (b) numerous   (c) partial   (d) wretched

3. The Latin word *vetus* means "old." The word **veterans** in paragraph 3 means
    (a) ex-army members   **(b) experienced people**   (c) novices   (d) assistants

4. Pick the word that best defines **blunders** as it is used in paragraph 3.
    (a) successes   (b) conclusions   **(c) errors**   (d) doubts

*An interrogative sentence asks a question. It ends with a question mark. For example, **Do you know about black bears?** Underline an example of an interrogative sentence in "Hibernation Lessons."* **See paragraph 3.**

Write Your Own

Working with a partner, list the pros and cons of hibernation from a bear's point of view. Include three words from this unit in your list.

For more practice with kinds of sentences, see Grammar Workshop, Level Blue, Lesson 1.

Word Study   Dictionary: Multiple-Meaning Words

 A **multiple-meaning word** is a word with more than one meaning. One example from this unit is *veteran* (page 9). If you look up *veteran* in a dictionary, you will find an entry with numbers showing the word's different meanings.

veteran 1. *(n.)* a person who has served in the armed forces: *My father is a Gulf War veteran.* **2.** *(n.)* a person who has a lot of experience: *The respected soccer player is a veteran of his sport.*

Read this sentence: *My favorite baseball player was a ten-year* **veteran** *of the team.* You can tell from the definitions that the sentence illustrates meaning 2 of *veteran*.

Look at the chart to find other examples of multiple-meaning words.

coat	1. *(n.)* an item of clothing worn when it is cold 2. *(v.)* to cover a surface with something
drill	1. *(n.)* a practice of something such as a safety routine 2. *(n.)* a tool used to make holes in hard surfaces
uniform	1. *(n.)* an outfit worn by members of a group 2. *(adj.)* having hardly any or no difference

PRACTICE   *Write the multiple-meaning word from the chart above that completes each sentence. Using the part of speech can help you choose the word. Then write the number of the meaning.*

__1__   **1.** Be sure to put on your ______coat______ before you go out in the snow.

__2__   **2.** Our classroom is kept at a ______uniform______ temperature.

__1__   **3.** Our school has a fire ______drill______ at least once a month.

__2__   **4.** The cook will ______coat______ the pan with oil so the onions don't stick.

APPLY   *Complete each sentence so that it makes sense. Use the multiple-meaning word in* **boldface**. *You may have to change the word's ending.*
Accept reasonable answers that demonstrate the correct meaning.

5. drill   To hang the picture, we _____________________.

6. coat   The floor will look shiny and new if I _____________________.

7. uniform   To show that we are members of the glee club, we _____________________.

8. veteran   After teaching for twenty-four years, the teacher _____________________.

Think of the multiple meanings for each word below. Then use one of the words in a sentence. Ask your partner to tell what the word means.

Example: light (n.) / light (v.)   bend (n.) / bend (v.)

Shades of Meaning Similes

In the passage "Why Bear Sleeps So Much" on pages 6–7, you read this sentence: *Fortunately, at that moment, Eagle flew in **like a bolt of lightning**.* In this sentence, *like a bolt of lightning* is a simile.

A **simile** compares two unlike things using the word *like* or *as*. In the sentence from the passage, the simile *like a bolt of lightning* compares the way Eagle flew to a bolt of lightning. Since a bolt of lightning is known for how quickly it can strike, saying that Eagle flew like a bolt of lightning means that Eagle flew very quickly.

PRACTICE   *Complete each sentence with a simile at the right. Write the number of the sentence next to the simile.*

1. The sisters are identical twins. They are _____________.	__2__ like cats and dogs
2. My brother and I can never agree on anything. Our parents say that we fight ____________.	__1__ like two peas in a pod
3. I am very talkative, but my best friend is _____________.	__4__ as rough as sandpaper
4. The gardener's dry, chapped hands are _____________.	__3__ as quiet as a mouse

APPLY   *Complete each sentence so that it makes sense. Pay attention to the simile in **boldface**.* Accept answers that show an understanding of the simile.

5. When I am as **hungry as a bear**, I _______________________________________

____.

6. I think my grandmother is **as sweet as honey** because _____________________

____.

7. The student driver looked **like a deer caught in the headlights** when _________

____.

8. After gym, I moved **like a snail** because ____________________________________

____.

9. I felt **like a fish out of water** during my first _______________________________

____.

Introducing the Words

Read the following historical nonfiction passage about a hero of the American Revolution. Notice how the highlighted words are used. These are the words you will be learning in this unit.

Sybil Ludington's Ride

(Historical Nonfiction)

A differentiated version of this passage is available at **SadlierConnect.com**.

Listen, my children, and you shall hear of the midnight ride of . . . Sybil Ludington? Thanks to a very famous poem, almost everyone knows about Paul Revere. The name of Sybil Ludington, however, is probably unfamiliar. Yet like Revere, Ludington made an **impressive** midnight ride to warn American patriots—those fighting for independence—of an approaching British army.

In April 1777, two years after Revere's famous ride, British soldiers made an **assault** on Danbury, Connecticut, not too far from where sixteen-year-old Sybil Ludington lived. The Continental Army, as the army of the Americans was called, stored supplies in Danbury, and the British **strategy** was to burn them. Once the supplies were destroyed, the British began to burn the homes and workplaces of **numerous** patriots in Danbury. The **villain** in this raid was the British general William Tryon, who lost control of his soldiers and allowed them to hurt innocent citizens.

A messenger quickly rode out from Danbury with news of the attack. His destination was the mill of Colonel Henry Ludington in nearby New York State. Only Ludington, the leader of about four hundred patriot volunteers, could fight off the British. After hearing the news, Ludington quickly agreed to help, but his men were spread out for miles. Who would alert them?

This postage stamp honors Sybil Ludington's contribution to the cause of American freedom.

The messenger from Danbury did not know his way around the area. Ludington himself had to stay at home to assemble his soldiers as they arrived. Perhaps that's when Ludington's daughter Sybil volunteered to make the ride, or perhaps Ludington asked her to go. Either way, it was a shrewd choice. No one could dispute that Sybil was a skillful rider, and she knew the local roads well. Also, as the oldest of twelve children, she was used to responsibility. Sending Sybil was a decision that would be easy to justify.

Sybil quickly mounted her horse and rode off on her mission. It was after 9:00 p.m. and raining when she left, and in the darkness, the rough unmarked trails could be misleading. Sybil never lost her way though, galloping from farm to village and calling out the news. In all, she rode forty miles that night, twice as far as Paul Revere. Along the way, she had to avoid British spies and soldiers. According to one account, she even used a type of gun called a musket to scare away some outlaws who preyed on travelers at night.

Sybil had a productive ride that night! When she arrived back home at dawn, more than four hundred patriot volunteers were gathering at her father's mill. Under Colonel Ludington, they were quickly converted into a regular fighting force. By now, the British had burned and abandoned Danbury and were marching inland. Ludington's forces, however, stopped the British advance. Later, at the Battle of Ridgefield, the patriots fought the British invaders, who eventually retreated to their boats on Long Island Sound.

In the months that followed, Sybil's father and the volunteers he led often praised and thanked Sybil for her heroic ride. Even General George Washington sent his congratulations for a job well done. Like so many other patriots, Sybil Ludington had come to the aid of her country.

Definitions

You were introduced to these words in the passage. Study the pronunciation, part of speech, definition, and example sentence for each word. Then read the synonyms and antonyms.

1. abandon
(ə ban′ dən)
(uh-BAN-duhn)

(v.) to give up on completely; to leave with no intention of returning

The captain gave the order to abandon ship.

SYNONYMS: to desert, forsake, cease, surrender
ANTONYMS: to continue, stay, remain, occupy

2. assault
(ə sôlt′)
(uh-SAWLT)

(n.) a violent attack

The victim was injured in the assault.

(v.) to attack violently or suddenly

Dad dared us to assault his snow fort.

SYNONYMS: (n.) an invasion, raid, mugging, beating; (v.) to besiege, storm
ANTONYMS: (v.) to protect, defend, resist

3. convert
(v., kən vûrt′)
(kuhn-VURT)
(n., kän′ vûrt)
(KON-vert)

(v.) to change from one form to another

A drop in temperature to 32˚ F will convert water to ice.

(n.) a person who has changed from one opinion, belief, or religion to another

The new convert was introduced to the congregation.

SYNONYMS: (v.) to transform, turn, alter, switch
ANTONYMS: (v.) to maintain, conserve, remain

 Use each definition of **convert** in a sentence.

4. dispute
(di spyüt′)
(di-SPYOOT)

(v.) to argue, debate, quarrel over; to question or doubt the truth of

The committee did not dispute the merits of the bill.

(n.) an argument, quarrel, debate

Why not try to resolve the dispute peacefully?

SYNONYMS: (v.) to differ, disagree; contest, challenge; (n.) a conflict, disagreement, controversy
ANTONYMS: (v.) to agree, harmonize; (n.) an agreement, understanding, accord

 Discuss with your partner a fair way to resolve a **dispute**.

5. impressive
(im pre′ siv)
(im-PRE-siv)

(adj.) having a strong effect, commanding attention

The skater gave an impressive performance.

SYNONYMS: memorable, striking, stirring, thrilling, awesome, splendid
ANTONYMS: inferior, mediocre

6. justify
(jus′ tə fī)
(JUHSS-tuh-fye)

(v.) to show to be fair or right; to give good reasons for

Be prepared to justify your behavior.

SYNONYMS: to defend, explain, support, excuse
ANTONYMS: to convict, blame, accuse

7. misleading
(mis lē′ diŋ)
(miss-LEE-ding)

(adj.) tending to give a wrong idea, often on purpose

The lawyer called the statement misleading.

SYNONYMS: deceptive, false, tricky, inaccurate
ANTONYMS: direct, honest, true, accurate, straightforward

8. numerous
(nüm′ rəs)
(NOOM-ruhss)

(adj.) many or very many

Numerous aunts and uncles came to our family reunion.

SYNONYMS: several, plenty, plentiful; ANTONYM: few

9. productive
(prə duk′ tiv)
(pruh-DUHK-tiv)

(adj.) making or capable of making large amounts of; giving good results

With care, it may become a productive orchard.

SYNONYMS: energetic, effective, fruitful, efficient, worthwhile
ANTONYMS: unproductive, idle, useless, inactive

10. shrewd
(shrüd)
(SHROOD)

(adj.) showing clever judgment and practical understanding

My aunt is a shrewd businesswoman.

SYNONYMS: artful, wise, sharp, crafty, wily, cunning
ANTONYMS: slow, stupid, dull-witted

11. strategy
(stra′ tə jē)
(STRA-tuh-jee)

(n.) a carefully made plan or plot; a plan of military operations

Our teacher suggested a test-taking strategy.

SYNONYMS: an approach, design, method, scheme

Tell your partner about a **strategy** you use to remember things you need to do.

12. villain
(vi′ lən)
(VI-luhn)

(n.) an evil or wicked person or character, especially in a story or play

In old movies, the villain often wore a black hat.

SYNONYMS: a scoundrel, rascal, outlaw, criminal
ANTONYMS: a hero, heroine, champion

In your opinion, who is the most evil film or television **villain**?

 As time allows, have partners complete graphic organizers for select words, available at **SadlierConnect.com**.

Synonyms

*Choose the word that is most nearly the **same** in meaning
as the word or phrase in **boldface**. Then write your choice
on the line provided.*

1. **change** starch to sugar
   a. abandon   b. assault   c. dispute   d. convert   **convert**

2. **supported** the decision
   a. abandoned   b. assaulted   c. justified   d. converted   **justified**

3. a **thrilling** performance
   a. misleading   b. numerous   c. shrewd   d. impressive   **impressive**

4. tried to be more **effective**
   a. numerous   b. misleading   c. productive   d. shrewd   **productive**

5. a problem-solving **approach**
   a. strategy   b. assault   c. dispute   d. villain   **strategy**

6. a **crafty** move
   a. misleading   b. impressive   c. shrewd   d. productive   **shrewd**

Antonyms

*Choose the word that is most nearly **opposite** in meaning
to the word or phrase in **boldface**. Then write your choice
on the line provided.*

1. **agreed** with the umpire's call
   a. disputed   b. assaulted   c. converted   d. justified   **disputed**

2. **few** paint colors
   a. shrewd   b. misleading   c. numerous   d. productive   **numerous**

3. **occupy** the old shack
   a. assault   b. convert   c. abandon   d. justify   **abandon**

4. **defended** the bridge
   a. converted   b. assaulted   c. disputed   d. justified   **assaulted**

5. the **hero** of the movie
   a. convert   b. assault   c. strategy   d. villain   **villain**

6. gave **accurate** directions to the tourist
   a. impressive   b. misleading   c. numerous   d. productive   **misleading**

Completing the Sentence

Choose the word from the box that best completes each item. Then write the word on the line provided. (You may have to change the word's ending.)

abandon	assault	convert
dispute	impressive	justify
misleading	numerous	productive
shrewd	strategy	villain

Greeks and Trojans at War

■ Both the Greek poet Homer and the Roman poet Virgil wrote of the ten-year siege of Troy by the Greeks and of the heroes and __villains__ who did battle there.

■ One of the most famous stories describes the sly __strategy__ that the Greeks thought up to defeat the Trojans.

■ The Greeks had tried not once but on __numerous__ occasions to force the Trojans to surrender the fortress city.

■ Several times the Greeks had __assaulted__ the walls of Troy, but all of the attacks had failed.

■ Finally, the Greeks came up with a __shrewd__ plan: They left at the gates of Troy a huge wooden horse as a pretended peace offering. The Trojans brought the horse inside the city walls.

■ But the wooden horse was a __misleading__ gift, for hidden inside was a small army of Greeks, who at nightfall climbed from the horse and opened the gates to the city.

A False Science

■ Alchemists were people who believed that it was possible to __convert__ ordinary metals, such as iron and lead, into gold. The best-known alchemists are those who practiced in Europe during the Middle Ages.

■ They staged very __impressive__ experiments to try to convince others that they could do as they promised.

■ Some people believed that the possibility of great wealth __justified__ even the most far-fetched experiments.

■ Scientists today would __dispute__ the ideas of the alchemists, but centuries ago many people believed that their ideas were sound. In fact, it was not until the 1800s that scientists proved that base metals cannot be turned into gold.

■ Failure upon failure finally persuaded most alchemists to __abandon__ their dreams of wealth and glory.

■ In a way, the work that the alchemists did was __productive__ because it sometimes led to advances in chemistry. During the Middle Ages, for example, alchemists were responsible for the discovery of mineral acids.

Word Associations

*Circle the letter next to the word or phrase that best completes the sentence or answers the question. Pay special attention to the word in **boldface**.*

1. You might expect a **villain** to
   a. volunteer in a soup kitchen.
   b. receive an award.
   c. play the piano.
   d. break the law.

2. On a **productive** day you would
   a. play outside.
   b. get a lot done.
   c. stay inside.
   d. get nothing done.

3. If your friends are **numerous**,
   a. you have very few of them.
   b. they live nearby.
   c. you have a lot of them.
   d. they live far away.

4. When I **justify** my opinion,
   a. I take it back.
   b. I form it.
   c. I defend it.
   d. I change it.

Words with Latin Roots

The unit word **convert** comes from the Latin prefix **con-**, meaning "with," and the Latin root **vert** or **vers**, which means "to turn." Together, the word parts mean "to change from one form to another." The root **vert** or **vers** is used in the following words:

- avert (v.): to avoid (*to turn away*)
- revert (v.): to go back to (*to turn back*)
- advertise (v.): to make known or make public (*to turn attention toward*)
- diversion (n.): the act of turning aside (*a turning aside*)
- versatile (adj.): able to change (*able to turn to something new*)

Choose two of the words from the list. Write a sentence for each word to show you understand its meaning.

1. Accept answers that show an understanding of the vocabulary.

2. ____

Read the passage. Then answer each question.

Deborah Sampson: Revolutionary War Soldier

1   No one can **dispute** the fact that men played important roles in the Revolutionary War. However, women were also **productive** in the war effort. One woman named Deborah Sampson contributed in a particularly **impressive** way.

2   Deborah Sampson was born in Massachusetts in 1760. She was a young adult during the Revolutionary War. As a woman, Sampson was not permitted to be a soldier. So instead, she came up with a **strategy** to disguise herself as a man and joined the Fourth Massachusetts Regiment. She scouted land and led raids for the American Patriot forces. She even survived a cannon **assault**. Sampson and two sergeants demonstrated **shrewd** judgment when they led an expedition to scout out enemy resources in New York in June of 1782.

3   Sampson served as a soldier for two years before her fellow soldiers discovered she was female. Many male soldiers who previously believed that women could not be soldiers became **converts** when they learned about her identity. Deborah Sampson was the only woman to receive a military pension for service in the Revolutionary War.

1. What is the meaning of the word **dispute** as is it used in paragraph 1?
- (a) argument
- (b) belief
- (c) to challenge
- (d) to solve

2. What does the word **strategy** mean as it is used in paragraph 2?
- (a) a careful plan
- (b) an instruction
- (c) a military operation
- (d) a special routine

3. What does the word **assault** mean as it is used in paragraph 2?
- (a) a long journey
- (b) a violent attack
- (c) to attack violently
- (d) to journey

4. The Latin word *convertere* means "to turn around." The word **converts** in paragraph 3 describes people with
- (a) changed opinions
- (b) changed religions
- (c) new jobs
- (d) new names

 *A compound subject has two or more simple subjects that have the **same** predicate. The subjects are joined by the coordinating conjunction **and** or **or**. For example:* **Men and women** *supported the Revolutionary War. Underline a compound subject in "Deborah Sampson: Revolutionary War Soldier."* **See paragraph 2.**

  ## Write Your Own

Write 3–5 sentences about a time you wore a disguise or a costume, using at least three words from this unit. Share your story with a partner. Then have your partner write a sentence using at least one word from this unit explaining why someone might wear a costume or disguise.

 *For more practice with compound subjects, see* Grammar Workshop, Level Blue, Lesson 5.

Word Study Context Clues I

When you read, you may come across words that you do not know. When this happens, look for context clues in the sentence or surrounding sentences to help you figure out the word's meaning.

Read the sentences and explanations below to learn about three types of context clues.

Definition	*The house has an **extensive** yard, covering a large area.* The words *covering a large area* define *extensive*.
Example	*I like **condiments** such as ketchup, mustard, and relish on a burger.* The examples are "ketchup, mustard, and relish." This helps you understand that a *condiment* is something added to a food for flavor.
Restatement	*Very few plants grow well in **arid**, or dry, places.* The synonym *dry* explains the meaning of *arid*.

PRACTICE *Read each sentence. Write the meaning of the **boldface** word on the line. Then underline the words that helped you figure out its meaning.*
Accept reasonable answers. Possible answers are given.

1. I was **elated**, totally thrilled, when I won the bike race. _______ very happy _______

2. The **pesky** mosquitoes were causing trouble and annoying our guests.
   _______ troublesome, irritating _______

3. One day, I want to design **garments** such as dresses, suits, and skirts.
   _______ clothes _______

4. The lost hiker was **bewildered**, unsure about which of the two paths to take.
   _______ greatly confused _______

APPLY *Rewrite each sentence. Add context clues so that a reader can figure out the meaning of the **boldface** word in the sentence.*
Accept reasonable answers that demonstrate the meaning.

5. I use different measuring **devices**.

   ____

6. The popular singer **shuns** photographers.

   ____

Make up a sentence using a unit word. The sentence should provide good context clues. Ask a partner to name the word and the clue to its meaning.

Shades of Meaning Adages and Proverbs 1

In the passage "Sybil Ludington's Ride" on pages 16–17, Sybil Ludington knew that her father was depending on her to make contact with the patriot volunteers. Sybil ran into several obstacles as she rode through the night, but she continued on until she accomplished her mission. Her success that night surely shows that she believed that **where there's a will, there's a way**.

A proverb or adage is a short, well-known expression or saying that states an obvious truth or gives advice. *Where there's a will, there's a way* is a proverb. It means that if you are determined to do something, you will figure out a way to make it happen.

PRACTICE   *Read each sentence. Decide which proverb best expresses a truth about the situation described. Write the number of the sentence next to the proverb.*

1. Dad insisted we arrive at the store just as the doors opened to take advantage of the sale.

2. No matter how many things the child had, he always thought his friends had more than he did.

3. I continued to look for my notebook long after my friends had stopped searching.

4. It always amazes me how much my sister is like my mother.

__4__ The apple doesn't fall far from the tree.

__1__ The early bird gets the worm.

__3__ Leave no stone unturned.

__2__ The grass is always greener on the other side of the fence.

APPLY   *Discuss each proverb with a partner. Then write a sentence to tell what the proverb means.* Accept reasonable answers. Possible answers are given.

5. Don't bite off more than you can chew.

   Don't take on more than you can handle or accomplish.

6. Nothing ventured, nothing gained.

   If you don't try new things, you'll never know what you can accomplish.

7. Home is where the heart is.

   Home is any place where you find the people you love.

8. Haste makes waste.

   When you rush, you may not do as good a job as when you plan and take your time.

Introducing the Words

Read the following magazine article about a spectacular journey. Notice how the highlighted words are used. These are the words you will be learning in this unit.

Monarchs begin their long migration.

The Flight of the Monarch

(Magazine Article)

A differentiated version of this passage is available at **SadlierConnect.com**.

They are the only butterflies known to migrate, or travel, at a particular time of year. Some fly as far as 3,000 miles to reach their winter homes. They are also among the most **vivid** of all insects. Their bright orange, white, and black bodies can be seen flashing brilliantly in the sunlight. Their name is also appropriate because the **monarch** "rules" over the vast territory that it passes during its annual migration.

When the first cold winds of autumn blow, monarch butterflies in the United States begin their long migration south. They cannot **postpone** this flight, or their bodies might freeze. Monarchs in the eastern states migrate to warm **havens** in Mexico. For monarchs west of the Rocky Mountains, the winter destination is southern California.

Monarchs tend to migrate south in large groups, but weaker ones often **straggle** far behind. At night, the butterflies roost together in tall fir, cedar, and pine trees. Monarchs usually cover from fifty to one hundred miles a day, and it can take them up to two months to complete the trip.

The long flight south can be **treacherous**. Cold weather and early snowstorms often take a toll on the travelers. Monarchs must be **cautious** and try to avoid danger. Many birds feed on monarchs, too. Some butterflies run into **obstacles**, such as cars and trucks. Others just weaken and die from the strain of the difficult flight.

The **bluffs** and peaks of the Sierra Madre, a mountain range in Mexico, make an ideal haven for the monarchs. The fir forests there

When its wings are open, the monarch is $3\frac{1}{2}$ to 4 inches wide.

High in the mountains of Mexico, monarchs wait out the winter.

provide the right temperature and humidity. The butterflies gather in a few small areas in colonies that consist of millions and millions of individuals. A single tree might be home for more than ten thousand of the insects. The monarchs are not active at this time. Like bears, they sleep away the winter months.

To help preserve the monarchs, the Mexican government has taken steps to protect their winter home. For example, logging, or the cutting down of trees, is prohibited. Environmentalists despise this illegal activity, which shrinks the monarchs' habitat. Also, as the forest thins, the butterflies are more likely to get wet and freeze during winter rainstorms.

When the warm days of March arrive, the monarchs wake up and flutter down from their trees. After mating, the females lay their eggs. The eggs, which look like miniature pearls, hatch as caterpillars in about four days. After two weeks, each caterpillar transforms itself into a chrysalis, an egglike pod. Ten days later, the adult monarch emerges.

We must be clear when describing the migration of monarchs. The butterflies that flew south do not return north themselves. Only their offspring will begin the return flight in spring. Also, since most monarchs live only six weeks, it takes about three generations of monarchs to reach the northernmost states from Mexico. The females of each generation will deposit eggs along the route. Once grown, the new generation resumes the journey begun by its parents.

Fortunately, the generation of monarchs that is alive in early autumn lives much longer— about seven months. So those butterflies have time to make the long flight south. In this way, monarchs have populated large areas and lived on throughout the years.

Definitions

You were introduced to these words in the passage. Study the pronunciation, part of speech, definition, and example sentence for each word. Then read the synonyms and antonyms.

1. bluff
(bluf)
(BLUHF)

(adj.) direct and outspoken in a good-natured way

> *He seemed a hearty, bluff fellow.*

(n.) a steep, high cliff or bank; an attempt to fool someone

> *A scout stood on a bluff overlooking the valley.*

(v.) to deceive or trick; to try to fool others by putting on a confident front

> *The thieves tried to bluff their way past the security guard.*

SYNONYMS: (adj.) hearty; (n.) a ridge; a trick, hoax; (v.) to mislead, pretend, fake
ANTONYMS: (adj.) insincere, artful, sly

 Use each definition of **bluff** in a sentence.

2. cautious
(kô′ shəs)
(KAW-shuhss)

(adj.) avoiding unnecessary risks or mistakes

> *A cautious traveler prepares for emergencies.*

SYNONYMS: careful, watchful, wary, guarded
ANTONYMS: daring, reckless, wild

 Describe to your partner three situations in which it is important to be **cautious**.

3. consist
(kən sist′)
(kuhn-SIST)

(v.) (used with *of*) to be made up of

> *Many salad dressings consist of oil, vinegar, and spices.*

SYNONYMS: to contain, include, involve, comprise

4. despise
(di spīz′)
(di-SPIZE)

(v.) to look down on intensely or feel contempt for, dislike strongly

> *I despise bullies.*

SYNONYMS: to hate, scorn, detest, loathe
ANTONYMS: to love, admire, esteem, adore, praise

 What are three foods that you **despise**? Tell your partner why you despise them.

5. haven
(hā′ vən)
(HAY-vuhn)

(n.) a safe place

> *The captain sought a haven from the storm.*

SYNONYMS: a harbor, port, refuge, retreat, shelter, sanctuary
ANTONYMS: a trap, snare, ambush

6. miniature
(mi′ nē ə chŭr)
(MI-nee-uh-chur)

(n.) a very small copy, model, or painting

Her collection of miniatures is quite valuable.

(adj.) on a very small scale

A miniature railroad was on display in the toy department of the store.

SYNONYMS: (adj.) little, tiny, minute; ANTONYMS: (adj.) huge, giant

Draw a **miniature** version of the classroom. Share it with your partner.

7. monarch
(mä′ nərk)
(MAH-nuhrk)

(n.) a person who rules over a kingdom or empire

Queen Victoria was Great Britain's monarch from 1837 to 1901.

SYNONYMS: a ruler, king, queen, emperor, empress, czar
ANTONYMS: a subject, follower, commoner

8. obstacle
(äb′ sti kəl)
(OB-sti-kuhl)

(n.) something that gets in the way

Shyness need not be an obstacle to success.

SYNONYMS: a hurdle, barrier, snag, hindrance
ANTONYMS: an aid, help, support, advantage

9. postpone
(pōst pōn′)
(pohst-PONE)

(v.) to put off until later

Coach decided to postpone the practice.

SYNONYMS: to delay, suspend, shelve, defer; ANTONYMS: to advance, move up

10. straggle
(stra′ gəl)
(STRA-guhl)

(v.) to stray off or trail behind; to spread out in a scattered fashion

Students who straggle from the group may get lost.

SYNONYMS: to ramble, drift, wander, roam, rove, detour

11. treacherous
(tre′ chə rəs)
(TRE-chuh-ruhss)

(adj.) likely to betray; seemingly safe but actually dangerous

That hill can be a treacherous climb in winter.

SYNONYMS: disloyal, untrustworthy, unreliable; chancy, deceptive, tricky, hazardous
ANTONYMS: faithful, trustworthy; safe, harmless

12. vivid
(vi′ vəd)
(VI-vuhd)

(adj.) bright and sharp, giving a clear picture; full of life

She gave a vivid description of her trip.

SYNONYMS: lively, intense, brilliant, dazzling, spirited, clear
ANTONYMS: lifeless, dull, drab, hazy, foggy

Tell your partner about a **vivid** memory from your childhood.

 As time allows, have partners complete graphic organizers for select words, available at **SadlierConnect.com**.

Synonyms

*Choose the word that is most nearly the **same** in meaning as the word or phrase in **boldface**. Then write your choice on the line provided.*

1. **fake** your way past the guard
   a. consist   b. despise   c. postpone   d. bluff   **bluff**

2. **wander** from the route
   a. bluff   b. straggle   c. postpone   d. despise   **straggle**

3. a peaceful **refuge** in the war-torn city
   a. haven   b. miniature   c. monarch   d. bluff   **haven**

4. a mix that **contained** flour, sugar, and baking powder
   a. bluffed   b. consisted of   c. despised   d. postponed   **consisted of**

5. a **watchful** driver
   a. miniature   b. treacherous   c. cautious   d. vivid   **cautious**

6. a noble, wise, and generous **ruler**
   a. monarch   b. haven   c. obstacle   d. miniature   **monarch**

Antonyms

*Choose the word that is most nearly **opposite** in meaning to the word or phrase in **boldface**. Then write your choice on the line provided.*

1. **adore** that kind of music
   a. consist   b. bluff   c. despise   d. straggle   **despise**

2. formed a **hazy** image
   a. treacherous   b. vivid   c. cautious   d. miniature   **vivid**

3. to **move up** the ceremony one month
   a. postpone   b. bluff   c. despise   d. straggle   **postpone**

4. a **huge** model of the castle
   a. cautious   b. treacherous   c. bluff   d. miniature   **miniature**

5. a **faithful** servant
   a. treacherous   b. cautious   c. miniature   d. vivid   **treacherous**

6. no **advantage** to winning the election
   a. haven   b. obstacle   c. miniature   d. monarch   **obstacle**

Completing the Sentence

Choose the word from the box that best completes each item. Then write the word on the line provided. (You may have to change the word's ending.)

bluff	cautious	consist
despise	haven	miniature
monarch	obstacle	postpone
straggle	treacherous	vivid

Americans Fight for Their Independence

■ King George III was the English **monarch** when American colonists began to grow impatient with English rule.

■ Even colonists who were eager for independence were **cautious** at first because they did not want a war.

■ But not all colonists **despised** British rule; nearly one-third of them believed they should stay loyal to the King.

■ The first fight took place between 700 British soldiers and a small army that **consisted** of 70 American volunteers called Minutemen.

■ In 1780, the American General Benedict Arnold took part in a **treacherous** plot that nearly cost the lives of three thousand American soldiers.

■ After overcoming many **obstacles**, the Americans defeated the British.

A View from High Above

■ As we looked down from the rocky **bluff**, we could see a small herd of wild ponies trotting in a field far below us.

■ We were so high above them that they looked like **miniature** horses.

■ One gray mare **straggled** behind the rest of the herd to protect her young foal.

A Getaway for Presidents

■ Since 1942, American presidents have used a quiet cabin retreat in Maryland as a **haven** from the summer heat of Washington, D.C.

■ My Uncle David has **vivid** memories of the occasion when President Eisenhower renamed the retreat Camp David to honor the President's grandson.

■ A crisis might cause the President to **postpone** a planned visit to Camp David until the situation is under control.

*Circle the letter next to the word or phrase that best completes the sentence or answers the question. Pay special attention to the word in **boldface**.*

1. A **cautious** person is one who
a. enjoys parties.
(b.) does not take risks.
c. is very curious.
d. eats a lot.

2. If you **despise** broccoli, you
(a.) won't ever want to eat it.
b. will put it on pizza.
c. prefer to eat it raw.
d. like it every once in a while.

3. Which of these is a **haven**?
a. a small meadow
b. a mountain lake
c. a thick forest
(d.) a safe place

4. Another name for a **monarch** is
a. moth.
(b.) ruler.
c. servant.
d. parent.

Words with Latin Roots

The unit word ***miniature***, meaning "a very small copy" or "on a very small scale," comes from the Latin root ***min***, which means "small, less, or least." The root is used in the following words:

- minor (adj.): lesser in size (*of small importance*)
- minority (n.): less than half (*a smaller number or part*)
- minimum (n.): the smallest possible number or amount for a given purpose (*a small part of the whole*)
- minimize (v.): to make as small as possible (*to make smallest*)
- diminish (v.): to decrease (*to make smaller*)
- diminutive (adj.): tiny (*very small*)

Choose two of the words from the list. Write a sentence for each word to show you understand its meaning.

1. Accept answers that show an understanding of the vocabulary.

2.

Read the passage. Then answer each question.

Butterfly Gardens

1   Creating a butterfly garden is an interesting and fun project. Almost any garden of this kind, however **miniature**, is pleasant to look at, while providing a **haven** for some of the planet's most beautiful insects. Plant selection and site selection are important to planning a butterfly garden.

2   Because butterflies have a unique life cycle, a butterfly garden needs to **consist** of two basic groups of plants. One is leafy food plants for caterpillars, and the other is nectar plants for adult butterflies. Don't try to **bluff** your way through the plant selection process. Visit local butterfly gardens or consult butterfly field guides. Find out as much as you can about the plants on which the butterflies in your area depend. If the butterflies find everything they need, they will be unlikely to **straggle** from your garden.

3   Planning the garden site also requires care. Trees and shrubs provide shelter from wind, but too much shade will create an **obstacle** to sunlight. Bright flowering plants in **vivid** colors need plenty of sunshine, after all, and so do butterflies.

1. What is the meaning of the word **miniature** as it is used in paragraph 1?
- (a) small
- (b) colorful
- (c) huge
- (d) personal

2. What does the word **bluff** mean as it is used in paragraph 2?
- (a) fake
- (b) hearty
- (c) ridge
- (d) hoax

3. The Latin word *vivere* means "to live." The word **vivid** in paragraph 3 means
- (a) drab
- (b) hazy
- (c) fortunate
- (d) lively

4. Pick the word that best defines **obstacle** as it is used in paragraph 3.
- (a) support
- (b) barrier
- (c) advantage
- (d) supply

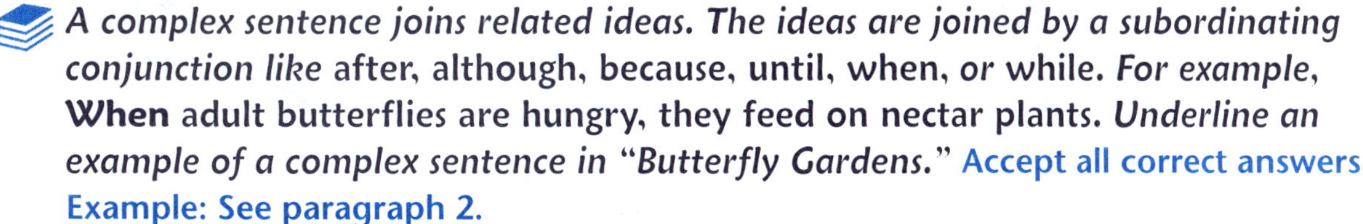

A complex sentence joins related ideas. The ideas are joined by a subordinating conjunction like after, although, because, until, when, *or* while. *For example,* **When** *adult butterflies are hungry, they feed on nectar plants. Underline an example of a complex sentence in "Butterfly Gardens."* Accept all correct answers. Example: See paragraph 2.

Write Your Own

With a partner, draw a sketch of a butterfly garden and write 3–5 sentences describing your garden. Include three vocabulary words from this unit in your description. Then exchange drawings and sentences with another pair. Have them replace the vocabulary words you used with synonyms.

For more practice with complex sentences, see Grammar Workshop, Level Blue, Lesson 8.

Vocabulary for Comprehension

*Read this passage in which some of the words you have studied in Units 1–3 appear in **boldface**. Then answer the questions.*

The Tallest Sailor in the World

1   Long ago, a thunderous wave crashed on the shores of Cape Cod. Moments later, a loud cry split the air. The villagers promptly **converted** their worry into action. They rushed to the **bluff** overlooking the beach. They were shocked to find that the noise had come from a baby. The child was no **miniature**, however. He was 6 feet tall! The locals put the giant baby in a cart and hauled him into town. They named him Alfred Bulltop Stormalong, but called him Stormy.

2   Stormy grew to love the sea. He loved swimming in the deep, sometimes even **treacherous**, water, and he rode sea monsters for fun. Fearless, he soon became a **veteran** sailor; once, he even turned an old house upside down and tried to sail away in it.

3   Stormy grew to be 36 feet tall, and Cape Cod became too small for him. He left Cape Cod and traveled to Boston. There he became the captain of a mighty, large ship called the *Courser*. Stormy was no ordinary captain, though: he ate stew from a rowboat and he slept in the mainsail.

4   In one adventure, Stormy was sailing his ship through the English Channel when he discovered that the waterway was barely wider than the ship. Expecting a tight fit and wanting to avoid a costly and careless **blunder**, Stormy ordered the crew to soap the sides of the ship. Although it slipped through, the huge vessel scraped the Dover cliffs, leaving behind a thick layer of soap. These cliffs have been pure white ever since. While some may say Stormy is just a **myth**, folks at Dover say the Channel is still foamy from the soap.

1. Which statement best describes a theme of this passage?
   - ⓐ Stormy was just like the average person.
   - **ⓑ Stormy was a very unusual person.**
   - ⓒ No one knows why the cliffs at Dover are white.
   - ⓓ Commanding a ship can be a difficult task.

2. The Latin word *convertere* means "to turn around." The word **converted** in paragraph 1 means
   - ⓐ maintained
   - ⓑ conserved
   - ⓒ rejected
   - **ⓓ transformed**

3. Which word has the opposite meaning of **miniature** in paragraph 1?
   - **ⓐ gigantic**
   - ⓑ evident
   - ⓒ vigorous
   - ⓓ humble

4. What does the use of the word **treacherous** in paragraph 2 suggest?
   - ⓐ excitement
   - ⓑ calm
   - **ⓒ danger**
   - ⓓ beauty

5. What does the word **veteran** mean as it is used in paragraph 2?
   - **ⓐ experienced**
   - ⓑ novice
   - ⓒ amateur
   - ⓓ lucky

6. What does the author mean by the word **blunder** in paragraph 4?
   - ⓐ achievement
   - **ⓑ mistake**
   - ⓒ certain order
   - ⓓ decision

7. Which phrase from the passage best shows the idea of **blunder**?
   - **ⓐ "costly and careless"**
   - ⓑ "soap the sides"
   - ⓒ "the Dover cliffs"
   - ⓓ "a thick layer"

8. What is the meaning of the word **myth** as it is used in paragraph 4?
   - ⓐ fact
   - ⓑ rumor
   - **ⓒ tale**
   - ⓓ gossip

Write Your Own

Think about other American myths and legends that you know. On a separate sheet of paper, write to retell a story about another favorite character from a myth or legend. Use at least three vocabulary words from Units 1–3.

Introducing the Words

Read the following diary entries about a girl's journey west during the time of the California Gold Rush. Notice how the highlighted words are used. These are the words you will be learning in this unit.

Wagon Train Diary

(Diary Entries)

A differentiated version of this passage is available at **SadlierConnect.com**.

May 1, 1849 Today, we said good-bye and started off to the land of gold. There are thirty wagons in our group and sixty people. We began with much laughter, but a **mishap** quickly spoiled the mood. While crossing the Missouri River, two wagons were swept away by the water, and the families inside barely escaped.

May 15 The oxen plod on, slowly and steadily. How I wish they moved at a more **aggressive** pace! When it rains, we barely cover two miles in a day. Will we ever reach California? Everyone who **emigrates** wonders this, for the hours drag slowly. The bumping wagon bruises my bones, so usually I walk. My feet are sore, but the prairie flowers are beautiful, and I would not see them so well from the wagon.

May 18 Just before noon, the sky looked **hazy**. I thought it must be full of smoke, but then we heard the buzzing and knew it was a swarm of grasshoppers in flight. There were more of them than anyone could imagine. The giant cloud of grasshoppers **overwhelmed** us,

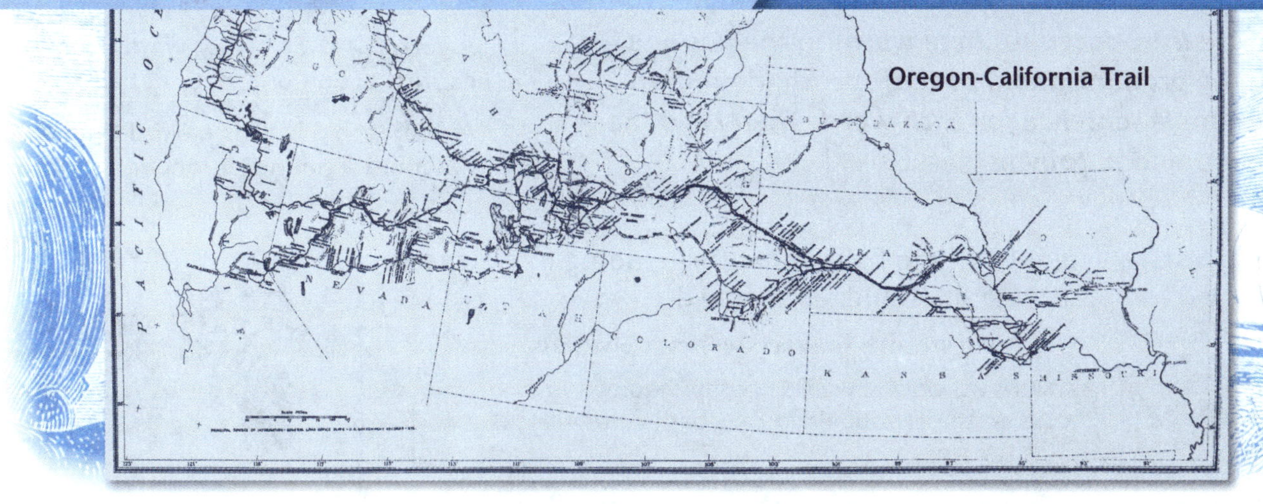

turning day to night. We did all we could to keep the pests off our faces until, mercifully, they moved on.

June 3   Hurrah! Today, we reached the Platte River. After weeks of dusty travel, how luxurious to sit in the water. The taste of fish is indeed a welcome change after salted pork. If only we could linger here, but we dare not. The wide span of a desert and the tall masses of a mountain range await us.

June 19   At Independence Rock, so many emigrants have cut their names into the granite that I could barely find a spot for my own.

Now my name will forever be associated with this landmark on the trail leading west.

July 6   We took a cutoff and got lost. At last, we are heading the right way, but the oxen need water. Once we thought we saw a stream, but it was a mirage—a trick of sunlight that deceived us.

August 6   It seemed like there would be no end to the wind and dust. Seven of our wagons turned back. Then there was a sight to behold at Soda Springs. Hot water puffed and spurted high into the air, leaving a trail of rainbows. I wouldn't have traded that beauty for the glamour of any big city.

August 20   Grass is scarce, and the oxen groan. We had to lighten our load, and Father dumped our stove and pots and books. Necessity has made us flexible, and we cannot be too attached to our belongings. The long trail is littered with lovely things.

September 8   Today, we traveled fourteen miles and had to cross the Truckee River twelve times.

September 15   Never did we believe that we'd make it up the rocky trail to the top of the Sierra Nevada, a mountain range in California, but here we are, and the majestic pines and peaks frame our first grand glimpse of California!

You were introduced to these words in the passage. Study the pronunciation, part of speech, definition, and example sentence for each word. Then read the synonyms and antonyms.

1. aggressive
(ə gre′ siv)
(uh-GRE-siv)

(adj.) quick to fight or quarrel, tending to violence; bold and forceful, determined

An aggressive salesperson never gives up.

SYNONYMS: violent, warlike; pushy, vigorous
ANTONYMS: peaceful, timid; shy, bashful, retiring

2. associate
(v., ə sō′ shē āt)
(uh-SOH-shee-ate)
(n., adj., ə sō′ shē ət)
(uh-SOH-shee-uht)

(v.) to join or be together as partners, allies, or friends; to link in one's mind, connect

I will always associate peaches with summer.

(n.) a partner, friend

The businessman introduced his associate.

(adj.) having less than full rank

She was hired as an associate professor in the science department.

SYNONYMS: (v.) to unite, mingle, combine, mix, relate; (n.) a companion, teammate, coworker; (adj.) assistant
ANTONYMS: (v.) to separate, distance, divorce; (n.) an enemy, foe, rival, stranger

 Use each definition of **associate** in a sentence.

3. deceive
(di sēv′)
(di-SEEV)

(v.) to trick or lead a person into believing something that is not true

It is wrong to deceive the customer with false advertising.

SYNONYMS: to fool, swindle, mislead, double-cross, cheat

4. emigrate
(e′ mə grāt)
(E-muh-grate)

(v.) to leave one's home country or area to live in another

Henri hopes to emigrate from Haiti to the United States.

SYNONYMS: to relocate, resettle, move, migrate

 Talk to your partner about reasons people might **emigrate** to another country.

5. flexible
(flek′ sə bəl)
(FLEK-suh-buhl)

(adj.) able to bend without breaking; able to change or to take in new ideas

I brought in a box of flexible straws.

SYNONYMS: bendable, limber, elastic, springy; adaptable, adjustable
ANTONYMS: stiff, rigid, unbendable; inflexible

 As time allows, have partners complete graphic organizers for select words, available at **SadlierConnect.com**.

6. glamour
(gla′ mər)
(GLA-mur)

(n.) mysterious charm, beauty, or attractiveness

The movie captures the glamour of Paris.

SYNONYMS: style, sparkle, magic, enchantment, romance, fascination

7. hazy
(hā′ zē)
(HAY-zee)

(adj.) unclear, misty; not readily seen or understandable

Another hot and hazy day is forecast.

SYNONYMS: cloudy, smoggy, foggy, blurry, dim; vague
ANTONYMS: bright, clear; precise

8. linger
(liŋ′ gər)
(LING-gur)

(v.) to stay longer than expected, be slow in leaving; to go slowly or take one's time

We like to linger over breakfast on Saturdays.

SYNONYMS: to delay, stall, remain, stay, lag, persist; to dawdle
ANTONYMS: to hurry, rush, charge, hasten

9. luxurious
(ləg zhùr′ ē əs)
(luhk-SHUR-ee-uhss)

(adj.) providing ease and comfort far beyond what is ordinary or necessary

They took a luxurious vacation.

SYNONYMS: rich, elegant, pleasurable, lavish, extravagant, fancy
ANTONYMS: poor, plain, simple, modest

 **Describe** to your partner one **luxurious** item you wish you could buy.

10. mishap
(mis′ hap)
(MISS-hap)

(n.) an unfortunate but minor accident

The waiters chuckled over the mishap.

SYNONYMS: a misfortune, mistake, blunder, slipup

11. overwhelm
(ō vər welm′)
(oh-vur-WELM)

(v.) to overcome by superior force, crush; to affect so deeply as to make helpless

Fresh troops threatened to overwhelm the weakened defenders.

SYNONYMS: to overpower, destroy, crush; to stun, shock, stagger, astound

12. span
(span)
(SPAN)

(n.) the full reach or length, especially between two points in space or time

The span of most insects' lives is very brief.

(v.) to stretch or reach across

A new bridge will be built to span the Golden Gate, which is the opening of San Francisco Bay.

SYNONYMS: (n.) extent, distance, length, scope, period;
(v.) to bridge, cross, last

 **Measure** the **span** of your hand. **Compare** your measurements to your partner's.

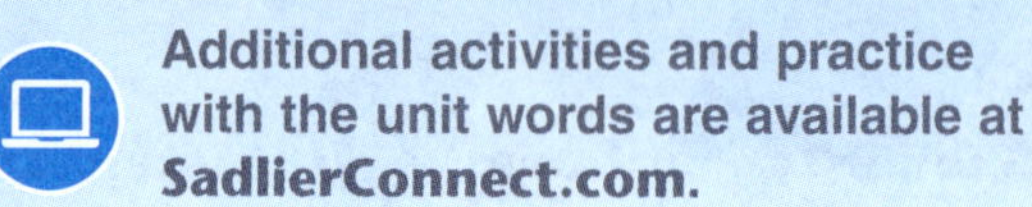

Synonyms

*Choose the word that is most nearly the **same** in meaning as the word or phrase in **boldface**. Then write your choice on the line provided.*

1. the **magic** of Hollywood
   a. mishap   b. span   c. glamour   d. associate   *glamour*

2. **crush** our opponents
   a. deceive   b. emigrate   c. linger   d. overwhelm   *overwhelm*

3. told us about the **slipup**
   a. glamour   b. span   c. mishap   d. associate   *mishap*

4. **move** from Egypt to Italy
   a. overwhelm   b. linger   c. deceive   d. emigrate   *emigrate*

5. **mislead** the enemy
   a. associate   b. deceive   c. overwhelm   d. emigrate   *deceive*

6. over the **period** of a year
   a. associate   b. mishap   c. span   d. glamour   *span*

Antonyms

*Choose the word that is most nearly **opposite** in meaning to the word or phrase in **boldface**. Then write your choice on the line provided.*

1. **timid** base runners
   a. associate   b. aggressive   c. luxurious   d. hazy   *aggressive*

2. introduced her **rival**
   a. glamour   b. associate   c. span   d. mishap   *associate*

3. **hurry** over our good-byes
   a. span   b. emigrate   c. overwhelm   d. linger   *linger*

4. a **rigid** point of view
   a. flexible   b. aggressive   c. hazy   d. luxurious   *flexible*

5. a **simple** meal with friends
   a. aggressive   b. flexible   c. luxurious   d. hazy   *luxurious*

6. a **clear** sky
   a. flexible   b. luxurious   c. aggressive   d. hazy   *hazy*

Completing the Sentence

Choose the word from the box that best completes each item. Then write the word on the line provided. (You may have to change the word's ending.)

A New Life in America

■ Poor conditions in their homeland have driven many Mexicans to __________**emigrate**__________ to the United States. Many have settled in the Southwest, but others have traveled to big cities in the Midwest and Northeast in search of work.

■ Some dishonest agents __________**deceive**__________ travelers by taking their money in exchange for legal documents that they never provide.

■ Over the __________**span**__________ of the past fifty years, more immigrants have come to the United States from Mexico than from any other country.

■ Many immigrants have only a(n) __________**hazy**__________ notion of what life will be like in the new country they have heard so much about.

■ Mix-ups over language or local customs often lead to __________**mishaps**__________ and misunderstandings.

■ Despite facing some __________**overwhelming**__________ problems, most immigrants manage to build better lives for themselves and their families.

A Legal Brief

■ It is a lawyer's duty to act in a(n) __________**aggressive**__________ fashion in order to protect the interests of his or her clients. Trial lawyers especially cannot afford to be timid or shy.

■ Most lawyers have to keep __________**flexible**__________ hours to serve their clients well.

■ From the newest __________**associate**__________ to senior partners, lawyers must research past cases to find ways to support their arguments.

■ Media attention lends some legal cases more __________**glamour**__________ than they really deserve. Some especially newsworthy trials are now televised from start to finish.

■ The impact of such cases may __________**linger**__________ in the public mind long after all the lawyers, the judge, and the jurors have left the courtroom.

■ Lawyers on television and in movies are often seen to drive __________**luxurious**__________ cars and wear expensive clothes. In fact, most real-life lawyers work long, hard hours and rarely enjoy the spotlight of celebrity.

*Circle the letter next to the word or phrase that best completes the sentence or answers the question. Pay special attention to the word in **boldface**.*

1. You might **linger** if you are
   a. in a hurry.
   b. late for an appointment.
   c. having a great time.
   d. bored to tears.

2. **Aggressive** ballplayers would
   a. lose interest in the game.
   b. play as hard as they can.
   c. let their opponents win.
   d. ask to sit out the game.

3. If a movie **overwhelms** you, you
   a. might feel as if you will cry.
   b. might ask for a refund.
   c. might refuse to applaud.
   d. might get very hungry.

4. The "**span** of a lifetime" means
   a. from Monday to Friday.
   b. from birth to death.
   c. from kindergarten to college.
   d. from breakfast to dinner.

Words with Latin Roots

The unit word *associate* comes from the Latin prefix *ad-*, meaning "to," and the Latin root *soc*, which means "friend, companion, or ally." Together, the word parts mean "to join together with others as friends or companions." The root *soc* is used in the following words:

- social (adj.): living or interacting together with others (*acting as allies or friends with others*)
- sociable (adj.): enjoying other people's company (*drawn to others as friends*)
- society (n.): group of people living as a community (*group of companions or allies*)
- socialize (v.): to interact with other people (*to enjoy others as friends*)
- socialite (n.): a person prominent in fashionable circles (*someone friendly with wealthy or famous people*)

Choose two of the words from the list. Write a sentence for each word to show you understand its meaning.

1. Accept answers that show an understanding of the vocabulary.

2. ____

Read the passage. Then answer each question.

Sutter's Mill, 1848

1   In 1841, John Sutter built a settlement and a fort to protect it on a **span** of land that is known today as Sacramento, California. Sutter's settlement provided **luxurious** hospitality to people arriving in the harsh, rough landscape.

2   Then, in 1848, James W. Marshall, a carpenter employed by Sutter, found gold flakes in a stream bed while building a water-powered sawmill. Sutter and Marshall agreed to become partners and tried to keep their discovery a secret. However, word of the gold flakes spread quickly. Gold prospectors traveled from all parts of the world to California. They were known as the "forty-niners" since most came to California in 1849.

3   Sutter's luck ran out with the arrival of the forty-niners. These **aggressive** fortune seekers **overwhelmed** Sutter's Fort. By 1852, Sutter and his **associates** found themselves penniless. Most of their goods had been stolen or destroyed.

4   The rush for gold also led to **hazy** futures for many of the forty-niners. Searching for gold was hard work, and living conditions were primitive. Prospectors had to be tough, **flexible**, and lucky to adapt and strike it rich on the rugged frontier.

1. What is meaning of the word **luxurious** as it is used in paragraph 1?
(a) cheap   (b) simple   (c) fancy   (d) famous

2. What does the word **overwhelmed** mean as it is used in paragraph 3?
(a) prevented   (b) overpowered   (c) encircled   (d) enriched

3. The Latin word *associāre* means "to work with." The word **associates** in paragraph 3 means
(a) partners   (b) mingles   (c) enemies   (d) relates

4. Pick the word that best defines **flexible** as it is used in paragraph 4.
(a) strong   (b) bendable   (c) adaptable   (d) experienced

*A common noun names a person, place, or thing. A proper noun names a specific person, place, or thing. For example, the word **gold** is a common noun, and **Sacramento** is a proper noun. Underline a common noun and a proper noun in "Sutter's Mill, 1848."*
Accept all correct answers. Example: See paragraph 1.

Write Your Own

Imagine you and your partner are prospectors. Together, you have just arrived in California in 1849 from the eastern United States. Write a 3–5 sentence story that uses at least three vocabulary words from the unit about your experiences searching for gold. Then share your story with another pair.

For more practice with common and proper nouns, see Grammar Workshop, Level Blue, Lesson 10.

Word Study Analogies

An **analogy** is a statement that shows how two pairs of words are related. Here is an analogy with the word *flexible* (page 38): *wire* is to *flexible* as *cotton* is to *soft*.

In this analogy, the first word in each pair names an object, and the second word gives a description of the object. *Wire* can be described as *flexible*, and *cotton* can be described as *soft*.

The chart at the right shows other types of relationships that analogies can have.

Object/ Description	*wire* is to *flexible* as *cotton* is to *soft*
Synonyms	*vivid* is to *bright* as *dull* is to *boring*
Antonyms	*left* is to *right* as *even* is to *odd*
Object/Class	*rose* is to *flower* as *pine* is to *tree*
Object/Function	*fork* is to *eat* as *pencil* is to *write*

PRACTICE *Match the word pairs to form a complete analogy. Write the number of the first pair next to the pair with the* **same** *relationship.*

1. *keyboard* is to *type* as

2. *lemon* is to *sour* as

3. *linger* is to *rush* as

4. *robin* is to *bird* as

___4___ *trout* is to *fish*

___3___ *luxurious* is to *plain*

___1___ *scissors* is to *cut*

___2___ *honey* is to *sweet*

APPLY *Complete each analogy. Explain the relationship on the lines provided.*
Accept reasonable answers. Possible answers are given.

5. *strawberry* is to *fruit* as *carrot* is to ____vegetable____

A strawberry is a type of fruit, and a carrot is a type of vegetable.

6. *ruler* is to *measure* as *microscope* is to ____magnify____

A ruler is used to measure, and a microscope is used to magnify.

7. *cheetah* is to *fast* as *snail* is to ____slow____

A cheetah can be described as fast, and a snail can be described as slow.

8. *fearless* is to *timid* as *hazy* is to ____clear____

The pairs of words are antonyms.

9. *justify* is to *defend* as *deceive* is to ____fool____

The pairs of words are synonyms.

Create an analogy using a word from Units 1–4. Have a partner complete the analogy. Talk about the relationship between the words.

Shades of Meaning Words That Describe Behavior

In the passage "Wagon Train Diary" on pages 36–37, you read: *How I wish they moved at a more **aggressive** pace!* Here, *aggressive* describes the way the narrator would like the oxen to move. She wishes that they would move with more energy.

Aggressive can also be used to describe behavior, the way in which a person or animal acts. Look at the words in the chart. Each describes a particular behavior.

aggressive	A person who is **aggressive** is quick to attack or start a fight.
arrogant	A person who is **arrogant** feels very proud, believing that others are much less important.
assertive	A person who is **assertive** stands up for himself or herself and tells others what he or she thinks or wants.
impulsive	A person who is **impulsive** acts without thinking carefully first.

PRACTICE *Write the word from the chart that best describes each behavior.*

1. She jumped right into the pool without taking her shoes off. ___impulsive___

2. The dog growled and bared its teeth when we walked by. ___aggressive___

3. He always thinks his ideas are the best in the class. ___arrogant___

4. She won the student council election because she is not afraid to speak her mind. ___assertive___

5. The athlete defended his request for practice time on the basketball court. ___assertive___

6. At the auction, the woman bid on an item she didn't even want. ___impulsive___

7. Because he believed he had the best plan, the candidate thought everyone would vote for him. ___arrogant___

APPLY *Give an example of when you have shown or seen each of the behaviors below.* Accept answers that students can justify.

8. aggressive ____

9. arrogant ____

10. assertive ____

11. impulsive ____

Introducing the Words

Read the following ancient myth about what happens after a poor couple meets a pair of travelers. Notice how the highlighted words are used. These are the words you will be learning in this unit.

Baucis and Philemon

(Ancient Myth)

A differentiated version of this passage is available at **SadlierConnect.com**.

In his palace on Mount Olympus, Jupiter, the supreme Roman god, was furious. "People are so corrupt!" he told his grandson Mercury. "They lie, they cheat, they steal—it's a disgrace."

"Is it really that bad?" asked Mercury.

"Worse," replied Jupiter. "People don't even show hospitality to strangers anymore." This last blemish on the character of humans bothered Jupiter the most. Welcoming guests kindly was important to the king of the gods. "I have to teach people a lesson!" the great god continued.

"Before you unjustly accuse people and persecute them, let's travel to Earth and see for ourselves," suggested Mercury. "Maybe there are more good people than you think."

Using Mercury's winged sandals, the two gods transported themselves to the city of Phrygia. There, they disguised themselves in ragged cloaks so that no one would know they were gods. Looking at them, you would conclude that they were poor travelers.

From house to house, the two nomads wandered, asking for water and bread. Sad to say, the situation was as bad as Jupiter had predicted. No one welcomed the travelers.

"On your way!" one farmer warned, threatening to turn his dogs loose on them.

"Get out of here!" a woman shouted, waving a blunt ax.

So it went at every house in the city until at last the travelers came to Baucis and Philemon. Their one-room hut was falling down, for Baucis and Philemon were poor. They were also old, in their eighties, and had been married sixty years.

"Come in, come in!" Philemon welcomed the strangers. "You have walked a long way, for I can see the dust and the fatigue on your faces."

"Will you stay for dinner?" Philemon's wife Baucis asked. "It isn't much—fruit, bread and olives—but you're welcome to share our meal with us."

The gods sat down at the rough wooden table, and Baucis lit candles to give the meal a festive atmosphere. As Philemon served the food, Baucis again apologized for the meal. "We live very simply," she said. "The important thing is that we love each other."

Philemon nodded, but he had just detected something very strange. He brought his guests more food and drink every time their plates were empty, yet the serving pot and jug remained full. Only a god was capable of such a miracle!

Reading Philemon's mind, Jupiter and Mercury threw off their cloaks and shone in all their glory. "In this entire city," Jupiter said, "only this house has shown us hospitality."

As he spoke, another wonder occurred. The wooden hut fell away and in its place stood a shining marble house. "Tell me what you wish for most," said Jupiter, "and I will give it to you."

"Let this building be your temple, and let us be the priests here," Philemon began.

"And let us die together, so neither ever has to live without the other," Baucis concluded.

And so it was. Baucis and Philemon served in the temple for many years, and when they were about to die, Jupiter turned them into trees—an oak and a linden. Remarkably, both trees grew from the same trunk. Together, their long branches shaded the temple for generations.

Definitions

You were introduced to these words in the passage. Study the pronunciation, part of speech, definition, and example sentence for each word. Then read the synonyms and antonyms.

1. blemish
(ble′ mish)
(BLE-mish)

(n.) a mark or stain that damages the appearance of something; a weakness or flaw

> *The carpenter noticed a blemish in the finish of the cabinet.*

SYNONYMS: a scar, spot, smudge; a defect, weak spot

2. blunt
(blunt)
(BLUHNT)

(adj.) having a dull point or edge, not sharp; honest but insensitive in manner

> *My uncle gave me some blunt advice.*

(v.) to make less sharp

> *Misuse will blunt a knife blade.*

SYNONYMS: (adj.) dull; outspoken, frank, direct
ANTONYMS: (adj.) sharp, keen; tactful, diplomatic; (v.) to sharpen

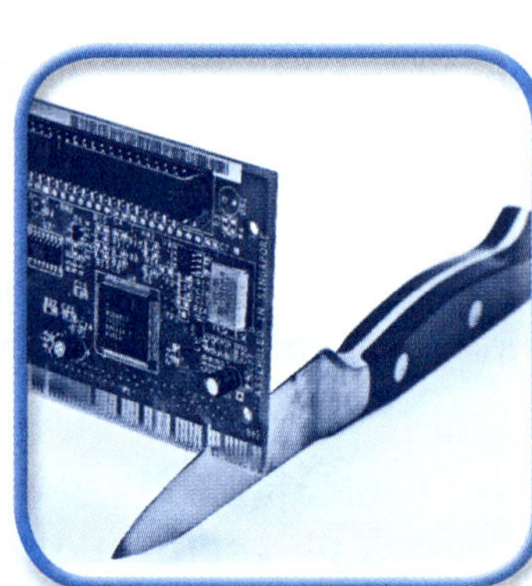

 Use each definition of **blunt** in a sentence.

3. capable
(kā′ pə bəl)
(KAY-puh-buhl)

(adj.) able and prepared to do something; fit or skilled

> *A capable teacher should be rewarded.*

SYNONYM: qualified
ANTONYMS: unqualified, incapable, unfit

 Who are two people in your life who are **capable** of making you laugh?

4. conclude
(kən klüd′)
(kuhn-KLOOD)

(v.) to finish; to bring something to an end; to decide after careful thought

> *After electing a new secretary, the committee voted to conclude the meeting.*

SYNONYMS: to close, complete, stop; to reason, judge
ANTONYMS: to open, begin, start, commence

5. detect
(di tekt′)
(di-TEKT)

(v.) to find or discover something, notice

> *A test may detect chemicals in the water supply.*

SYNONYMS: to observe, spot
ANTONYMS: to miss, overlook

As time allows, have partners complete graphic organizers for select words, available at **SadlierConnect.com**.

6. fatigue
(fə tēg')
(fuh-TEEG)

(n.) weariness or exhaustion from work or lack of sleep

By the end of the day, I felt overcome with fatigue.

(v.) to make very tired

The riders were warned not to fatigue the horses.

SYNONYMS: (n.) tiredness, sleepiness, weakness; (v.) to tire
ANTONYMS: (n.) liveliness, energy; (v.) to energize, perk up

💬 **Tell your partner two activities that make you feel fatigue.**

7. festive
(fes' tiv)
(FESS-tiv)

(adj.) having to do with a feast or celebration

Decorations will help lend a festive atmosphere.

SYNONYMS: happy, merry, playful; ANTONYMS: sad, gloomy, somber

💬 **What are the most festive occasions in your house?**

8. hospitality
(häs pə ta' lə tē)
(hoss-puh-TA-
luh-tee)

(n.) a friendly welcome and treatment of guests

The innkeepers were famous for their hospitality.

SYNONYMS: friendliness, generosity, warmth; ANTONYMS: unfriendliness, hostility

9. nomad
(nō' mad)
(NOH-mad)

(n.) a member of a people who move from place to place; a person who roams aimlessly

The adventurer lived the life of a nomad.

SYNONYMS: a wanderer, roamer, rover

10. persecute
(pûr' si kyüt)
(PUR-si-kyoot)

(v.) to treat unjustly or cause to suffer

The dictator may try to persecute the minority group.

SYNONYMS: to torment, hurt, annoy
ANTONYMS: to reward, favor, comfort, help, protect

11. supreme
(sə prēm')
(suh-PREEM)

(adj.) highest in power, rank, authority, quality, or degree

He acted as if giving up his seat were the supreme sacrifice.

SYNONYMS: first, greatest, dominant, outstanding
ANTONYMS: low, lowly, worst

12. transport
(v., trans pôrt')
(transs-PORT)
(n., trans' pôrt)
(TRANSS-port)

(v.) to move or carry from one place to another

A mover was hired to transport the furniture.

(n.) a vehicle used to move things from place to place; the act or process of moving something from one place to another

The ocean liner was used as a troop transport during the war.

SYNONYMS: (v.) to haul, cart, send, convey

💬 **Tell your partner how you are transported to school each day.**

Synonyms

*Choose the word that is most nearly the **same** in meaning
as the word or phrase in **boldface**. Then write your choice
on the line provided.*

1. her **outstanding** accomplishment
a. blunt   b. festive   c. supreme   d. capable   _supreme_

2. tried to conceal the **flaw**
a. blemish   b. nomad   c. fatigue   d. hospitality   _blemish_

3. **carry** the grain to distant markets
a. conclude   b. detect   c. blunt   d. transport   _transport_

4. a **skilled** performer, but not a star
a. supreme   b. capable   c. blunt   d. festive   _capable_

5. followed the trail of **wanderers**
a. transports   b. blemishes   c. nomads   d. hospitalities   _nomads_

6. a **happy** atmosphere
a. festive   b. capable   c. supreme   d. blunt   _festive_

Antonyms

*Choose the word that is most nearly **opposite** in meaning
to the word or phrase in **boldface**. Then write your choice
on the line provided.*

1. **overlook** the danger
a. detect   b. conclude   c. persecute   d. transport   _detect_

2. spoke in a **diplomatic** manner
a. supreme   b. festive   c. blunt   d. capable   _blunt_

3. **begin** the homework project
a. detect   b. persecute   c. transport   d. conclude   _conclude_

4. **protected** the strangers
a. blunted   b. persecuted   c. concluded   d. detected   _persecuted_

5. surprised by their **liveliness**
a. nomad   b. blemish   c. fatigue   d. hospitality   _fatigue_

6. showed **unfriendliness** to the visitors
a. fatigue   b. hospitality   c. transports   d. blemishes   _hospitality_

Completing the Sentence

Choose the word from the box that best completes each item. Then write the word on the line provided. (You may have to change the word's ending.)

blemish	blunt	capable
conclude	detect	fatigue
festive	hospitality	nomad
persecute	supreme	transport

Speaking Out Against Bias

■ The principal did not mince her words but spoke in __________**blunt**__________ terms on the subject of prejudice to the students assembled in the school auditorium.

■ She described the ugly insult that had been written on a wall as a __________**blemish**__________ on the school's honor.

■ She went on to warn that she would not allow a handful of students to be __________**persecuted**__________ just because they held different religious beliefs from most.

■ "Sometimes it requires a __________**supreme**__________ effort," she said, "to overcome our prejudices and respect the dignity of others."

■ She asked that everyone work together to make ours a school that is known for the __________**hospitality**__________ it shows to all.

On the Move

■ Though many Native American peoples lived in settled villages and farmed the land, many others lived the life of __________**nomads**__________.

■ The nomadic tribes of the Great Plains marked successful buffalo hunts with __________**festive**__________ ceremonies of thanks.

■ In Asia the nomadic Kazakhs use camels to __________**transport**__________ their tents, called *yurts*, and other belongings from place to place.

■ Because they lose body water very slowly, camels are __________**capable**__________ of traveling for days, even in extreme heat, without drinking a drop.

A Train Derails

■ The safety panel looking into the train crash __________**concluded**__________ that the most likely cause was human error.

■ The engineer had not slept in 36 hours and suffered from extreme __________**fatigue**__________.

■ Furthermore, tests of the equipment did not __________**detect**__________ any signs of failure in the train's braking system.

*Circle the letter next to the word or phrase that best completes the sentence or answers the question. Pay special attention to the word in **boldface**.*

1. If you feel **fatigue**, you might
a. take a nap.
b. run three miles.
c. swim 50 laps.
d. clean up the kitchen.

2. Which is a **festive** event?
a. a final exam
b. a terrible tragedy
c. a birthday party
d. a criminal trial

3. A good detective might **conclude** a robbery case by
a. turning in her badge.
b. looking for clues.
c. having a cup of coffee.
d. arresting the thief.

4. A **nomad's** home might be
a. an apartment.
b. a castle.
c. a tent.
d. a farmhouse.

Words with Latin Roots

The unit word *persecute* comes from the Latin prefix *per-*, meaning "through," and the Latin root *sec* or *seq*, which means "to follow." Together these two word parts mean "to treat unjustly or cause to suffer (*to cause suffering to follow*)." The root *sec* or *seq* is used in the following words:

- sequence (n.): orderly arrangement or pattern (*one part following another in order*)
- consecutive (adj.): proceeding in a logical order (*following in order*)
- consequence (n.): result or outcome (*a result that follows a cause*)
- consequential (adj.): important, significant (*having significant results that follow*)
- prosecute (v.): to take legal action against an accused person (*to cause legal action to follow*)

Choose two of the words from the list above. Write a sentence for each word to show you understand its meaning.

1. Accept answers that show an understanding of the vocabulary.

2. ____

Words in Context

Read the passage. Then answer each question.

Hosts and Guests

1   Sometimes word histories give us a chance to ask interesting questions about history and culture. Take the word "**hospitality**," for example. This word comes from the Latin root word *hospes*. The same root gave us the words *host*, *hospital*, *hostel*, and *hotel*. But the fascinating thing is that *hospes* can mean "guest" and "stranger," as well as "host." How could this be?

2   The answer may be **detected** in the widespread connection between hosts, guests, and strangers in different cultures throughout the world. This link probably dates back many centuries to the days when travel was far more risky than it is today. Wandering **nomads** in ancient times had to depend for their lives on the kindness of hosts. Most journeys involved great discomfort and **fatigue**. A warm welcome would **blunt** these hardships. At the same time, most hosts could probably **conclude** that, sooner or later, they might be in a guest's shoes. Hosts thus had an instinctive sympathy with guests as they **transported** themselves across strange lands.

1. What is the meaning of the word **detected** as it is used in paragraph 2?
(a) ignored   (b) repeated   (c) discovered   (d) released

2. Pick the word that best defines **fatigue** as it is used in paragraph 2.
(a) to tire   (b) to travel   (c) distance   (d) weariness

3. The Latin word *claudere* means "to close." The word **conclude** in paragraph 2 means
(a) doubt   (b) imagine   (c) request   (d) decide

4. Pick the word that best defines **transported** as it is used in paragraph 2.
(a) moved   (b) threw   (c) a vehicle   (d) a process

 *Some nouns have irregular plurals. There are special rules for forming these plurals. For example, the word **leaf** changes to **leaves** when it is plural. Underline an example of an irregular plural noun in "Hosts and Guests."* **Accept all correct answers. Example: See paragraph 2.**

Write Your Own

Working with a partner, write 3–5 sentences about hosts and guests. One partner should describe a perfect host, and one should describe a perfect guest. Include three vocabulary words from this unit in your descriptions.

 *For more practice with irregular plural nouns, see* Grammar Workshop, Level Blue, Lesson 12.

Word Study — Words That Are Often Confused

Words that look similar and have similar pronunciations but that have different meanings often cause confusion. For example, the word *persecute* (page 49) is often confused with the word *prosecute*. Read this sentence: *The king who had* **persecuted** *the peasants was* **prosecuted** *for his crimes.* Here, *persecuted* means "caused to suffer" and *prosecuted* means "to bring legal action against."

Look at the chart to find other examples of words that are often confused.

access	(*n.*) an entrance or approach
excess	(*adj.*) beyond what is needed; extra
advice	(*n.*) an idea that is offered
advise	(*v.*) to give help and information
cease	(*v.*) to stop
seize	(*v.*) to take hold of

PRACTICE   *Underline the word in* **boldface** *that best completes the sentence.*

1. During a trip to the restaurant, our class was given (**access**, **excess**) to the kitchen.

2. At closing time each day, the workers store (**access**, **excess**) food in large refrigerators.

3. When I could not decide which club to join, I asked my friend for (**advise**, **advice**).

4. "Please (**advise**, **advice**) me on what to do," I said.

5. The wind blew so hard I had to (**cease**, **seize**) the rail to keep from falling.

6. The windstorm did not (**cease**, **seize**) for the rest of the day.

APPLY   *Complete each sentence using a* **boldface** *word from the chart above.*

7. I ______advise______ you to ______seize______ my arm if you feel as if you might fall.

8. Before we gain ______access______ to the beach, we must wait for the storms to ______cease______.

9. The business owner hired an accountant to give her ______advice______ about spending the ______excess______ funds.

Here are two more word pairs that can cause confusion. Write a sentence for each of the words. Then look in a dictionary to make sure you used each word correctly.
Accept sentences that show an understanding of the word meanings.
Word Pairs: picture / pitcher   costume / custom

Shades of Meaning — Words That Name Travelers

In the passage "Baucis and Philemon" on pages 46–47, you read this sentence: *From house to house, the two **nomads** wandered, asking for water and bread.* In the passage, Jupiter and Mercury are the *nomads*. They are travelers wandering the city of Phrygia and looking for someone to show them hospitality.

Here are some other words that name travelers. Notice that one difference among the travelers is their purpose for traveling.

nomad	A **nomad** roams from place to place.
commuter	A **commuter** travels a long distance between home and work.
tourist	A **tourist** travels to visit a place for pleasure.
pilgrim	A **pilgrim** journeys to a sacred place, usually for religious reasons.

PRACTICE *Write the word from the chart that best names the person making each statement.*

1. I traveled a great distance to visit a holy shrine. _____pilgrim_____

2. I take the train to work every day. _____commuter_____

3. I never live in one place for a long time. _____nomad_____

4. I went to the Grand Canyon to see the sights. _____tourist_____

5. Each year, I travel with my family to visit the origins of my religion. _____pilgrim_____

6. The job requires me to be in Boston every month. _____commuter_____

APPLY *Answer each question to show the meaning of the word in* **boldface.** *Be sure to use the* **boldfaced** *word in your answer.* Accept answers that students can justify.

7. Who is a **commuter** you know? Why is that person a commuter?

____

8. What might a **tourist** do in your area?

____

9. What are some examples of places a **pilgrim** might travel to?

____

10. What reasons might a person have for being a **nomad**?

____

Introducing the Words

Read the following biography about a famous American poet. Notice how the highlighted words are used. These are the words you will be learning in this unit.

The Surprising Life of Emily Dickinson

(Biography)

A differentiated version of this passage is available at **SadlierConnect.com**.

Once upon a time, in the town of Amherst, Massachusetts, lived a young girl named Emily Dickinson. She was a lively, happy child who lived with her parents, sister, and brother in a big house near the village green. At school, Emily learned to read and write, and at home, she learned to cook and sew. Like many of her friends, she no doubt had a great **capacity** for fun as well, sledding in the cold New England winter and going on picnics in the green and flowering summertime.

There was nothing unusual about young Emily. It seemed **apparent** that she would get married one day. Eventually, she would have her own house and raise her own children, perhaps in Amherst. In many ways, she would **duplicate** the life that her mother had lived. After all, that's what most girls did in the 1800s.

When she was older, Emily went away to college for a while. She took a few trips, too, once traveling to Washington, D.C., where her father was a congressman. At home, she took part in town and church activities. When the Civil War began, she worked with other **civilians** to find ways to support the soldiers.

Then, suddenly, everything changed. For some reason, Emily decided to **withdraw** from everyday life. She stopped seeing almost everyone, never traveled, and rarely went outside. Eventually, she didn't leave her parents' house at all, and that's how she lived for the rest of her life.

What **provoked** Emily Dickinson to take this course of action? Even today, no one can say for sure. While the **undoing** of her normal social life must have caused loneliness and pain, it also enabled the young woman to **accomplish** something great. In the years that followed, Emily Dickinson wrote 1,775 poems!

Emily Dickinson
(1830–1886)

Sometimes, Emily might send a poem to a friend, but she didn't try to publish her poetry. If anything, she concealed it, tying her poems in bundles and hiding them in her dresser drawers.

Fortunately, Emily's poetry didn't stay hidden from the world. After her death, the poems were finally published. When they appeared in print, readers couldn't believe how rich—and vast—her output had been. Although she never left the shelter of her house, Emily Dickinson had a keen imagination. In a drop of water, she could see a flood; in a grain of sand, she saw a desert.

To write so many poems, Emily Dickinson must have experienced many spurts of inspiration. Yet she crafted each poem carefully, choosing the exact words, rhythms, and punctuation to express her meaning. Some of the poems do reflect her loneliness, but they are inspiring too. Somehow, Dickinson could use a simple image—the wind in the trees, a robin on a garden path, a train in the valley— to suggest life's endless possibilities.

Simply put, Emily Dickinson was one of America's finest poets. From the stillness of her quiet room in Amherst, her delicate yet powerful words echoed across the land.

Emily Dickinson's home is now a museum.

Definitions

You were introduced to these words in the passage. Study the pronunciation, part of speech, definition, and example sentence for each word. Then read the synonyms and antonyms.

1. **accomplish**
(ə käm′ plish)
(uh-KOM-plish)

(v.) to do, make happen, succeed in, carry through
Let's work together to accomplish the task.
SYNONYMS: to perform, fulfill, achieve, complete; ANTONYMS: to fail, undo, fall short

2. **apparent**
(ə par′ ənt)
(uh-PAR-uhnt)

(adj.) open to view; easy to understand; seeming to be true or real
Speeding was the apparent cause of the accident.
SYNONYMS: clear, obvious, visible; plain; likely
ANTONYMS: hidden, concealed; difficult, uncertain

3. **capacity**
(kə pa′ sə tē)
(kuh-PA-suh-tee)

(n.) the amount of space that can be filled; ability or skill; office or role
The stadium was filled to capacity for the championship game.
SYNONYMS: volume, size, room; gift; position, job

With your partner, decide on the best way to figure out the **capacity** of your backpack.

4. **civilian**
(sə vil′ yən)
(suh-VIL-yuhn)

(n.) a person not in a military, police, or firefighting force
A team of civilians investigated the accident.
(adj.) nonmilitary
No civilian casualties were reported.
SYNONYM: (n. & adj.) nonmilitary; ANTONYM: (n. & adj.) military

5. **conceal**
(kən sēl′)
(kuhn-SEEL)

(v.) to hide or keep secret, to place out of sight
I tried to conceal my disappointment with a smile.
SYNONYMS: to cover, disguise, mask, tuck away; ANTONYMS: to uncover, open, reveal

6. **duplicate**
(v., dü′ pli kāt)
(DOO-pli-kate)
(n., adj., dü′ pli kət)
(DOO-pli-kuht)

(v.) to copy exactly; to produce something equal to
A locksmith can duplicate almost any key.
(adj.) exactly like something else
My friend and I came up with duplicate plans.
(n.) an exact copy
He hung up a framed duplicate of a famous painting in his office.
SYNONYMS: (v.) to reproduce, clone; (adj.) identical; (n.) a reproduction, replica
ANTONYM: (n.) an original

7. keen
(kēn)
(KEEN)

(adj.) having a sharpened edge; quick and sharp in thought or in sight, hearing, or smell; eager

Birds of prey have keen eyesight.

SYNONYMS: razor-edged; acute, alert; ready; ANTONYMS: dull, blunt; lazy, unwilling

> **Name some animals whose senses are keener than humans' senses. Tell your partner about the animal and the sense.**

8. provoke
(prə vōk′)
(pruh-VOKE)

(v.) to annoy or make angry, stir up; to do something in order to get a response

Name-calling is bound to provoke an argument.

SYNONYMS: to excite, enrage, madden, goad; ANTONYMS: to calm, soothe, pacify, quiet

> **What might happen if you provoke a wild animal? Describe these possible consequences to your partner.**

9. spurt
(spûrt)
(SPURT)

(v.) to shoot out quickly in a stream; to show a burst of energy

We watched the runners spurt for the finish line.

(n.) a sudden, short stream of fluid; a quick burst of activity

My shirt was stained by a spurt of ketchup.

SYNONYMS: (v.) to squirt, gush, flow; (n.) a jet, surge

10. undoing
(ən dü′ iŋ)
(uhn-DOO-ing)

(n.) a bringing to ruin or destruction; the cause of ruin; unfastening or loosening

Idle gossip was the cause of their undoing.

SYNONYMS: downfall, misfortune, trouble; an opening
ANTONYMS: good luck, fortune, success; fastening

11. vast
(vast)
(VAST)

(adj.) very great or very large

A vast ocean stretched into the distance.

SYNONYMS: huge, enormous, spacious; ANTONYMS: tiny, small, little, narrow

> **Use gestures to show how you would describe something vast.**

12. withdraw
(with drô′)
(with-DRAW)

(v.) to pull out or remove; to move back or away, retreat

Is it too late to withdraw from the race?

SYNONYMS: to subtract; to leave, depart; ANTONYMS: to deposit, enter; to attack

>  **As time allows, have partners complete graphic organizers for select words, available at SadlierConnect.com.**

Synonyms

*Choose the word that is most nearly the **same** in meaning as the word or phrase in **boldface**. Then write your choice on the line provided.*

1. create an **identical** set of plans
   a. vast   b. duplicate   c. keen   d. apparent   _duplicate_

2. measured the trunk's **room**
   a. capacity   b. spurt   c. civilian   d. undoing   _capacity_

3. **complete** the mission in two weeks
   a. provoke   b. duplicate   c. accomplish   d. withdraw   _accomplish_

4. led to the **downfall** of the dictator
   a. civilian   b. spurt   c. capacity   d. undoing   _undoing_

5. **depart** from the battlefield
   a. withdraw   b. provoke   c. spurt   d. conceal   _withdraw_

6. water that **squirted** from the hose
   a. concealed   b. spurted   c. withdrew   d. provoked   _spurted_

Antonyms

*Choose the word that is most nearly **opposite** in meaning to the word or phrase in **boldface**. Then write your choice on the line provided.*

1. **hidden** reasons
   a. apparent   b. keen   c. vast   d. civilian   _apparent_

2. a **military** operation
   a. vast   b. civilian   c. apparent   d. keen   _civilian_

3. a **small** field
   a. keen   b. duplicate   c. civilian   d. vast   _vast_

4. **calm** the animal
   a. provoke   b. conceal   c. duplicate   d. accomplish   _provoke_

5. **reveal** the answers
   a. duplicate   b. provoke   c. conceal   d. withdraw   _conceal_

6. a **dull** sense of humor
   a. vast   b. civilian   c. duplicate   d. keen   _keen_

Completing the Sentence

Choose the word from the box that best completes each item. Then write the word on the line provided. (You may have to change the word's ending.)

accomplish	apparent	capacity
civilian	conceal	duplicate
keen	provoke	spurt
undoing	vast	withdraw

Revolution in America and France

■ One of the events that led to the American Revolution was the Boston Massacre, when British soldiers fired into a crowd of __________ **civilians** __________.

■ Some historians say that the soldiers were __________ **provoked** __________ into firing by the insults and taunts of the crowd.

■ It soon became __________ **apparent** __________ to the British—even those who preferred not to see it—that the American colonies would settle for nothing less than full independence.

■ The leaders of the French Revolution were inspired by the American Revolution and hoped to __________ **duplicate** __________ its success.

■ The Revolution in France led to the death of King Louis and the __________ **undoing** __________ of the old order.

A California Desert

■ With an area of 25,000 square miles, the Mojave Desert covers a(n) __________ **vast** __________ portion of southern California.

■ During the daytime some animals, such as the kangaroo rat, __________ **withdraw** __________ from the hot desert floor to cooler underground burrows.

■ Though the desert roadrunner is a poor flier, it can run in quick __________ **spurts** __________ to capture its prey. The roadrunner feeds on lizards, snakes, and insects.

The Sixteenth President

■ In his __________ **capacity** __________ as commander in chief, Abraham Lincoln played an important part in choosing the generals of the Union armies.

■ General Ulysses S. Grant __________ **accomplished** __________ what no other Union general before him had been able to do—force the surrender of Robert E. Lee.

■ Lincoln's aides so feared for his safety that they often went to great lengths to __________ **conceal** __________ his movements.

■ The many examples of his jokes and stories show that Lincoln possessed a(n) __________ **keen** __________ sense of humor.

*Circle the letter next to the word or phrase that best completes the sentence or answers the question. Pay special attention to the word in **boldface**.*

1. Which might you **conceal**?
- a. the sky
- (b.) a secret
- c. good news
- d. the air

2. A hawk with **keen** eyes has
- a. difficulty hunting.
- b. eyes of a dark color.
- (c.) excellent vision.
- d. eyes set far apart

3. A **withdrawn** objection would be
- a. voiced loudly.
- b. repeated.
- c. considered.
- (d.) taken away.

4. To **duplicate** a page, you
- a. edit it.
- (b.) make a copy.
- c. extend it.
- d. write a summary.

Words with Latin Roots

The unit word *provoke* comes from the Latin prefix *pro-*, meaning "forward," and the Latin root *voc*, which means "to call." Together, the word parts mean "to call forth a response, such as anger or annoyance." The root *voc* is used in the following words:

- revoke (v.): to cancel (*to call back*)
- provocation (n.) a cause of anger or irritation (*calling forth annoyance*)
- evoke (v.): draw forth (*to call out of*)
- vocation (n.): profession, line of work (*calling*)
- convocation (n.): meeting or official assembly (*a calling together*)

Choose two of the words from the list. Write a sentence for each word to show you understand its meaning.

1. Accept answers that show an understanding of the vocabulary.

2. ____

 *Read the passage. Then answer each question.*

Emily Dickinson and Carlo

1   Emily Dickinson, the great American poet, spent most of her days inside her home in Amherst, Massachusetts. To ease her loneliness, her father gave her a Newfoundland puppy. Emily could not **conceal** her delight, and she named him Carlo. Carlo required plenty of exercise, so Emily would take him to some nearby woods. She loved to watch him take off in a **spurt** and chase after squirrels as they raced away to safety. Sometimes friends would join them. If military officers were among them, they were careful to wear **civilian** clothes. Carlo's muddy pawprints could ruin their uniforms.

2   Emily's decision to **withdraw** from society might have led to her **undoing**, but in many ways she thrived. She devoted herself to her poetry, and even wrote many poems about Carlo. The large black dog lived for 17 years by Emily's side. When he died, she was heartbroken. Carlo had revealed her loving heart and **capacity** to nurture. Emily might have hoped to find a **duplicate** of her beloved companion. But it is not known that she ever had another dog.

1. What is the meaning of the word **conceal** as it is used in paragraph 1?
ⓐ match   ⓑ reveal   **ⓒ mask**   ⓓ postpone

2. Pick the word that best defines **civilian** as it is used in paragraph 1.
ⓐ military   **ⓑ nonmilitary**   ⓒ a soldier   ⓓ an employee

3. What does the word **undoing** mean as it is used in paragraph 2?
ⓐ poor health   ⓑ problem   ⓒ success   **ⓓ downfall**

4. The Latin word *duplicare* means "to double." The word **duplicate** in paragraph 2 means
ⓐ replica   ⓑ original   ⓒ relative   ⓓ illusion

 *An appositive is a word or phrase that identifies or explains a noun. For example: "A Bird Came Down the Walk,"* **a famous poem,** *was published in 1891. The appositive* **a famous poem** *identifies "A Bird Came Down the Walk." Underline an appositive in the passage.* See paragraph 1.

 ## Write Your Own

Using at least three vocabulary words from the unit, write a 3–5 sentence story describing but not naming a favorite animal. Use as much detail as you can without giving away what it is. Then share your story with a partner and ask your partner to try to guess what the animal is.

 *For more practice with appositives, see* Grammar Workshop, Level Blue, Lesson 14.

Vocabulary for Comprehension

*Read this passage in which some of the words you have studied in Units 1–6 appear in **boldface**. Then answer the questions.*

Trouble in Paradise

1   Far from anywhere, in the middle of the **vast** Pacific Ocean, lies the beautiful island nation of Nauru. Sandy beaches, swaying palm trees, and clear blue water circle the island.

2   Nauru is **miniature** compared to other nations on Earth. It is only about 8 square miles in size and home to about 14,000 people. Nauru used to be very rich because its land held a lot of phosphate. Phosphate is a natural material used for farming and making new products. The phosphate on Nauru formed from droppings of birds flying over the island. It was then dug from the ground, loaded onto ships and **transported** to countries that **span** the world. There is no **dispute** that this is an unusual but profitable treasure.

3   The **aggressive** digging and selling of phosphate made Nauru very rich. For a while, its people were some of the richest in the world. Unfortunately, the vigorous digging was a **blunder** and destroyed Nauru's land. Around the year 2000, the phosphate ran out and suddenly the islanders had a big problem. Not only was its land ruined, but Nauru also had no way to earn money.

4   Today, the people of Nauru struggle to build a new future for their country. They must now **convert** from selling phosphate to earning money in new ways. One idea is to attract visitors in search of **luxurious** beach vacations. This will be a hard goal to **accomplish** because the island is so remote from most places. However, the people of Nauru hope that visitors will **associate** their beautiful island with a great beach vacation. It is an easy connection to make. Although Nauru may not be able to **duplicate** their past success, they hope that their new ideas will create jobs for their **civilians**.

Fill in the circle next to the choice that best completes the sentence or answers the question.

1. What is a main idea of the passage?
   (a) Bird droppings were responsible for creating phosphate that Nauru sold for profit.
   (b) Nauru is one of the smallest islands on Earth with a population of 14,000.
   (c) Nauru dug for phosphate and sold it all around the world.
   (d) It is difficult for a country to depend on one natural resource for income.

2. As it is used in paragraph 1, what does the word **vast** show about the Pacific Ocean?
   (a) It is continuous.
   (b) It is large.
   (c) It is dangerous.
   (d) It is beautiful.

3. What does the use of the word **miniature** in paragraph 2 suggest?
   (a) Nauru is very rich.
   (b) Nauru is very small.
   (c) Nauru is very large.
   (d) Nauru is a small copy of another island.

4. The Latin word *disputāre* means "examine." The word **dispute** in paragraph 2 means
   (a) sermon
   (b) complaint
   (c) agreement
   (d) debate

5. What does **span** mean as it is used in paragraph 2?
   (a) to occupy a short space
   (b) a small amount of time
   (c) to stretch or reach across
   (d) the full reach

6. What does the author mean by the word **associate** in paragraph 4?
   (a) to link in one's mind
   (b) to be aware of
   (c) a partner or friend
   (d) having less than full rank

7. Which phrase from the passage best shows the idea of **associate**?
   (a) "a new future"
   (b) "easy connection"
   (c) "create jobs"
   (d) "attract visitors"

8. What is the meaning of **duplicate** as it is used in paragraph 4?
   (a) forget
   (b) copy
   (c) innovate
   (d) form

Write Your Own

Many people in Nauru want to encourage travelers to vacation on their island. Imagine you are writing a travel brochure for the area you live in. Write to persuade others to come visit. Use at least three vocabulary words from Units 1–6.

Classifying

Choose the word from the box that goes best with each group of words. Write the word in the space provided. Then explain what the words have in common. The first one has been done for you.

bluff	capacity	cautious
conceal	~~continuous~~	detect
document	hazy	monarch
productive	supreme	vast

1. continue, continual, __continuous__, continuation
The words belong to the same word family.

2. blunt, __bluff__, blood, blanket, blade
The words begin with the same initial sounds.

3. crazy, daisy, __hazy__, lazy
The words rhyme.

4. enormous, immense, massive, __vast__
The words are synonyms.

5. spot, observe, notice, __detect__
The words are synonyms.

6. article, essay, report, __document__
The words name types of written material.

7. produce, product, __productive__, production
The words belong to the same word family.

8. horrible, mediocre, good, __supreme__
The words are descriptions of quality, in order from worst to best.

9. president, dictator, emperor, __monarch__
The words name heads of government.

10. mask, hide, disguise, __conceal__
The words are synonyms.

11. reckless, daring, wild, __cautious__
The words describe behavior.

12. length, width, weight, __capacity__
The words name attributes that can be measured.

*Complete each sentence so that it makes sense. Pay attention to the word in **boldface**.* **Accept answers that show an understanding of the vocabulary.**

1. When I clean a **fragile** vase, I ________________________________.

2. To **justify** my opinion, I ________________________________.

3. My favorite meal **consists** of ________________________________.

4. We were able to **overwhelm** the other team because ________________.

5. To prepare for the **festive** event, we ________________________.

6. A dog with a **keen** sense of smell can ____________________.

7. Our class had to **cancel** our trip because ____________________.

8. In order to settle our **dispute**, we ________________________.

9. Whenever I face an **obstacle**, I ________________________.

10. A **flexible** person is able to ________________________.

11. A **miniature** train set takes up ________________________.

12. I had to **withdraw** from the competition because ________________.

13. The **veteran** spoke to our class about ____________________.

14. The advertisement is **misleading** because ____________________.

15. Whenever a **mishap** occurs, I try to ________________________.

16. The athlete felt **fatigue** after ________________________.

17. The **apparent** cause of the fire was ____________________.

Writing Challenge
Check that vocabulary is used correctly and that each sentence is written correctly.

*Write two sentences using the word **associate**. In the first sentence, use **associate** as a verb. In the second sentence, use **associate** as an adjective.*

1. ____

2. ____

Introducing the Words

Read the following biography about the career and travels of a modern-day explorer. Notice how the highlighted words are used. These are the words you will be learning in this unit.

Eugenie Clark: Swimming with Sharks

(Biography)

A differentiated version of this passage is available at **SadlierConnect.com**.

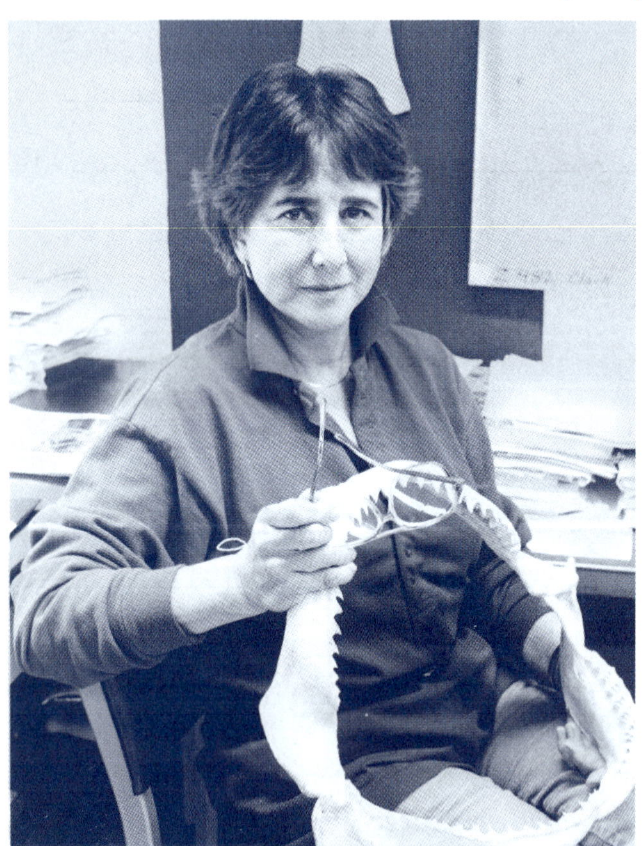

Dr. Eugenie Clark

Nine-year-old Genie leaned against the glass barrier and stared at the fish. This was her first visit to the aquarium, and she couldn't keep her eyes off the underwater scene. Neon fish flashed by, and an octopus waved. Genie, however, stared mainly at the sharks. Imagine swimming with these graceful creatures!

After that, Genie became a reliable visitor to the New York City Aquarium. She went back week after week, always learning more about ocean life. Soon she decided to become an *ichthyologist*, a scientist who studies fish. She was only in fourth grade, but Eugenie Clark calculated that there was nothing else that she would rather do than swim with the sharks.

Years later, Genie's dream came true, when, in her twenties, she became Dr. Eugenie Clark. She had degrees in marine biology and experience studying fish all over the world. Since diving was the best way to study fish, Dr. Clark obtained some scuba gear. On one early dive, a large shark appeared and gave her a jolt. Not frightened, Clark simply admired the shark's beauty.

Swimming with sharks was fun, but Eugenie Clark also wanted to learn about them through experiments. To pursue this kind of work, she started a marine laboratory in Florida. Doing so made her the first woman in the United States to run her own marine biology lab, a considerable achievement.

Over the years, Clark composed many articles and even wrote a book about her adventures that was called *The Lady and the Sharks*. The book became a best-seller, and people started calling her "Shark Lady." Clark also helped teach people about ocean life through films and television shows. Always on the go, she did not appoint deputies to do the filming. Instead, she traveled the world to take part in it herself.

During her travels, Clark often called attention to threats to the ocean environment. For example, she often dived in the Red Sea in Egypt. There, the Ras Muhammad reefs, like many of the world's coral reefs, were being harmed by pollution. To save the reefs, Eugenie Clark teamed with Egyptian scientists and divers. Together, these experts made the Egyptian government and public aware of the problem. Many Egyptians rejoiced when, as a result of their efforts, Ras Muhammad became Egypt's first national park.

Eugenie Clark wasn't about to retire when she turned sixty-five. Instead, she began to dive in submersibles, or mini-submarines. For Clark, the subs safely opened up new areas of the ocean for study. After all, diving deep down or for long periods of time in scuba gear can be unhealthy and dangerous. Exposure to salt water can shrivel a person's skin. The intense pressure of the water can leave a diver unconscious and senseless. By contrast, a diver in a submersible can descend thousands of feet with no harmful physical effects.

Industrious as ever, Dr. Clark keeps studying sharks and writing books. Diving in submersibles, she continues to live her childhood dream of exploring the treasures of the sea. To her, of course, that doesn't mean sunken treasure chests and pirate loot, but rather the wonders of underwater life.

Dr. Clark swimming
with a shark

Definitions

You were introduced to these words in the passage. Study the pronunciation, part of speech, definition, and example sentence for each word. Then read the synonyms and antonyms.

1. barrier
(bar′ ē ər)
(BAR-ee-ur)

(n.) something that blocks the way; an obstacle

Firefighters often construct a barrier to stop a forest fire.

SYNONYMS: an obstruction, fence, wall, blockade, safeguard
ANTONYMS: an opening, passage

---

2. calculate
(kal′ kyə lāt)
(KAL-kyuh-late)

(v.) to find out by using mathematics or reasoning; to reckon, estimate

The math teacher asked us to calculate the number of hours we spend on homework each week.

SYNONYMS: to gauge, figure, determine, judge

 **Calculate** the number of hours you slept last night. **Share this number with your partner.**

---

3. compose
(kəm pōz′)
(kuhm-POZE)

(v.) to be or make up the parts of, form; to create or write; to calm or quiet one's mind

Before you compose the essay, you might write an outline.

SYNONYMS: to produce, invent; to still, settle
ANTONYMS: to annoy, disturb

 **Compose** a silly story with your partner. Take turns writing sentences.

---

4. considerable
(kən sid′ ər ə bəl)
(kuhn-SID-ur-uh-buhl)

(adj.) fairly large in size or extent; worthy of attention

It will take a considerable amount of time to complete the science project.

SYNONYMS: great, sizable, major, important; ANTONYMS: small, slight, negligible

---

5. deputy
(de′ pyə tē)
(DE-pyuh-tee)

(n.) one chosen to help or take the place of another or to act in that person's absence

The sheriff's first act after winning the election was to appoint a deputy.

SYNONYMS: an assistant, aide, substitute

---

6. industrious
(in dus′ trē əs)
(in-DUHSS-tree-uhss)

(adj.) busy, working steadily

The crew that gathered to clean up the vacant lot was as industrious as an ant colony.

SYNONYMS: active, occupied, energetic, untiring; ANTONYMS: lazy, idle, loafing, slow

---

 As time allows, have partners complete graphic organizers for select words, available at **SadlierConnect.com.**

7. jolt
(jōlt)
(JOHLT)

(v.) to shake up roughly; to move along in a jerky or bumpy fashion

It was fun to jolt down the dirt road in the wagon.

(n.) a sudden bump or jerk; a shock or surprise

We felt a jolt as the Ferris wheel started.

SYNONYMS: (v.) to jar, rattle, hit; (n.) a lurch, bounce

💬 Use each definition of **jolt** in a sentence.

8. loot
(lüt)
(LOOT)

(v.) to rob by force or violence, especially during war or time of unrest

The soldiers were warned not to loot the villages.

(n.) valuable things that have been stolen or taken by force

Detectives found loot from a dozen robberies.

SYNONYMS: (v.) to steal, plunder; (n.) prize, spoils

9. rejoice
(ri jois')
(ri-JOISS)

(v.) to feel joy or great delight; to make joyful

The whole town will rejoice if the team wins the championship.

SYNONYMS: to celebrate, cheer; ANTONYMS: to grieve, mourn

 Show your partner how you look when you **rejoice**.

10. reliable
(re līʹ ə bəl)
(re-LYE-uh-buhl)

(adj.) deserving trust, dependable

It is not easy to find a reliable baby-sitter.

SYNONYMS: faithful, proven, trustworthy; ANTONYMS: unreliable, questionable, fickle

💬 Why is it important to be **reliable**? Explain your answer to your partner.

11. senseless
(sensʹ ləs)
(SENSS-luhss)

(adj.) lacking meaning, stupid or foolish; without use of the senses

The boxer was knocked senseless by the blow.

SYNONYMS: ridiculous, silly, illogical, birdbrained; unconscious
ANTONYMS: brilliant, clever, smart

12. shrivel
(shrivʹ əl)
(SHRIV-uhl)

(v.) to shrink and wrinkle, especially from heat, cold, or dryness

Exposed skin will shrivel in the frosty air.

SYNONYMS: to wither, dry, contract; ANTONYMS: to expand, enlarge, swell

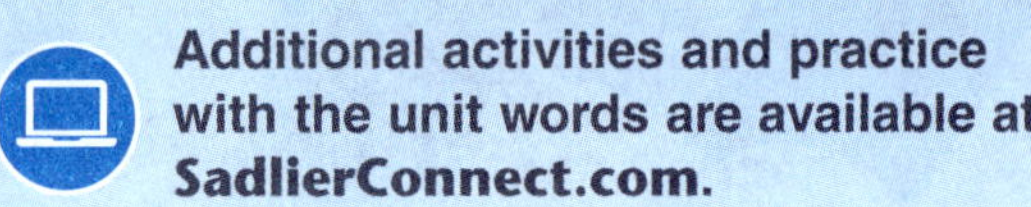

Synonyms

*Choose the word that is most nearly the **same** in meaning as the word or phrase in **boldface**. Then write your choice on the line provided.*

1. knocked **unconscious** when I fell off the ladder
   a. industrious   b. senseless   c. considerable   d. reliable   __senseless__

2. **jarred** by the rough landing
   a. jolted   b. composed   c. shriveled   d. looted   __jolted__

3. **produce** a long poem
   a. jolt   b. calculate   c. compose   d. rejoice   __compose__

4. call the **assistant** for help
   a. barrier   b. loot   c. deputy   d. jolt   __deputy__

5. **determine** the cost of painting the apartment
   a. compose   b. rejoice   c. jolt   d. calculate   __calculate__

6. would **plunder** the house while the owners were away
   a. jolt   b. compose   c. loot   d. calculate   __loot__

Antonyms

*Choose the word that is most nearly **opposite** in meaning to the word or phrase in **boldface**. Then write your choice on the line provided.*

1. the **idle** carpenter
   a. considerable   b. industrious   c. reliable   d. senseless   __industrious__

2. **swell** in the heat
   a. calculate   b. jolt   c. compose   d. shrivel   __shrivel__

3. **mourn** over the election results
   a. loot   b. calculate   c. rejoice   d. shrivel   __rejoice__

4. made a **slight** difference
   a. considerable   b. industrious   c. senseless   d. reliable   __considerable__

5. a **questionable** source of information
   a. industrious   b. considerable   c. reliable   d. senseless   __reliable__

6. found an **opening**
   a. deputy   b. loot   c. jolt   d. barrier   __barrier__

Choose the word from the box that best completes each item. Then write the word on the line provided. (You may have to change the word's ending.)

barrier	**calculate**	**compose**
considerable	**deputy**	**industrious**
jolt	**loot**	**rejoice**
reliable	**senseless**	**shrivel**

Earthquake!

■ The powerful earthquake that hit the San Francisco Bay area on October 17, 1989, did **considerable** damage to the city, though not nearly so much as was done by the terrible earthquake and fire of 1906.

■ The mighty **jolt**, which registered 7.1 on the Richter scale, shook buildings and buckled elevated highways.

■ Safety officials put up **barriers** to keep people away from unsafe areas.

■ Scientists **calculated** that the loss of life and property would have been far greater if the earthquake had hit during the day instead of early evening.

A Great Artist

■ Vincent van Gogh was an ambitious and **industrious** artist who made hundreds of paintings and drawings. He moved to southern France in 1888, and there he produced many of his masterpieces. Van Gogh died in 1890 at the age of 37.

■ Van Gogh **rejoiced** at the completion of each new painting but despaired that his work never sold.

■ As the summer heat **shriveled** the olives on the trees near his home, van Gogh wrote sad letters to his brother Theo.

■ He **composed** works of great beauty that were not appreciated until after his death. Today his paintings are in museums and are sold for millions of dollars.

Sirens in the Night

■ When a power blackout darkened part of the city, some criminals roamed the streets. They broke windows and **looted** neighborhood stores.

■ Community leaders spoke out against this **senseless** violence and urged people to act responsibly during the emergency.

■ Several sheriff's **deputies** arrived to restore order and interview witnesses.

■ One witness offered information about the robberies, but the police officers paid him little mind because they knew he was not **reliable**.

Circle the letter next to the word or phrase that best completes the sentence or answers the question. Pay special attention to the word in **boldface.**

1. Which is a **barrier** to success in school?
   a. poor study habits
   b. encouragement from friends
   c. a tall fence
   d. eating breakfast every day

2. You might **rejoice** if you
   a. found your lost dog.
   b. ruined your favorite shirt.
   c. failed a spelling test.
   d. saw a popular movie.

3. People who **loot** are
   a. winning a prize.
   b. breaking the law.
   c. running in circles.
   d. taking pictures.

4. A **reliable** friend is one who
   a. doesn't let you down.
   b. makes fun of you.
   c. is never on time.
   d. always makes you laugh.

Words with Latin Roots

The unit word *compose* comes from the Latin prefix *com-*, meaning "with," and the Latin root *pos*, which means "to put or place." Together, the word parts mean "to form, to put together" or "to create or write." The root *pos* is used in the following words:

- composition (n.): something formed to make a whole (*something put together*)
- impose (v.): to put a burden or requirement on (*to put or place something on*)
- oppose (v.): to be against someone or something (*to put or place against*)
- transpose (v.): to switch or shift (*to place in a different order*)
- posture (n.): position of the body (*the way the body is placed*)

Choose two of the words from the list above. Write a sentence for each word to show you understand its meaning.

1. Accept answers that show an understanding of the vocabulary.

2. ____

 ## Words in Context

Read the passage. Then answer each question.

The Coral Reefs of Aqaba

1   The rapid disappearance of coral reefs around the world is a **jolt** to scientists. Experts **calculate** that 25 to 50 percent of reefs have vanished. Up to 90 percent are endangered. But **considerable** evidence suggests that some coral reefs are different. They can resist the harsh conditions that **loot** other coral reefs and rob them of their health. These conditions are rising sea temperatures and increasing acidity in the oceans.

2   The "heat-resistant" reefs are located in the Red Sea's Gulf of Aqaba. They are off the coast of Jordan. The seawaters here are among the world's warmest. Scientists have **composed** and performed sets of **reliable** experiments to closely observe the Aqaba reefs' special qualities. Their tests show that the corals—the small living things that build the reefs—possess heat resistance at both the adult and early-life stages.

3   People now wonder if knowledge about the Aqaba reefs might be used to help save or rebuild reefs in other waters. However, they also point out that it would be **senseless** to regard the new information as a cure-all. Any rebuilt reefs will still have to cope with other threats, such as water pollution.

1. What is the meaning of the word **jolt** as it is used in paragraph 1?
 (a) to annoy   (b) to rattle   (c) a shock   (d) a gift

2. What does the word **loot** mean as it is used in paragraph 1?
 (a) plunder   (b) nourish   (c) break   (d) condemn

3. The Latin word *componere* means "to put or place with." The word **composed** in paragraph 2 means
 (a) checked   (b) borrowed   (c) questioned   (d) created

4. Choose the word that best defines **senseless** as it is used in paragraph 3.
 (a) foolish   (b) clever   (c) emotional   (d) rational

 *A direct object is a noun or pronoun that receives the action of the verb. A direct object answers the question **what** or **whom** after an action verb. For example: A boat took **us** out to the ocean. Underline an example of a direct object in "The Coral Reefs of Aqaba."* Accept all correct answers. Example: See paragraph 1.

 ## Write Your Own

With a partner, develop a short script for a podcast that informs listeners about coral reefs. Include at least three vocabulary words from this unit in your script.

For more practice with direct objects, see Grammar Workshop, Level Blue, Lesson 16.

Word Study — Prefixes *pre-, in-, im-, ir-, il-*

A **prefix** is a word part that is added to the beginning of a **base word** to make a new word. You can add the prefix *pre-* to *calculate* (page 70) to make a new word.

The prefix **pre-** means "before."	
pre + calculate = **pre**calculate → means "calculate before"	
The prefixes **in-**, **im-**, **ir-**, and **il-** often mean "not" or "without."	
in + capable = **in**capable → means "not have the ability to"	
im + mobile = **im**mobile → means "not able to move"	
ir + replaceable = **ir**replaceable → means "cannot be replaced"	
il + legal = **il**legal → means "not legal"	

PRACTICE *Write the missing prefix and base word. Then write the meaning of the new word.*

	Prefix	Base Word	New Word	Meaning
1.	im	proper	= improper →	not proper
2.	in	complete	= incomplete →	not finished
3.	ir	relevant	= irrelevant →	not relevant
4.	il	legible	= illegible →	not readable
5.	pre	date	= predate →	exist before in time

APPLY *Complete each sentence with a word that contains the prefix pre-, in-, im-, ir, or il-. Choose from the words above.*

6. My teacher said my messy handwriting was ____illegible____.

7. The phones in our house ____predate____ the cell phone that I carry.

8. After I broke my leg, I was ____immobile____ for a few weeks.

9. I tried not to include any ____irrelevant____ details in my report.

10. My brother was ____incapable____ of giving me a good reason for skipping breakfast.

11. It is ____improper____ to talk while someone is giving a speech.

✎ *Write two words that begin with each of the prefixes pre-, in-, im-, ir-, and il-. Then consult a dictionary, either in a book or online, to check the meanings.*

Shades of Meaning   Metaphors

In the passage "Eugenie Clark: Swimming with Sharks" on pages 68–69, you read about Eugenie Clark's love of fish, especially the shark, and her love of the ocean environment. She loved swimming with the ocean's creatures and exploring their world. To Eugenie, these creatures and their surroundings *are treasures of the sea*. In this sentence, *are treasures of the sea* is a metaphor.

A **metaphor** compares two unlike things without using the word *like* or *as*. A metaphor doesn't say that one thing is *like* another. It says that one thing *is* another. Saying that the ocean's creatures and their surroundings are *treasures of the sea* means that the ocean's creatures and their surroundings are amazing underwater sights.

PRACTICE   *Read each sentence. Figure out the meaning of each metaphor in **boldface**. Write the number of each sentence next to its meaning.*

1. The assignment **was a breeze**. I was able to finish it in only ten minutes.

2. These lovely earrings **are twinkling stars**.

3. I eat so much that my mother thinks my stomach is **a bottomless pit**.

4. The boom of fireworks **was thunder in the night**. It could be heard a mile away.

___4___ very loud

___1___ easy

___2___ sparkly

___3___ without end or limit

APPLY   *Read each sentence. Figure out the meaning of each metaphor in **boldface**. Write the meaning on the line provided.* Accept reasonable answers. Possible answers are given.

5. The shopping center **was a sea of people**.

   a large crowd of people

6. During the heat of the summer, the attic **is a sauna**.

   extremely hot

7. By the time we unpacked our camping gear, the garage **was a disaster area**.

   a messy place

8. Even though they are brothers, their personalities **are night and day**.

   completely opposite

9. On election night, the candidate's office was **a whirlwind of activity**.

   extremely busy

Introducing the Words

Read the following essay about a building from New York City's past. Notice how the highlighted words are used. These are the words you will be learning in this unit.

What Happened to Pennsylvania Station?

(Essay)

A differentiated version of this passage is available at **SadlierConnect.com**.

Cars and taxis passed the eighty-four pink granite columns that stood like guards at the front of the station. Pedestrians approached along an elegant arched passageway. The waiting room was fifteen stories high and a block and a half long. In many ways, Pennsylvania Station, also known as Penn Station, was the heart of New York City.

Built in 1910, the station was an **energetic** place. Filled with bustling crowds, Penn Station welcomed travelers with its bright and **hearty** atmosphere. Getting on or off a train here was an exciting thing to do.

By the 1950s, however, fewer people were traveling by train. They had found **alternate** ways to travel. Airlines carried more and more passengers. New superhighways made driving long distances easier.

By the end of the decade, the owners of Penn Station made a fateful decision. They would **demolish** the famous landmark. In its place, they would build an office building and a sports arena. The plan seemed to make financial sense, but little thought was given to train passengers. People would now have to board trains underground from small waiting areas near the train tunnels.

Demolish Penn Station? When New Yorkers heard the plan, they couldn't believe their ears. One of the city's finest public places had been given a death sentence, and New Yorkers didn't like the **verdict**!

Citizens joined together to save the landmark. For months, they would **strive** to rescue it from the wrecking ball. They pointed out that the station was an architectural treasure. It had played a key role in the life and history of the city. What's more, the new underground station would be cramped and uncomfortable. A person didn't have to be very **observant** to see that.

Unfortunately, no one could stop the tragedy. City officials **enforced** the wishes of the owners, and in 1963, the wrecking balls

The Clock in Penn Station was a popular meeting place.

went to work. Onlookers gazed in horror as an architectural masterpiece crashed to the ground in dust.

In the end, New Yorkers resigned themselves to the loss of Penn Station. They had, however, learned a lesson: Landmark buildings had to be saved. A special landmarks commission was formed. Its primary purpose was to identify and protect the city's finest architecture. Its members recognized that as a city changes and matures, some older buildings do have to be demolished to make room for new ones. Landmarks, however, must be preserved.

Ironically, by the 1990s, train travel had picked up at Penn Station, especially among commuters from surrounding towns. The underground station had difficulty handling the raging river of traffic. As predicted, few liked the cramped replacement.

Some New Yorkers hope to convert a grand old post office into a new train station. The post office is in the right place, and in some ways, it resembles the old Pennsylvania Station. The plan may work, but the overhaul will be a very difficult and costly feat. So the tragedy teaches another lesson: Sometimes, it's better to preserve what we have than to try to replace it.

Main Waiting Room at Pennsylvania Station

Pennsylvania Station was one of New York City's most beautiful structures.

Definitions

You were introduced to these words in the passage. Study the pronunciation, part of speech, definition, and example sentence for each word. Then read the synonyms and antonyms.

1. alternate
(v., ôl′ tər nāt)
(AWL-tur-nate)
(n., adj., ôl′ tər nət)
(AWL-tur-nuht)

(v.) to do, use, or happen in successive turns; to take turns

We chose two students to alternate in the lead role for our class play.

(n.) a person acting or prepared to act in place of another; a substitute

Juries usually include two or more alternates.

(adj.) happening or appearing in turns; every other; being a choice between two or more things

The bus driver took an alternate route.

SYNONYMS: (v.) to rotate, change; (n.) a replacement, deputy

 **Use each definition of alternate in a sentence.**

2. demolish
(di mäl′ ish)
(di-MOL-ish)

(v.) to tear down, break to pieces

A wrecking crew arrived to demolish the old building.

SYNONYMS: to raze, destroy, wreck, smash, level
ANTONYMS: to construct, build, restore, mend

3. energetic
(e nər je′ tik)
(e-nur-JE-tik)

(adj.) active and vigorous, full of energy, forceful

Our teacher has an energetic assistant.

SYNONYMS: hardworking, tireless, peppy
ANTONYMS: idle, lazy, inactive

Demonstrate what it looks like when you feel energetic.

4. enforce
(en fôrs′)
(en-FORSS)

(v.) to force obedience to

It is the duty of the police to protect citizens and enforce the laws.

SYNONYM: to carry out
ANTONYMS: to overlook, abandon, disregard

Is it important for a community to enforce rules and laws? Explain your answer to your partner.

5. feat
(fēt)
(FEET)

(n.) an act or deed that shows daring, skill, or strength

The crowd cheered when the circus strongman performed a mighty feat.

SYNONYMS: an achievement, exploit, effort

As time allows, have partners complete graphic organizers for select words, available at SadlierConnect.com.

6. hearty
(härt′ ē)
(HART-ee)

(adj.) warm and friendly; healthy, lively, and strong; large and satisfying to the appetite

We all sat down to a hearty meal.

SYNONYMS: cheerful, friendly; fit, healthy; plentiful
ANTONYMS: insincere, phony; sickly

7. mature
(mə tür′)
(muh-TYUR)

(v.) to bring to or reach full development or growth

The puppy will mature over the summer.

(adj.) fully grown or developed

A field of mature oats waved in the breeze.

SYNONYMS: (v.) to grow, develop, age, ripen; (adj.) complete, ripe
ANTONYMS: (adj.) immature, inexperienced, raw, green

8. observant
(əb zûr′ vənt)
(uhb-ZUR-vuhnt)

(adj.) watchful, quick to notice; careful and diligent

An observant guard spotted the vandals.

SYNONYMS: aware, attentive, alert, sharp; dutiful, mindful
ANTONYMS: inattentive, careless

9. primary
(prī′ mer ē)
(PRYE-mer-ee)

(adj.) first in importance, first in time or order; basic, fundamental

Raising money was our primary order of business.

(n.) an early election that narrows the choice of candidates who will run in a final election

The challenger won the primary.

SYNONYMS: (adj.) highest, main, prime; ANTONYMS: (adj.) secondary, last

What is the **primary** reason students attend school?

10. resign
(ri zīn′)
(ri-ZINE)

(v.) to give up a job, an office, or a right or claim

Richard Nixon was the first president to resign from office.

SYNONYMS: to quit, abandon, leave, surrender

11. strive
(strīv)
(STRIVE)

(v.) to devote much energy or effort, try hard

You must strive to finish your homework on time.

SYNONYMS: to attempt, struggle, labor, slave, strain

What are two goals that you **strive** to achieve?

12. verdict
(vûr′ dikt)
(VUR-dikt)

(n.) the decision of a jury at the end of a trial or legal case; any decision

The jury brought in a guilty verdict.

SYNONYMS: a ruling, judgment, finding

Synonyms

*Choose the word that is most nearly the **same** in meaning as the word or phrase in **boldface**. Then write your choice on the line provided.*

1. handed down the **ruling**
a. primary   b. feat   c. alternate   d. verdict   _____verdict_____

2. a **cheerful** laugh that made his shoulders jiggle
a. alternate   b. hearty   c. mature   d. observant   _____hearty_____

3. read about the daring **achievement**
a. feat   b. verdict   c. primary   d. alternate   _____feat_____

4. packed a **replacement** camera as a backup
a. observant   b. hearty   c. primary   d. alternate   _____alternate_____

5. **abandon** the job of manager
a. alternate   b. demolish   c. strive   d. resign   _____resign_____

6. **attempt** to learn to read Japanese
a. demolish   b. alternate   c. strive   d. resign   _____strive_____

Antonyms

*Choose the word that is most nearly **opposite** in meaning to the word or phrase in **boldface**. Then write your choice on the line provided.*

1. **construct** a covered bridge
a. demolish   b. strive   c. alternate   d. enforce   _____demolish_____

2. **idle** workers
a. mature   b. energetic   c. observant   d. primary   _____energetic_____

3. showed an **inexperienced** outlook
a. alternate   b. hearty   c. mature   d. primary   _____mature_____

4. an **inattentive** reader
a. alternate   b. mature   c. observant   d. hearty   _____observant_____

5. **overlook** the "No Smoking" laws
a. alternate   b. strive   c. resign   d. enforce   _____enforce_____

6. a **secondary** cause of blindness
a. hearty   b. observant   c. primary   d. energetic   _____primary_____

Choose the word from the box that best completes each item. Then write the word on the line provided. (You may have to change the word's ending.)

alternate	**demolish**	**energetic**
enforce	**feat**	**hearty**
mature	**observant**	**primary**
resign	**strive**	**verdict**

Raising a New House

■ The storm so badly damaged the house that it was unsafe to live in. The owner decided to __________ **demolish** __________ it and build a new one.

■ It was quite a(n) __________ **feat** __________ to tear down the house, clear the land, and build another house in only ten weeks!

■ Two crews __________ **alternated** __________ in the building work. When one finished, the other began, so that construction went on from break of day until after the sun went down.

■ All of the workers were encouraged to __________ **strive** __________ as hard as they could to finish the job ahead of schedule.

■ Luckily, a(n) __________ **observant** __________ worker spotted a mistake in the building plans before it caused a delay. The worker was rewarded for his attention and diligence.

An After-School Job

■ My sister says that the responsibilities of a part-time job can help teens develop into more __________ **mature** __________ individuals.

■ The managers at Burger Barn, where she works after school, __________ **enforce** __________ three rules: be on time, be honest, and be polite.

■ As long as she follows those rules, the managers greet her each day with a cheerful smile and a __________ **hearty** __________ handshake.

To the Polls!

■ The __________ **primary** __________ election in September decided which candidates would run for state assembly in the general election in November. In the Democratic race, two politicians challenged the two-term assemblyman for a place on the ballot.

■ Many young, __________ **energetic** __________ volunteers worked tirelessly to get out the vote.

■ After ballots were counted, the __________ **verdict** __________ was clear: Voters wanted the two-term assemblyman to run again.

■ However, health problems in October forced him to __________ **resign** __________ his office and pull out of the election.

Word Associations

*Circle the letter next to the word or phrase that best completes
the sentence or answers the question. Pay special attention to the
word in* **boldface.**

1. If you and your sister **alternate**
   walking the dog, then you must
   a. do twice as much walking.
   b. walk the dog every other time.
   c. walk the dog two times in a row.
   d. walk farther than your sister.

2. People who **strive**
   a. give up easily.
   b. always succeed.
   c. do their very best.
   d. prefer to be outdoors.

3. An **energetic** performer might
   a. do three shows a day.
   b. nap during intermission.
   c. not answer fan mail.
   d. sing softly.

4. Which would be the hardest to
   demolish?
   a. a snow fort
   b. a house made of cards
   c. a brick wall
   d. a dollhouse

Words with Latin Roots

The unit word *primary*, meaning "first in importance" or "basic,"
comes from the Latin root *prim*, which means "first." The root is used
in the following words:

- prime (adj.): very important or high in quality (*first in importance or rank*)
- primarily (adv.): mainly, most importantly (*first of all*)
- primitive (adj.): early in terms of development or style; basic or very simple
  (*first in time*)
- primeval (adj.): of the earliest ages (*first in time or chronology*)
- primordial (adj.): existing from the beginning (*first among the ages or in sequence*)

*Choose two of the words from the list. Write a sentence for each word
to show you understand its meaning.*

1. Accept answers that show an understanding of the vocabulary.

2.

 *Read the passage. Then answer each question.*

The Atlanta Beltline

1   The Atlanta Beltline is revitalizing the city of Atlanta with a network of walking and biking trails. The project's **primary** aim is to create an **alternate** use for an old railway line surrounding the city. When complete, the Beltline Park will have 33 miles of trails that connect neighborhoods, parks, and exhibits.

2   A Georgia Tech student first had the idea for the Beltline in 1999. The idea then **matured** into a campaign by **energetic** city residents. They wanted a city with parks and transportation. They also wanted better planning for the city's land use and growth. As a result, the Beltline is a **hearty** combination of housing, dining, healthy activities, and transportation all within one area.

3   Today, large parts of the Atlanta Beltline are complete. The city will **strive** to finish the project by 2030. The Beltline has 2 million visitors each year with more than $4.1 billion in funding. Not surprisingly, the **verdict** from residents and visitors has so far been very positive.

1. What is the meaning of the word **primary** as it is used in paragraph 1?
   ⓐ main   ⓑ largest   ⓒ president   ⓓ election

2. What does the word **alternate** mean as it is used in paragraph 1?
   ⓐ to rotate   ⓑ clever   ⓒ replacement   ⓓ to take turns

3. The Latin word *maturus* means "ripe." The word **matured** in paragraph 2 means
   ⓐ shrank   ⓑ inexperienced   ⓒ youthful   ⓓ developed

4. Pick the word that best defines **strive** as it is used in paragraph 3.
   ⓐ resign   ⓑ walk   ⓒ support   ⓓ attempt

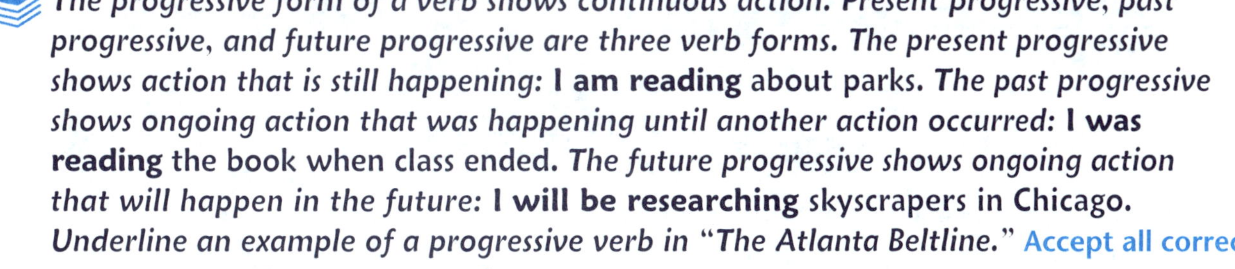

The progressive form of a verb shows continuous action. Present progressive, past progressive, and future progressive are three verb forms. The present progressive shows action that is still happening: **I am reading** *about parks. The past progressive shows ongoing action that was happening until another action occurred:* **I was reading** *the book when class ended. The future progressive shows ongoing action that will happen in the future:* **I will be researching** *skyscrapers in Chicago. Underline an example of a progressive verb in "The Atlanta Beltline."* Accept all correct answers. Example: See paragraph 1.

Write Your Own

 *How would you improve your town or city? With a partner, use at least three vocabulary words from this unit in a description of your idea for an improvement. Then share your idea with another pair of students.*

 *For more practice with progressive forms of verbs, see* Grammar Workshop, Level Blue, Lesson 22.

Word Study — Using a Thesaurus

A **thesaurus** is a reference book that lists words with their synonyms. Sometimes it also lists antonyms. You can use a thesaurus to find more interesting or more exact words for a given word. Read this sentence: *The man will **leave** his job as a teacher to retire.* Then look at the thesaurus entry for *leave*. Look for a synonym that can replace *leave* to improve the sentence.

Think about the synonyms *depart* and *resign*. *Depart* means "to go away, typically to start a journey," and *resign* (page 81) means "to give up a job or position." Of these two synonyms, *resign* is the better replacement for *leave*.

PRACTICE   *Look up each **boldface** entry word in a thesaurus. Then write two additional synonyms for the entry.* **Possible answers are given.**

1. **cold**   chilly, wintry, frosty,   __freezing__, __frigid__

2. **make**   build, create, assemble,   __construct__, __produce__

3. **surprise**   amaze, startle, astound,   __shock__, __stun__

4. **leave**   depart, desert, resign,   __abandon__, __quit__

APPLY   *Replace each **boldface** word with a synonym from the thesaurus entries above. Write the word on the line.* **Accept reasonable answers. Possible answers are given.**

5. It was **cold** the week before my swimming party. __chilly__

6. If I accidentally drop a book, I will **surprise** the readers in the library.
__startle__

7. The artist likes to **make** works of art out of wire. __create__

8. The buses **leave** the terminal at 9:10 p.m. __depart__

9. The weather turned **cold** as the autumn season came to an end.
__wintry__

10. The gardener will **make** a shed for all her gardening tools. __build__

Write a sentence about something that you did today. Then exchange sentences with a partner. Look for words in the sentence that could be more exact or more interesting. Use a thesaurus if you need to.

Shades of Meaning Words That Describe People

In "What Happened to Pennsylvania Station?" on pages 78–79, you read a description about one of New York City's famous train stations. The text described it as an *energetic* place full of activity and an exciting place to be.

In the passage, *energetic* describes a place, but the word *energetic* can also describe a person. Look at the words in the chart. Learning the words will help you choose the right word to use when you describe people in speaking and writing.

energetic	People who are **energetic** are enthusiastic and full of energy.
finicky	People who are **finicky** are very fussy and difficult to please.
impatient	People who are **impatient** get annoyed easily, especially when waiting.
resourceful	People who are **resourceful** are clever and imaginative. They are effective, especially in difficult situations.

PRACTICE   *Read each description. Choose a word from the chart to identify the type of person described.*

1. A person who participates in several after-school activities _______ energetic _______

2. A person who complains about standing in line _______ impatient _______

3. A person who is particular about how something is done _______ finicky _______

4. A person who is able to solve a problem creatively _______ resourceful _______

5. A person who wants the corn and peas in separate dishes _______ finicky _______

6. A person who keeps checking a clock when waiting for a bus _______ impatient _______

APPLY   *Read each item. Write a response using the word in* **boldface.**
Accept answers that students can justify.

7. Think about a time you felt **impatient**. What made you feel impatient?

____

8. At what time of day do you feel most **energetic**? Why do you think this is so?

____

9. Some people are **finicky** about what they eat. What are you finicky about?

____

10. Do you think a cook should be **resourceful**? Explain your answer.

____

Introducing the Words

Read the following contemporary fiction passage about a young athlete. Notice how the highlighted words are used. These are the words you will be learning in this unit.

The Competitive Edge

(Contemporary Fiction)

A differentiated version of this passage is available at **SadlierConnect.com**.

My friend Denise was the best distance runner on our track team. At least, I always assumed she was. In spring, we both run in 3-kilometer races in the **vicinity** of our school. She comes in first, and I might come in fifth or so—on a good day. I'm just not that focused on winning, I guess, and I certainly never thought anyone would **displace** Denise as the team's top runner.

"Maya, you have to be more competitive!" Coach Karen told me after my last race. "Today, you looked like you were jogging downtown for an ice cream cone."

Coach isn't always **considerate** of my feelings. Still, there's truth to what she says. If you took a **poll**, most people would say athletes are naturally competitive, but for some reason, I wasn't. Not that there's anything bad or **improper** about wanting to win—especially in sports. In fact, a competitive spirit is a healthy thing. So why didn't I have more of it?

That's what was on my mind last Friday just before the 3-kilometer race in Gray Falls. When the race began, I watched Denise jump out to the lead as I fell back to the middle of

the pack. This was identical to what had happened at the beginning of my last two races. I had come in sixth and seventh in those, but suddenly, that wasn't good enough. All of a sudden, I felt like winning!

We were already running at a brisk pace, but I picked it up a bit. Running hard, I moved ahead of the two girls in front of me. This was risky because pacing is all-important in distance running. If I wasn't careful, I might not have enough energy to finish. I might come in last and humiliate myself.

One thing was obvious. I wasn't jogging for ice cream today. In fact, I was gaining on Denise. With each step, I saw the soles of her track shoes more clearly. Usually, my mind races faster than my body does in a race. I think about how far I've run and how far I have to go. I estimate how much energy I have left. I second-guess every move I make. This race, however, was different. This time, my

mind was completely empty except for one thought: I'm going to pull ahead!

Incredibly enough, I did. I crossed the finish line less than a meter ahead of Denise. I had won my first race!

"Good race!" I said to Denise after we had caught our breaths.

"Yeah," she muttered, looking like she was in shock after her unexpected downfall.

"Lucky win for me," I heard myself say. I guess I came up with that to soothe Denise's feelings.

Just then, Coach came over. "That was more than luck," she said. "You both ran a great race. It's just that Maya wanted the win more—finally!"

I have to admit that winning the race felt great. It's a memory I cherish. Also, now that I've won once, I want to prove that I can do it again. Maybe that's what competition is all about.

Definitions

You were introduced to these words in the passage. Study the pronunciation, part of speech, definition, and example sentence for each word. Then read the synonyms and antonyms.

1. **brisk**
(brisk)
(BRISK)

(adj.) energetic, lively, fast; cool and fresh

The flag snapped and fluttered in the brisk wind.

SYNONYMS: quick, active, peppy; refreshing, nippy
ANTONYMS: slow, dull, sluggish

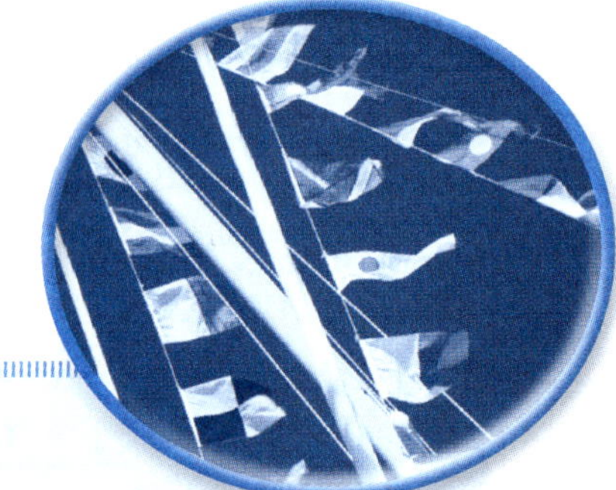

💬 What do you wear when it is **brisk** outside?

2. **cherish**
(cher′ ish)
(CHER-ish)

(v.) to feel or show great love for; to value highly; to take special care of

Our freedom is something we should always safeguard and cherish.

SYNONYMS: to treasure, hold dear, honor; to prize, preserve
ANTONYMS: to hate, despise, dishonor; to neglect

💬 What are two personal items that you **cherish**?

3. **considerate**
(kən si′ də rət)
(kuhn-SI-duh-ruht)

(adj.) showing concern for the needs or feelings of others

If you are a considerate guest, you might be invited back.

SYNONYMS: thoughtful, kind, giving, gracious
ANTONYMS: thoughtless, self-centered, selfish

4. **displace**
(dis plās′)
(diss-PLAYSS)

(v.) to force to move or flee; to move out of position

Officials feared that the flood would displace the villagers from their homes.

SYNONYMS: to uproot, expel, evict, dislodge; ANTONYMS: to settle, plant, install

5. **downfall**
(daủn′ fôl)
(DOUN-fawl)

(n.) a sudden fall from power or position; a sudden, heavy snow or rain

To this day, historians argue over what caused the Roman Empire's downfall.

SYNONYMS: collapse, ruin; ANTONYMS: triumph, success

6. **estimate**
(v., es′ tə māt)
(ESS-tuh-mate)
(n., es′ tə mət)
(ESS-tuh-muht)

(v.) to form a rough judgment about size, quantity, or value

I would estimate the number of people at the concert at about 15,000.

(n.) a rough calculation; a careful guess

The mechanic gave us an estimate for the auto repairs.

SYNONYMS: (v.) to figure, judge; (n.) a calculation, opinion

7. humiliate
(hyü mi′ lē āt)
(hyoo-MI-lee-ate)

(v.) to hurt someone's self-respect or pride

Our opponents accused us of trying to humiliate them by running up the score.

SYNONYMS: to shame, disgrace, dishonor, embarrass
ANTONYMS: to honor, applaud, praise

8. identical
(ī den′ ti kəl)
(eye-DEN-ti-kuhl)

(adj.) exactly the same, alike in every way

The twins liked to wear identical outfits.

SYNONYM: matching; ANTONYMS: unlike, different, opposite

9. improper
(im prä′ pər)
(im-PRAH-pur)

(adj.) not correct; showing bad manners or taste

The principal reminded us that improper behavior is not acceptable.

SYNONYMS: incorrect, wrong; impolite, unsuitable, rude
ANTONYMS: proper, right; appropriate, polite

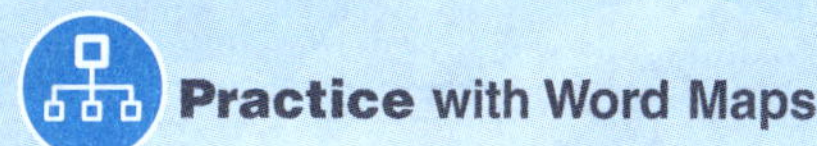

10. poll
(pōl)
(POHL)

(n.) a collecting of votes; (usually plural) a place where voting takes place; a collecting of opinions

Where did you see the results of the poll?

(v.) to receive votes; to vote; to question people to collect opinions

We are going to poll our classmates about their favorite movies.

SYNONYMS: (n.) an election; a survey, tally; (v.) to interview, tally up

11. soothe
(süth)
(SOOTH)

(v.) to make calm; to ease pain or sorrow

A nurse tried to soothe the fussy child.

SYNONYMS: to quiet, pacify; to comfort, relieve
ANTONYMS: to excite, upset; to hurt, worsen

Discuss with your partner some ways to **soothe** a bruised knee.

12. vicinity
(və si′ nə tē)
(vuh-SI-nuh-tee)

(n.) the area near a place, the surrounding region

There is a park in the vicinity of our school.

SYNONYMS: neighborhood, area, surroundings

With your partner, make a map that shows three rooms in the **vicinity** of your classroom.

As time allows, have partners complete graphic organizers for select words, available at **SadlierConnect.com**.

Synonyms

*Choose the word that is most nearly the **same** in meaning as the word or phrase in **boldface**. Then write your choice on the line provided.*

1. **dislodged** by the earthquake
   a. cherished   b. displaced   c. polled   d. soothed   __displaced__

2. **embarrassed** by a failing grade
   a. cherished   b. soothed   c. humiliated   d. displaced   __humiliated__

3. **treasure** the memory of my first home run
   a. estimate   b. poll   c. cherish   d. humiliate   __cherish__

4. **survey** voters on their choice for senator
   a. humiliate   b. estimate   c. poll   d. soothe   __poll__

5. recommended a restaurant in the **area**
   a. downfall   b. vicinity   c. poll   d. estimate   __vicinity__

6. **judged** the distance to be thirty feet
   a. polled   b. estimated   c. cherished   d. humiliated   __estimated__

Antonyms

*Choose the word that is most nearly **opposite** in meaning to the word or phrase in **boldface**. Then write your choice on the line provided.*

1. the general's **triumph**
   a. downfall   b. estimate   c. poll   d. vicinity   __downfall__

2. set a **slow** pace
   a. identical   b. brisk   c. improper   d. considerate   __brisk__

3. held **different** views
   a. improper   b. brisk   c. identical   d. considerate   __identical__

4. truly **thoughtless** behavior
   a. considerate   b. brisk   c. identical   d. improper   __considerate__

5. **worsened** the pain
   a. humiliated   b. estimated   c. polled   d. soothed   __soothed__

6. **correct** use of the word
   a. brisk   b. considerate   c. improper   d. identical   __improper__

Completing the Sentence

Choose the word from the box that best completes each item. Then write the word on the line provided. (You may have to change the word's ending.)

brisk	cherish	considerate
displace	downfall	estimate
humiliate	identical	improper
poll	soothe	vicinity

A Political Charge Backfires

■ In a heated speech late in the campaign, the mayor's opponent accused her of the __________**improper**__________ use of public funds. The mayor immediately denied the charge, declaring that she had never personally profited from her office.

■ A local newspaper conducted a __________**poll**__________ of likely voters. The results showed that 75% of those surveyed did not believe the charge against the mayor.

■ Rather than be __________**humiliated**__________ by what would almost certainly be a lopsided defeat, her opponent pulled out of the race. The mayor went on to win by a landslide.

The Buffalo Trail

■ Before they were forcibly __________**displaced**__________ by federal troops and European settlers, hundreds of thousands of Native Americans dwelled on the Great Plains.

■ __________**Brisk**__________ autumn winds and deep winter snows made warm clothing and shelter essential to survival on the Great Plains. Some of these robes and the tents were made from buffalo hides.

■ Because they were so dependent upon the buffalo for food as well, many tribes never strayed very far from the __________**vicinity**__________ of the huge herds that grazed the prairie.

■ Experts __________**estimate**__________ that as many as 30 million buffalo once roamed the vast open stretches of the northern Plains.

■ The Great Plains tribes __________**cherished**__________ their traditions and way of life. To dishonor these customs was a serious offense.

■ The destruction of the buffalo herds in the late 1800s was one of the factors that led to the __________**downfall**__________ of these tribes.

A Friend's Good Turn

■ I was very upset to learn that a friend planned to come to the party in a costume __________**identical**__________ to mine.

■ To __________**soothe**__________ my hurt feelings, she offered to wear a different costume.

■ It was very __________**considerate**__________ of her to do that for me, don't you think?

Word Associations

*Circle the letter next to the word or phrase that best completes the sentence or answers the question. Pay special attention to the word in **boldface.***

1. Which might you **cherish**?
   a. a thunderstorm
   b. a terrible cold
   c. a bathroom mirror
   d. a beloved pet

2. You're **considerate** if you show
   a. concern for others.
   b. your stamp collection to friends.
   c. off your new bicycle.
   d. pride in your work.

3. Which is most likely to **soothe**?
   a. a buzzing bee
   b. a fast dance
   c. soft music
   d. a hockey game

4. People who live in your **vicinity** are
   a. strangers.
   b. voters.
   c. neighbors.
   d. teachers.

Words with Latin Roots

The unit word *identical*, meaning "the same, alike in every way," comes from the Latin root *idem* or *iden*, which means "same." The root is used in the following words:

- identify (v.): to show to be a certain person or thing (*to show to be the same as expected*)
- identification (n.): something by which a person or thing can be named or shown (*proof that a person or thing is the same as expected*)
- identity (n.): being a specific person or thing (*being the selfsame*)
- identifiable (adj.): able to be named as a specific person or thing (*able to be shown to be the same as expected*)

Choose two of the words from the list. Write a sentence for each word to show you understand its meaning.

1. Accept answers that show an understanding of the vocabulary.

2. ____

 *Read the passage. Then answer each question.*

Preparing for a Marathon

1   A marathon is an exhausting 26.2-mile run. First-time runners should plan on taking the following steps before, during, and after the race.

2   Before signing up, runners must visit a doctor. The doctor will ensure that running such a long distance will not cause any harm. The next step is to select a race from those held all over the country. Runners can **poll** other marathoners about their favorite races.

3   Runners must then choose a training program. Experts **estimate** that it takes several months for runners to train, regardless of whether an athlete runs at a **brisk** or a slow pace.

4   Closer to race day, runners should research the weather in the **vicinity** of the event. If a **downfall** is predicted, they must have the proper clothing. Runners must also get plenty of sleep in the days before the race. Those who have slept enough will tire less quickly.

5   After months of training, it is race day. Runners should be aware of their competitors so as not to **displace** them on the course. After the marathon is over, runners can **soothe** their tired muscles in a hot bath.

1. What does the word **poll** mean as it is used in paragraph 2?
(a) a survey   (b) an election   (c) to vote   (d) to interview

2. The Latin word *aestimare* means "to value." The word **estimate** in paragraph 3 means
(a) to judge   (b) a calculation   (c) a guess   (d) to know

3. What does the word **downfall** mean as it is used in paragraph 4?
(a) fall from power   (b) heavy rain   (c) an unexpected change   (d) a sudden illness

4. What is the meaning of **displace** as it is used in paragraph 5?
(a) to force to flee   (b) to force to move   (c) to keep   (d) to disqualify

 *Regular verbs form the past tense by adding **-ed**. The regular verb **train** becomes **trained**. Irregular verbs change their spelling in the past tense or with the helping verbs has, have, and had. For example, **drive** is an irregular verb. The past forms are **drove** and **has/have/had driven**. Underline a past-tense irregular verb in "Preparing for a Marathon." See paragraph 4.*

Write Your Own

Write a 3–5 sentence story about someone training for a challenge, using at least three words from this unit. Do not write the opening sentence of the story. Share the story with a partner and have your partner write the opening sentence using one word from this unit.

 *For more practice with irregular verbs, see Grammar Workshop, Level Blue, Lesson 25.*

Vocabulary for Comprehension

*Read this passage in which some of the words you have studied in Units 7–9 appear in **boldface**. Then answer the questions.*

America's First Female Doctor

1   Elizabeth Blackwell (1821–1910) didn't always enjoy medicine. But once she chose to become a doctor, she let nothing stop her. In the mid-1800s, medical schools did not accept female students. People believed then that women could never become capable doctors, and this view made Elizabeth irate. Though she hadn't conducted formal **polls**, she knew that many women would feel more at ease consulting a woman about their health instead of a man. Despite public opinion, she decided she would strive to become a doctor.

2   Elizabeth applied to many medical schools, but she was rejected by each and every one. Refusing to be discouraged, Elizabeth **composed** herself after each rejection. Then she made **alternate** plans for her education. She was **industrious** as she read medical textbooks on her own and convinced an understanding doctor to be her private tutor. Finally, in 1847, a small college in upstate New York admitted Elizabeth into its medical program. When she got there, she learned that her acceptance was a joke. Some teachers and classmates tried to **humiliate** her, but Elizabeth did not let such behavior keep her from accomplishing her **primary** goal.

3   In January 1849, Elizabeth Blackwell graduated at the head of her class. She became the first woman in the United States to receive a medical degree. At her graduation, she said, "It shall be the effort of my life to shed honor on this diploma." In so doing, she broke down the barriers that prevented women from practicing medicine. Blackwell never lived to see how her early effort to bring women into medicine matured; by 2017, an **estimated** 50 percent of medical school graduates were women.

Fill in the circle next to the choice that best completes the sentence or answers the question.

1. What is a main idea of the passage?
   - (a) Blackwell became the first female doctor.
   - (b) Blackwell wanted to become a doctor.
   - (c) Blackwell applied to medical school.
   - (d) Blackwell went to college in New York.

2. What does the word **polls** mean as it is used in paragraph 1?
   - (a) collection of votes
   - (b) voting places
   - (c) to receive votes
   - (d) to vote

3. What does the use of the word **composed** in paragraph 2 suggest?
   - (a) Blackwell was neutral.
   - (b) Blackwell calmed down.
   - (c) Blackwell became upset.
   - (d) Blackwell asked questions.

4. What does the author mean by the word **industrious** in paragraph 2?
   - (a) annoyed
   - (b) confused
   - (c) working steadily
   - (d) getting tired

5. Which phrase from the passage best shows the idea of **industrious**?
   - (a) "alternate plans"
   - (b) "read medical textbooks"
   - (c) "small college"
   - (d) "its medical program"

6. As it is used in paragraph 2, what does the word **humiliate** show about the behavior of Blackwell's teachers and classmates?
   - (a) They made her feel accomplished.
   - (b) They made her feel better.
   - (c) They made her feel confident.
   - (d) They made her feel hurt.

7. What is the meaning of **primary** as it is used in paragraph 2?
   - (a) first in time or order
   - (b) fundamental
   - (c) first in importance
   - (d) an early election

8. The Latin word **aestimare** means "to value." The word **estimated** in paragraph 3 means
   - (a) a judgment about quantity
   - (b) a rough calculation
   - (c) a careful guess
   - (d) calculated carefully

Write Your Own

Elizabeth Blackwell accomplished a difficult goal despite many barriers. Think of a time when you worked hard to accomplish a goal. Write to tell what you accomplished and how you were able to do it. Use at least three words from Units 7–9.

Introducing the Words

Read the following textbook entry about a disaster that struck Ireland in the mid-1800s. Notice how the highlighted words are used. These are the words you will be learning in this unit.

Ireland's Great Famine

(Textbook Entry)

A differentiated version of this passage is available at **SadlierConnect.com**.

High in the Andes Mountains of Peru, in a climate too cold for corn, the Inca people grew the first potatoes. The Spanish who arrived in Peru in 1532 were interested in gold and silver, not potatoes. Nevertheless, when they **descended** the Andes and left Peru, they carried some of the strange new vegetables with them and later brought them back to Spain. From there, the potato spread to other parts of Europe. Many people who grew and ate potatoes enjoyed the new food, but some doctors and scientists had serious doubts. They **condemned** potatoes, claiming they caused disease. In France, some even tried to **abolish** the planting of the new crop, claiming it ruined the soil. Despite these extreme reactions, however, most Europeans eventually realized that potatoes were a good source of nutrition.

Nowhere were potatoes grown more widely than in Ireland. In the 1600s, Ireland was a very poor country, controlled by an English parliament that acted like a **dictator**. Most Irish farmers could only afford to rent small plots of land. Raising enough food for a family was a

A farmer needed only a shovel to plant potatoes.

constant challenge. The thrifty Irish farmers saw that they could grow more potatoes on their land than they could wheat, oats, or barley. Also, potato fields did not need to be plowed. As a result, a farmer did not need a horse and plow—only a shovel—to plant potatoes. For these reasons, potatoes became Ireland's main source of food.

For over a century, the new crop helped feed a growing population. Then, in 1845, disaster struck. A fungus, which is a type of plant growth, attacked the crop. On a visual level, its effects were horrifying. It could turn a healthy green potato field into a dark, wilted mess. On a practical level, the harm it could cause soon became clear as well. The fungus destroyed half of Ireland's potato crop that year. Although this occurrence caused widespread hunger, most people survived and looked forward to the next harvest. In fact, many farmers expanded their fields, hoping to grow more potatoes the following year to make up for their losses.

Sadly, the farmers' hopes were in vain. In the summer of 1846, the fungus reappeared. This time, Ireland's entire potato crop was lost. The nation's food supply chain, already fragile and brittle, snapped. Food prices shot up, and a serious famine gripped the land. To survive, people appealed to friends and relatives for help. They sold whatever portable possessions they had on hand in order to buy food. Eventually, they had nothing left that could be carried away. Even worse, after a time, there was no food left to buy.

The potato fungus was like a predator, and the Irish people were its prey. Weak from hunger, many were unable to fight off disease. To make matters worse, the normally mild Irish winter turned bitterly cold in the winter of 1846–1847. By 1848, about a million people had died of hunger or disease. Another million had left Ireland to start new lives in North America. In the years that followed, good potato harvests returned, but for the estimated one-quarter of the population that had died or emigrated, it was too late.

By 1848, about one million Irish emigrants had sailed to North America.

In 1845, a fungus destroyed much of Ireland's potato crop.

Definitions

You were introduced to these words in the passage. Study the pronunciation, part of speech, definition, and example sentence for each word. Then read the synonyms and antonyms.

1. abolish
(ə bä′ lish)
(uh-BAH-lish)

(v.) to do away completely with something; to put an end to

Will human beings ever be able to abolish war?

SYNONYMS: to outlaw, ban, repeal, stamp out
ANTONYMS: to establish, restore

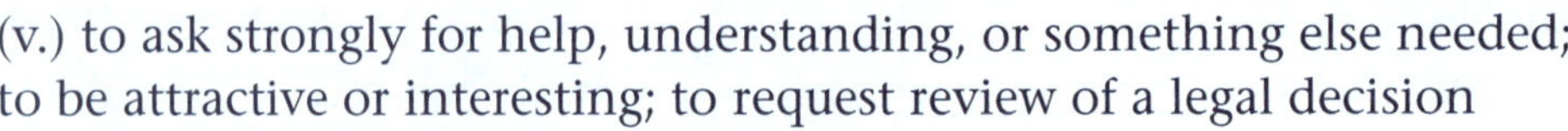

2. appeal
(ə pēl′)
(uh-PEEL)

(n.) a sincere or strong request for something that is needed; a quality or ability that attracts or interests people; a request to a higher court for review of a legal decision

Some people don't understand the appeal of video games.

(v.) to ask strongly for help, understanding, or something else needed; to be attractive or interesting; to request review of a legal decision

Our class will appeal for aid for the homeless.

SYNONYMS: (n.) a plea, petition; charm, attraction; (v.) to plead, implore, beg
ANTONYMS: (v.) to repel, disgust, repulse

 Make an **appeal** to your partner for something you want to borrow.

3. brittle
(bri′ təl)
(BRI-tuhl)

(adj.) easily broken, snapped, or cracked; not flexible

The pages of the old book had turned brittle.

SYNONYMS: breakable, stiff, unbending, fragile
ANTONYMS: bendable, flexible, elastic, rugged

What will happen if you drop something that is **brittle**?

4. condemn
(kən dem′)
(kuhn-DEM)

(v.) to criticize a person or action as wrong, guilty, or evil; to judge as guilty and to punish

The judge is expected to condemn the defendant to life in prison.

SYNONYMS: to disapprove, denounce, blame
ANTONYMS: to praise, admire, honor, applaud, approve

5. descend
(di send′)
(di-SEND)

(v.) to move to a lower place from a higher one; to come or be handed down from the past

We watched the climber descend the cliff.

SYNONYMS: to drop, fall, plunge, climb down; to stem, derive
ANTONYMS: to rise, climb, scale, ascend

6. dictator
(dik′ tā tər)
(DIK-tay-tur)

(n.) a ruler or leader who has total power

Sometimes my older brother acts like a dictator.

SYNONYMS: tyrant, master, despot, oppressor

7. expand
(ik spand′)
(ik-SPAND)

(v.) to open up, make or grow larger; to develop

The principal plans to expand our classroom.

SYNONYMS: to spread, stretch, swell, enlarge
ANTONYMS: to shrink, reduce, contract, abridge

Name two objects that **expand** when you put air in them.

8. famine
(fa′ mən)
(FA-muhn)

(n.) a severe shortage of food over a large area

Children especially suffered during the famine.

SYNONYMS: hunger, starvation, scarcity, want; ANTONYMS: feast, plenty

9. portable
(pôr′ tə bəl)
(POR-tuh-buhl)

(adj.) easily moved or carried

Dad put a portable crib in the trunk.

SYNONYMS: movable, transportable; ANTONYMS: immovable, fixed, rooted

With your partner, list three items in the classroom that are **portable**.

10. prey
(prā)
(PRAY)

(n.) an animal hunted as food by another; someone or something that is helpless against attack

The documentary showed a lion stalking its prey.

(v.) to hunt for food; to harm, rob, or take advantage of

Only a bully would prey upon the weak.

SYNONYMS: (n.) a victim; quarry; (v.) to devour; to bully, victimize, cheat
ANTONYMS: (n.) a hunter, predator

Use each definition of **prey** in a sentence.

11. thrifty
(thrif′ tē)
(THRIF-tee)

(adj.) careful about spending money; tending to save money; managing money well

My parents are teaching me to be a thrifty shopper.

SYNONYMS: economical, frugal, tightfisted
ANTONYMS: wasteful, careless, extravagant

12. visual
(vi′ zhə wəl)
(VI-zhuh-wuhl)

(adj.) having to do with sight or seeing

The math teacher likes to use visual aids.

SYNONYMS: visible, pictured, shown, illustrated

As time allows, have partners complete graphic organizers for select words, available at **SadlierConnect.com**.

Synonyms

*Choose the word that is most nearly the **same** in meaning as the word or phrase in **boldface**. Then write your choice on the line provided.*

1. a **movable** television
   a. brittle　　b. portable　　c. thrifty　　d. visual　　**portable**

2. reported on the terrible **scarcity**
   a. appeal　　b. prey　　c. dictator　　d. famine　　**famine**

3. a powerful and selfish **tyrant**
   a. prey　　b. famine　　c. appeal　　d. dictator　　**dictator**

4. **plead** for help
   a. abolish　　b. descend　　c. appeal　　d. prey　　**appeal**

5. **visible** proof of the break-in
   a. visual　　b. brittle　　c. thrifty　　d. portable　　**visual**

6. turned **stiff** by the cold
   a. brittle　　b. visual　　c. portable　　d. thrifty　　**brittle**

Antonyms

*Choose the word that is most nearly **opposite** in meaning to the word or phrase in **boldface**. Then write your choice on the line provided.*

1. **shrink** the size of the project
   a. expand　　b. descend　　c. appeal　　d. condemn　　**expand**

2. tracked the **predator**
   a. dictator　　b. prey　　c. appeal　　d. famine　　**prey**

3. **restore** the tax on medicine
   a. condemn　　b. descend　　c. abolish　　d. expand　　**abolish**

4. **praised** the decision
   a. appealed　　b. descended　　c. abolished　　d. condemned　　**condemned**

5. a **wasteful** consumer
   a. portable　　b. visual　　c. thrifty　　d. brittle　　**thrifty**

6. **ascend** the mountain
   a. prey upon　　b. descend　　c. abolish　　d. expand　　**descend**

Completing the Sentence

Choose the word from the box that best completes each item. Then write the word on the line provided. (You may have to change the word's ending.)

abolish	**appeal**	**brittle**
condemn	**descend**	**dictator**
expand	**famine**	**portable**
prey	**thrifty**	**visual**

An End to Slavery

■ Before the Civil War, many northerners ____**condemned**____ slavery as a terrible evil, but few wanted to go to war because of it. Abraham Lincoln, too, personally hated slavery but was prepared to accept it if by doing so the Union could be preserved.

■ Once the war began, however, many in the North argued that the time had come to ____**abolish**____ slavery once and for all. In 1863 Lincoln issued the Emancipation Proclamation, freeing the enslaved in the states of the Confederacy.

■ Abraham Lincoln's enemies called him a(n) ____**dictator**____ because he exercised so much power during the war.

■ Illustrators and photographers accompanied Union troops during some of the war's bloodiest campaigns, leaving us an important ____**visual**____ record of the horrors experienced by the soldiers on both sides of the conflict.

■ Some African Americans who have ____**descended**____ from enslaved families have passed along dramatic stories of their ancestors' experiences.

Drought Leads to Hunger

■ Without enough water, plant fibers dry out and become ____**brittle**____. If a drought lasts for a long time, plants and crops die.

■ If too many plants die, insects have no food, and the birds and animals that ____**prey**____ on insects then lose their food supply, too.

■ The threat of ____**famine**____ can drive animals great distances in search of food.

■ If these animals do not ____**expand**____ their hunting area, they too will starve.

A Teacher on a Budget

■ It would help our teacher a lot to have a laptop, a ____**portable**____ computer, that she could take back and forth between school and her home.

■ She has asked businesses to donate equipment that they no longer need. So far, many businesses have answered her ____**appeal**____ with computers for our classroom.

■ It has been a very ____**thrifty**____ way of modernizing our classroom because it has cost hardly anything at all.

Word Associations

Circle the letter next to the word or phrase that best completes the sentence or answers the question. Pay special attention to the word in **boldface.**

1. A **dictator** is most likely
   a. to be loved.
   b. to be honored.
   c. to be elected.
   d. to be feared.

2. If a book **appeals** to you,
   a. you will probably read it.
   b. it is probably very long.
   c. it is probably boring.
   d. you will never read it.

3. A **thrifty** person would
   a. give all her money away.
   b. never buy anything on sale.
   c. spend money wisely.
   d. leave a generous tip.

4. If something is **brittle**,
   a. it breaks easily.
   b. it freezes quickly.
   c. it is hard to see.
   d. it is easy to carry.

Words with Latin Roots

The unit word *portable*, meaning "easily moved or carried," comes from the root *port*. **Port** is a Latin root meaning "to carry." The root *port* is used in the following words:

- import (v.): to bring in from a foreign country (*to carry in*)
- export (v.): to send out to a foreign country (*to carry out*)
- transport (v.): to move something from one place to another (*to carry across*)
- transportation (n.): the act of moving something from one place to another (*carrying across*)
- support (v.): to prop up or help (*to carry from below*)

Choose two of the words from the list. Write a sentence for each word to show you understand its meaning.

1. Accept answers that show an understanding of the vocabulary. ______________

2. ____

 *Read the passage. Then answer each question.*

The Incas and Farming

1   The Andes Mountains, in South America, are one of the world's tallest mountain ranges. The ground can be dry, crusty, and **brittle**, and the mountain slopes are steep. Yet centuries ago, the Inca people adapted well to these mountains. They built a series of platforms, or terraces, for planting. Fields **descended** the mountain slopes, creating the **visual** effect of stair steps.

2   A terrace planting area was smaller than a typical farm field. But its stone wall, heated by the sun, would keep the plant roots warm, even on cold nights. This warming effect **expanded** the growing season and helped protect the Incas from **famine**.

3   The Inca diet consisted mostly of vegetables grown on the mountainside. The Incas developed strong breeds of crops like beans and corn, which still have **appeal** and value today. The Incas were better farmers than most civilizations. Sadly, however, their techniques were largely forgotten as these native people fell **prey** to the Spanish conquest of their land.

1. What is the meaning of the word **brittle** as it is used in paragraph 1?
   (a) flexible   (b) rugged   (c) breakable   (d) healthy

2. What does the word **descended** mean as it is used in paragraph 1?
   (a) went down   (b) fallen   (c) wrapped around   (d) went up

3. The Latin word *appellare* means "to call upon." The word **appeal** in paragraph 3 means
   (a) attraction   (b) tastiness   (c) high cost   (d) fame

4. Pick the word that best defines **prey** as it is used in paragraph 3.
   (a) bully   (b) devour   (c) victim   (d) hunter

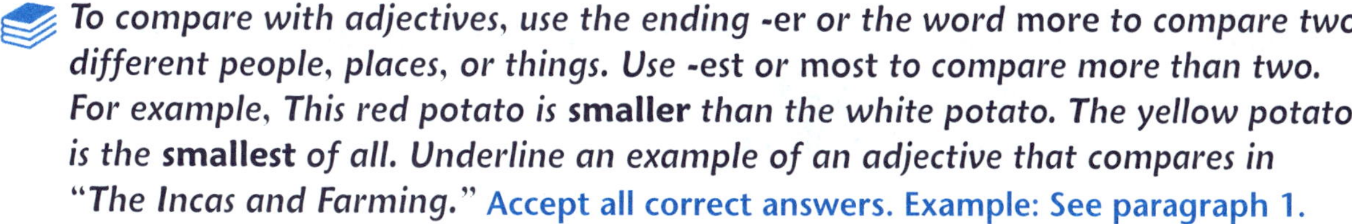 *To compare with adjectives, use the ending -er or the word* more *to compare two different people, places, or things. Use* -est *or* most *to compare more than two. For example,* This red potato is **smaller** than the white potato. The yellow potato is the **smallest** of all. *Underline an example of an adjective that compares in "The Incas and Farming."* Accept all correct answers. Example: See paragraph 1.

Write Your Own

Create flash cards for three of the vocabulary words used in the passage. Have your partner define the words on your flashcards. Challenge your partner to recall how the word is used in the passage.

 For more practice with comparing with adjectives, see Grammar Workshop, Level Blue, Lesson 31.

Word Study — Roots *port, mit*

A root is the main part of a word. Roots have meaning, but few roots can stand alone. Knowing the meaning of a root can sometimes help you figure out the meaning of a word. Often, the root comes from a different language, such as Latin or Greek.

The chart below shows the meanings of some words with the roots *port* and *mit*.

port—carry
The root **port** appears in **portable** (page 101). When something is **portable**, it is easily moved or carried.

mit—send
The root **mit** appears in **emit**. When buses **emit** fumes, they give off unhealthy smoke and gases.

import	to bring goods or materials into one country from another
porter	someone whose job it is to carry bags or other loads
submit	to send something in for consideration
transmit	to send out from one place or person to another; broadcast

PRACTICE *Complete each sentence with a word that contains the root* **port** *or* **mit**. *Choose from the words above.*

1. When do we have to ___submit___ our ideas for the science fair?

2. The ___porter___ helped us get our suitcases off the bus.

3. Many countries ___import___ bananas from Costa Rica.

4. Sneeze into a tissue so you don't ___transmit___ your cold.

5. Stores on an island ___import___ most of their merchandise.

6. The principal uses a microphone to ___transmit___ daily announcements.

APPLY *Complete each sentence to show you understand the meaning of the word in* **boldface**. **Accept reasonable answers. Possible answers are given.**

7. The hotel guest asked the **porter** to ___load the luggage in the car___.

8. If I don't **submit** my application by June 15, I'll ___miss the deadline___.

9. You can **transmit** information by ___sending an email___.

10. Some things our country might **import** are ___fruits and electronic equipment___.

Work with a partner to list other words that contain the roots **port** and **mit**. Write definitions for the words. Then consult a dictionary to check the meanings.

Shades of Meaning   Idioms I

In the passage "Ireland's Great Famine" on pages 98–99, you read this sentence: *Food prices shot up, and a serious **famine** gripped the land.* In this sentence, the word *famine* means "a severe shortage of food."

An **idiom** is an expression that has a special meaning. You cannot figure out its meaning from the individual words. Here is an example: *Along the boardwalk, business is **either feast or famine**. Business is robust when the weather is sunny and warm, but it is slow when it is rainy and cold.* Here, the idiom *either feast or famine* has nothing to do with food. Instead, the expression means "either too much or too little of something."

PRACTICE   *Read each sentence. Figure out the meaning of each idiom in* **boldface.** *Write the number of the sentence next to the meaning of the idiom.*

1. I was supposed to give my speech today, but I **got cold feet** and asked to be excused.

2. I worked **against the clock** to finish my book report.

3. Don't **add fuel to the fire** by criticizing how we played in the game that we lost.

4. I'm going **out on a limb** by giving her a second chance. After all, she did try hard.

4 put yourself in a tough position to support someone

3 make a bad situation worse than it is

2 rushed and short on time

1 became too nervous to go through with something

APPLY   *Read each sentence. Figure out the meaning of each idiom in* **boldface.** *Write the meaning on the line provided.* Accept reasonable answers. Possible answers are given.

5. You have become such a **couch potato** that we can't persuade you to do anything else.

   a lazy person who watches television all day

6. When my best friend also made the soccer team, it was the **icing on the cake**.

   when something goes well and then another good thing happens

7. While I was waiting to hear the test results, I was **on pins and needles**.

   very nervous, especially while waiting for something

8. Don't **spill the beans** about the party. It's a surprise.

   reveal a secret

Introducing the Words

Read the following magazine article about a daring rescue group. Notice how the highlighted words are used. These are the words you will be learning in this unit.

National Ski Patrol to the Rescue

(Magazine Article)

A differentiated version of this passage is available at SadlierConnect.com.

Avalanche! Without warning it happens. A mountainside of loose snow suddenly slides down a slope toward a downhill skier. As the skier looks up in horror, he loses his footing. It is as if a carpet has suddenly been pulled out from under his feet. Tons of snow knock him over and drag him down the hillside.

In seconds, the skier is buried. At first, he is angry with himself for not staying with his group and for getting himself into such a dangerous situation. Muttering tart comments about his bad luck, he tries to dig his way to the surface. He is too deeply buried for that, though. Instead, he decides to stay still and conserve the oxygen in the air pockets around him. Absurd as it sounds, the skier nestles into the snow, hoping that other members of his ski party will have seen the avalanche and notice that he is missing.

Fortunately, the buried skier is wearing a beacon. This electronic device sends out a regular signal to help rescuers locate him. There is no realistic way to avoid all the dangers of winter in the backcountry. Devices like beacons, however, reduce a skier's risk in the wilderness.

The skier's companions have seen the avalanche and realize that their partner is missing. As they race closer, they call in an urgent plea for help. Fortunately, members of the National Ski Patrol (NSP) are in the area. On snowmobiles, they navigate across the rugged landscape toward the disaster site.

Rescuers use beacons and poles to search for a skier under snow.

The National Ski Patrol is the largest winter rescue organization in the world. Since 1938, NSP volunteers have searched for and rescued thousands of skiers and hikers. The organization provides a sense of security for people who use the slopes. The guiding principle of the National Ski Patrol is to promote safe skiing and winter sports.

The National Ski Patrol classifies the country into different geographic regions. Volunteers patrol the ski slopes and wilderness ski areas in the region where they live. When choosing its volunteers, the organization is very selective. In addition to being in excellent physical shape, members must complete advanced training in outdoor emergency care. In areas where avalanches tend to occur, members receive special avalanche training, too. These steps help to ensure the success of rescue efforts.

Thanks to their high level of preparation, the NSP rescuers are able to help the skier buried by the avalanche. Immediately after arriving on the scene, they turn their own beacons to Receive. That lets them hear the signal from the skier's beacon. The rescuers also spot the ski mitten that the skier lost in the avalanche. That's another clue to his whereabouts.

The rescuers have identified the general area where the skier must be. Now they carefully probe the most likely areas with long aluminum poles. Methodically, they cover the area, probing every foot or so. Suddenly, they hear a muffled cry.

Fortunately, the snow is light and fluffy. It contains a lot of air. That lets the rescuers move it away quickly to reach the skier. More important, the buried man had enough air to breathe.

Soon a helicopter arrives to transport the skier to a hospital. It was a close call, but thanks to the National Ski Patrol, there was a happy ending!

Definitions

You were introduced to these words in the passage. Study the pronunciation, part of speech, definition, and example sentence for each word. Then read the synonyms and antonyms.

1. absurd
(əb sûrd')
(uhb-SURD)

(adj.) making no sense at all, going completely against or having no reason

> *No one is going to believe such an absurd story!*

SYNONYMS: silly, ridiculous, foolish, crazy, insane
ANTONYMS: sensible, wise, intelligent, sound

 With your partner, make up an **absurd** story about two animals that can speak.

2. avalanche
(a' və lanch)
(A-vuh-lanch)

(n.) a large mass of snow, ice, rocks, or other material sliding or falling swiftly down a mountainside; something resembling such an event

> *The skiers were almost buried by an avalanche that came roaring down the slope.*

SYNONYMS: a landslide, flood, cascade

3. classify
(kla' sə fī)
(KLA-suh-fye)

(v.) to group or label in an organized way

> *Libraries classify books by title, author, and subject.*

SYNONYMS: to order, arrange, sort, catalog, pigeonhole

 Make a list of ways grocery stores **classify** food.

4. ensure
(en shủr')
(en-SHUR)

(v.) to make sure, safe, or certain; to guarantee

> *The playground was designed to ensure the children's safety.*

SYNONYMS: to confirm, insure
ANTONYMS: to risk, endanger

5. navigate
(na' və gāt)
(NA-vuh-gate)

(v.) to plan and steer the course of a vessel or vehicle; to make one's way, get around

> *A pilot uses charts and instruments to navigate a helicopter.*

SYNONYMS: to guide, pilot, operate

 What is the best way to **navigate** your way to the main office?

 As time allows, have partners complete graphic organizers for select words, available at **SadlierConnect.com.**

6. nestle
(ne′ səl)
(NE-suhl)

(v.) to settle down comfortably; to hold lovingly

The child likes to nestle in her grandmother's lap.

SYNONYMS: to cuddle, snuggle

7. plea
(plē)
(PLEE)

(n.) an urgent request for help; the answer given in a law court by a person accused of a crime

The judge accepted the defendant's plea of not guilty.

SYNONYMS: an appeal, cry, petition, prayer

8. principle
(prin′ sə pəl)
(PRIN-suh-puhl)

(n.) a basic rule or law on which others are based; a belief used to tell right from wrong

A judge must be a person of high principles.

SYNONYMS: a standard, truth, guide, guideline, creed

9. realistic
(rē ə lis′ tik)
(ree-uh-LISS-tik)

(adj.) using facts and good sense to evaluate people, things, or situations; concerned with the practical; resembling real life

The painting was so realistic that it looked like a photograph.

SYNONYMS: achievable, reasonable, sensible; true-to-life
ANTONYMS: impractical, dreamy, unrealistic, pie-in-the-sky

💬 **What is a realistic number of books that you can read in one month? Explain to your partner why this number is realistic.**

10. security
(si kyůr′ ə tē)
(si-KYOOR-uh-tee)

(n.) freedom from danger, fear, or doubt; safety

There is always heavy security around the White House.

SYNONYMS: protection, safekeeping, confidence, assurance
ANTONYMS: doubt, insecurity, peril

11. selective
(sə lek′ tiv)
(suh-LEK-tiv)

(adj.) very careful about choosing or using

It pays to be a very selective shopper.

SYNONYMS: choosy, particular, picky, fussy, discriminating
ANTONYMS: unselective, careless

12. tart
(tärt)
(TART)

(adj.) having a sharp or sour taste; sharp in manner or tone

My sister replied with a very tart remark.

(n.) a small pie, usually filled with fruit

I had a peach tart for dessert.

SYNONYMS: (adj.) tangy, acid; biting, cutting, harsh; (n.) a pastry
ANTONYMS: (adj.) sweet; mild, gentle

💬 **Use each definition of tart in a sentence.**

Synonyms

*Choose the word that is most nearly the **same** in meaning as the word or phrase in **boldface**. Then write your choice on the line provided.*

1. questioned our **standards**
a. principles   b. securities   c. pleas   d. avalanches   _principles_

2. a **landslide** of mail at holiday time
a. plea   b. security   c. principle   d. avalanche   _avalanche_

3. **appeals** to save the rain forest
a. principles   b. avalanches   c. pleas   d. securities   _pleas_

4. **sort** the blocks by shape and color
a. navigate   b. ensure   c. nestle   d. classify   _classify_

5. **cuddle** in my mother's arms
a. classify   b. nestle   c. ensure   d. navigate   _nestle_

6. **pilot** a tanker through the canal
a. ensure   b. navigate   c. classify   d. nestle   _navigate_

Antonyms

*Choose the word that is most nearly **opposite** in meaning to the word or phrase in **boldface**. Then write your choice on the line provided.*

1. to **deny** safe passage
a. ensure   b. classify   c. navigate   d. nestle   _ensure_

2. a **sound** excuse for being absent
a. tart   b. absurd   c. realistic   d. selective   _absurd_

3. show very **careless** taste
a. selective   b. realistic   c. absurd   d. tart   _selective_

4. an **impractical** view of the situation
a. absurd   b. realistic   c. selective   d. tart   _realistic_

5. prefer **sweet** apples
a. selective   b. realistic   c. tart   d. absurd   _tart_

6. felt a sense of **danger**
a. avalanche   b. security   c. plea   d. principle   _security_

Completing the Sentence

Choose the word from the box that best completes each item. Then write the word on the line provided. (You may have to change the word's ending.)

absurd	avalanche	classify
ensure	navigate	nestle
plea	principle	realistic
security	selective	tart

A Dog's Life

■ Some dogs are grouped by breed or by the work that they do. Highly trained dogs that work to help people are __________**classified**__________ as assistance dogs.

■ Handlers of these animals have to be very __________**selective**__________ in choosing dogs for the demanding training. Some animals are simply not suited to the work.

■ Some dogs, such as police or guard dogs, offer __________**security**__________ from crime or trespassers, helping their owners feel safer in their homes.

■ Rescue dogs can go where humans cannot or dare not go. For example, these dogs can safely __________**navigate**__________ the ruins or rubble left by earthquakes or accidents, in search of survivors.

■ Large, strong dogs with thick fur, such as St. Bernards or huskies, are trained to rescue skiers or climbers trapped by __________**avalanches**__________.

■ Schools for these remarkable dogs make yearly __________**pleas**__________ for money and for volunteers who will help prepare puppies for "canine careers."

Clowning Around

■ Like other schools, the Ringling Brothers Clown College is guided by a philosophy of education. At the Clown College, the first and foremost __________**principle**__________ is that just about anyone can be taught the art of clowning.

■ To __________**ensure**__________ success as clowns, students must work hard to master many skills, including juggling, acrobatics, makeup design, and comedy writing.

■ Great clowns make sensible, ordinary tasks, like opening a box, somehow seem __________**absurd**__________ and wacky.

■ Sarcastic clowns use insults and __________**tart**__________ comments to get laughs. Occasionally they make fun of the audience, but they usually play jokes on themselves.

■ In one funny routine, a clown dressed as a porcupine __________**nestled**__________ against a cactus and called it "Mama."

■ The cactus looked quite __________**realistic**__________ and lifelike from a distance, but on closer inspection it proved to be made of rubber.

*Circle the letter next to the word or phrase that best completes the sentence or answers the question. Pay special attention to the word in **boldface.***

1. Where might you see an **avalanche**?
   a. on the ocean
   b. in the mountains
   c. in a desert
   d. in a suburb

2. Athletes with strong **principles**
   a. play by the rules.
   b. fight with the coach.
   c. hold out for more money.
   d. skip practice.

3. A movie about a **realistic** situation might be titled
   a. "I Married an Alligator!"
   b. "The Magic Eggplant."
   c. "Forest Fire!"
   d. "Martian Dance Party."

4. A sense of **security** makes you feel
   a. upset.
   b. nervous.
   c. safe.
   d. lucky.

Words with Latin Roots

The unit word *navigate*, meaning "to steer the course of a ship or vehicle," comes from the Latin *nav*. *Nav* is a Latin root meaning "ship." The root is used in the following words:

- navy (n.): armed forces based on ships (*a fleet of warships*)
- naval (adj.): having to do with a navy (*concerning warships*)
- navigation (n.): the act of steering a course (*the act of guiding a ship*)
- navigable (adj.): describing a body of water that can be traveled on or across (*suitable for ships to travel upon*)

Choose two of the words from the list. Write a sentence for each word to show you understand its meaning.

1. Accept answers that show an understanding of the vocabulary.

2.

Words in Context

Read the passage. Then answer each question.

What Causes an Avalanche?

1 We can **classify avalanches** in two ways, according to their cause: natural and artificial. Natural avalanches are caused by wind, sun, snow, or rain. These conditions can affect snowpack, or snow already packed on the ground, and cause some of the snow to slide. Artificial causes are created by humans. Skiers and snowmobiles have caused avalanches.

2 Avalanches are the most common during winter or spring, right after a storm bringing more than a foot of snowfall. Even though experts can sometimes predict an avalanche, one can wipe out an entire town when it occurs. It is almost impossible to **navigate** through the snow and ice after such an event.

3 When someone is caught in an avalanche, it is best to escape the moving snow. If people do get caught under snow, they should clear air space to breathe. It may not seem **realistic** or practical to scream out a **plea** for help because even a shrill, **tart** sound would be hard to hear. Still, make it a **principle** to stay calm. Many people are successfully rescued from avalanches each year.

1. What does the word **classify** mean as it is used in paragraph 1?
(a) to dig   (b) to escape   (c) to label   (d) to study

2. Pick the word that best defines **realistic** as it is used in paragraph 3.
(a) reasonable   (b) possible   (c) lifelike   (d) fictional

3. What does the word **tart** mean as it is used in paragraph 3?
(a) sour in taste   (b) sharp in tone   (c) small pie   (d) sharp object

4. The Latin word *principium* means "leader." The word **principle** in paragraph 3 means
(a) a name   (b) a verdict   (c) an idea   (d) a guideline

 *Coordinating conjunctions (**and, but,** and **or**) join sentences, subjects, and predicates. Subordinating conjunctions (**before, because,** and **when**) connect related ideas in complex sentences. Correlative conjunctions (**both/and, either/or, neither/nor, not only/but also**) work together in a sentence to connect two items. Underline one coordinating conjunction in a subject and underline one subordinating conjunction in a complex sentence in "What Causes an Avalanche?"*
Accept all correct answers. Examples: See paragraphs 1 and 3.

Write Your Own

Write 3–5 sentences about something that happened when you were outside in nature, using at least three words from this unit. Then leave out one sentence from the story and share the story with a partner. Have your partner fill in the missing sentence using at least one word from this unit.

 *For more practice with conjunctions, see Grammar Workshop, Level Blue, Lesson 37.*

Word Study Homophones

Homophones are words that sound alike, but have different spellings and meanings. For example, *principle* (page 111) and *principal* are homophones. A *principle* is a basic rule or law or a belief used to tell right from wrong. A *principal* is the head of a school or organization. *Principal* means "most important." Read this sentence: *The **principal** of our school believes in the **principle** of good sportsmanship.* Notice how the sentence illustrates two different meanings of the homophones.

Look at the chart to find the spellings and meanings of other homophones.

coarse	(*adj.*) rough in texture
course	(*n.*) a route followed by something
bolder	(*adj.*) braver than someone else
boulder	(*n.*) a large rock
hoard	(*v.*) to gather things and hide them away
horde	(*n.*) a large group of people

PRACTICE   *Underline the homophone that completes each sentence.*

1. The marathon runner finished the (**coarse, course**) in record time.

2. The man jumping off the high diving board is (**bolder, boulder**) than I am.

3. There was a (**hoard, horde**) of people around the famous movie star.

4. The (**bolder, boulder**) on the hiking trail was blocking our path.

5. Boars have (**coarse, course**) hair that is sometimes used in hairbrushes.

6. I (**hoard, horde**) my allowance money in a box under my bed.

APPLY   *Write a sentence using each homophone pair. Be sure to give the correct context for each word.* Accept answers that provide the correct context for each word.

7. bolder, boulder _______________________________

8. hoard, horde _______________________________

9. coarse, course _______________________________

Make up a riddle for one of the words in the homophone pairs below. Ask a partner to guess the word and spell it.

root/route   **pole/poll**

Example: I am the part of the plant that takes in food and water. What am I? (a root)

Shades of Meaning | Word Choice

request, plea, demand, interrogation

In the passage "National Ski Patrol to the Rescue" on pages 108–109, you read this sentence: *As they race closer, they call in an urgent **plea** for help.* The word **plea** is very specific. It tells you that the skiers are frightened and desperate for help. They are asking for help in an emotional way.

Words may have similar meanings, but no two words have exactly the same meaning. The words below all involve asking for something. Notice how they differ in meaning.

request	When you make a **request**, you ask for something politely or formally.
demand	A **demand** is more forceful than a request. When you make a demand, you speak in a firm way, as though you have a right to what you are asking for.
plea	A **plea** is an urgent call for help. You might make a plea if you are in a desperate, frightening, or intense situation.
interrogation	When a person conducts an **interrogation**, he or she asks questions of someone, sometimes for a long time, to get as much information as possible.

PRACTICE *Write whether each statement is making a **request**, a **demand**, or a **plea**, or whether it is an **interrogation**.*

1. Give me the money you owe me, right now! _____demand_____

2. Help me! I fell and twisted my ankle! _____plea_____

3. Could you please return the book to me tomorrow? _____request_____

4. Where were you at 10:00 p.m.? Why didn't you call? _____interrogation_____

APPLY *Decide how you will ask the question in each situation below. Be prepared to explain your answers.* Accept answers that students can justify.

5. You are angry that your sister borrowed your bike without asking. Would you make a **demand** or a **request** to get your bike back? Write what you would say.

____

6. You need your mother's permission to go to the premiere of the new movie. Would you make a **plea** or a **request** to get her to let you go? Write what you would say.

____

Introducing the Words

Read the following science fiction passage about a brave resident of a distant planet. Notice how the highlighted words are used. These are the words you will be learning in this unit.
A differentiated version of this passage is available at **SadlierConnect.com**.

A Message for Norrod

(Science Fiction)

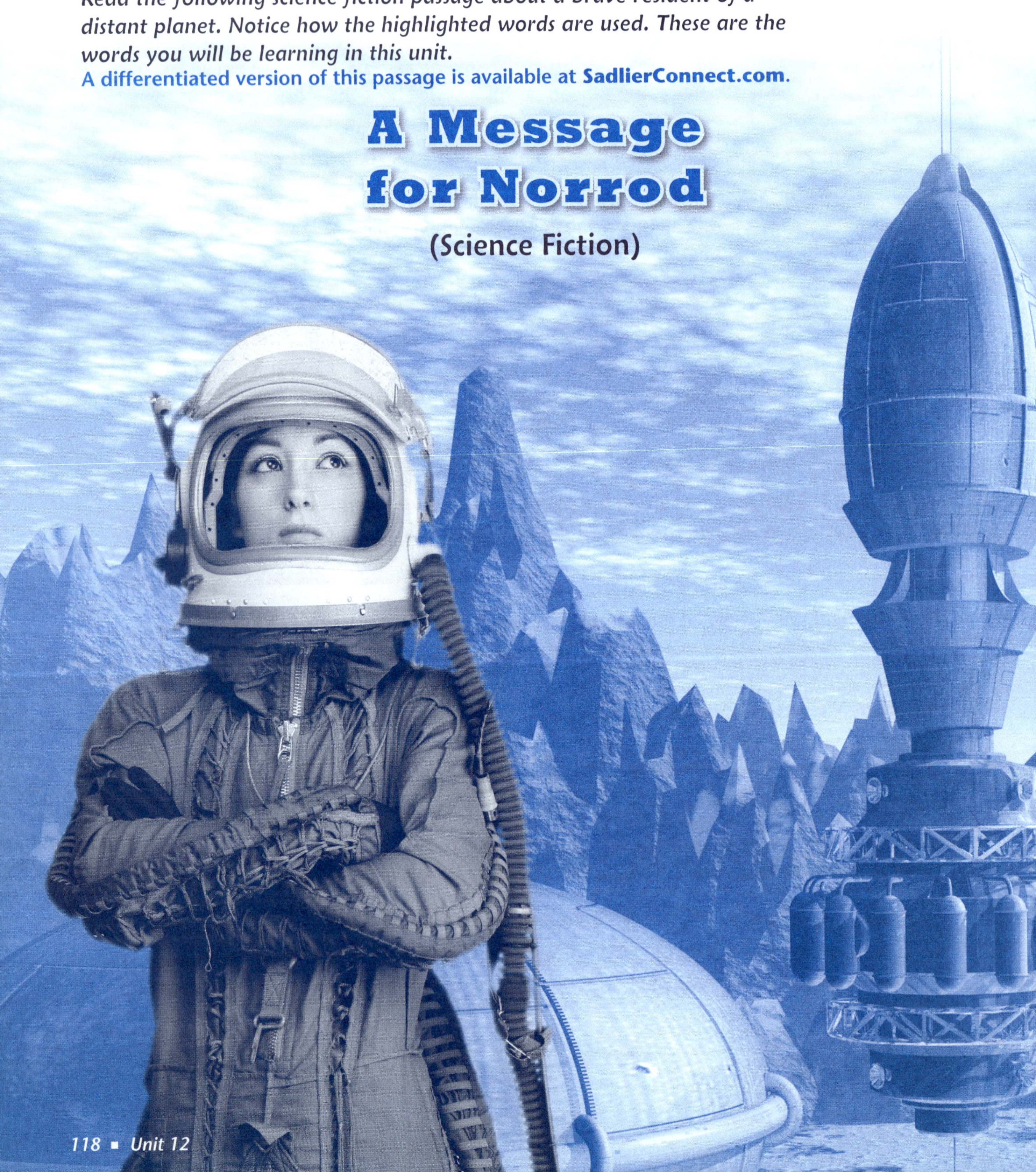

Zela had searched the dusty landscape for food all morning but found only a few shreds of wild dates and some tasteless roots. Food transports from the home planet had stopped two months earlier, and the colonists who had come to Norrod to live and work were hungry. The planet's pitiless climate—always hot and dry—made agriculture impossible. Besides, the Norrodian colonists weren't farmers, but miners who were digging up valuable minerals. The mineral transports to the home planet—along with communications—had also stopped. Colony officials had offered a few flimsy explanations for the halt, but these excuses lacked detail and were not convincing.

Zela walked back to her dome. The dwelling, in the shape of a half-sphere, was large but poorly furnished. Before she got there, she saw an unfamiliar spacecraft spinning above one of the landing pads. As it rotated, it also moved slowly downward. The strange-looking craft must be a migrant. Had it traveled from another solar system? It did not display the flag of Zela's home planet. Curious, Zela and a few other colonists approached it. A military patrol arrived but was unable to confirm the craft's identity.

"Follow the procedure for unidentified spacecraft!" Major Po barked to his soldiers. "Do not assume this craft is friendly or neutral." Some of the soldiers had turned on message devices, hoping to get a response from the spacecraft.

"If we receive no response in fifteen minutes," Major Po stated, "we will have to take action against it."

Thirteen minutes passed, and the strange spacecraft made no response. In a daze because of the tension and suspense, Zela watched and waited.

"Prepare to destroy the intruder," Major Po ordered.

"Wait!" Zela cried, springing into action and rushing forward. "For all you know, this craft may come from a friendly planet!"

A soldier grabbed Zela, shouting insults and words of abuse. "How dare a Class 3 miner interfere with Norrodian security!" he said, sneering at Zela's worn and dusty miner's suit.

Zela didn't care whether she looked presentable. She was gauging the distance to the spacecraft—about 100 meters. Breaking free from the soldier's grasp, she raced toward it. A ladder was built into the side of the craft, and Zela quickly scrambled up to the main hatch.

Behind her, Zela heard Major Po ordering his soldiers. "Raise the deflection screens!" Surely, they would not destroy the craft while she was on it. Or would they?

Now in the main hatch, Zela saw a large green light on a control panel. Instinctively, she placed her hand on it.

"Greetings to the colonists of Norrod," a loud message immediately began. The message was in Zela's language. "This is an unmanned craft from planet Earth. It comes in peace, bringing food and supplies for your survival." Then the craft's main cargo bay door opened, revealing crates of food as well as water purifiers, solar cookers, and other appliances.

Zela slowly climbed down from the craft and walked back toward the soldiers. The crowd had grown in size, and nearly everyone was cheering and thanking Zela.

"Yes, thank you, Zela," said Major Po, approaching her. "Thank you for keeping an open mind and not giving in to fear."

Definitions

You were introduced to these words in the passage. Study the pronunciation, part of speech, definition, and example sentence for each word. Then read the synonyms and antonyms.

1. abuse
(n., ə byüs′)
(uh-BYOOSS)
(v., ə byüz′)
(uh-BYOOZ)

(n.) improper, wrong, or cruel treatment; insulting language

The abuse of power is a danger in any government.

(v.) to put to bad use; to hurt or damage by treating badly

If you abuse your privileges, they may be taken away.

SYNONYMS: (n.) misuse, mistreatment; (v.) to harm, injure; to insult
ANTONYMS: (n.) care, support; (v.) to cherish, honor, praise

 Use each definition of **abuse** in a sentence.

2. appliance
(ə plī′ əns)
(uh-PLYE-uhnss)

(n.) a machine or tool used to do a household job

It seemed an awfully big claim for such a little appliance.

SYNONYMS: a device, utensil, contraption, gadget

 List three **appliances** that are often in a kitchen.

3. confirm
(kən fûrm′)
(kuhn-FURM)

(v.) to agree or prove that something is true; to make sure, remove any doubt

The press secretary refused to confirm the report.

SYNONYMS: to verify, support, assure; to check
ANTONYMS: to deny, disprove; to cancel

4. daze
(dāz)
(DAYZ)

(v.) to stun or confuse

Some predators daze their prey with a blow to the head.

(n.) a state of confusion

When I heard that I had won the prize, I walked around in a daze.

SYNONYMS: (v.) to numb, shock, astound, baffle, bewilder; (n.) a trance, stupor.

5. flimsy
(flim′ zē)
(FLIM-zee)

(adj.) not strong or solid; poorly made; not convincing

I don't think my teacher believed my flimsy excuse for not doing my homework.

SYNONYMS: thin, light, weak, rickety, feeble; shabby, shoddy
ANTONYMS: strong, sturdy, sound; convincing

 What will happen to a **flimsy** house in a strong storm?

 As time allows, have partners complete graphic organizers for select words, available at **SadlierConnect.com**.

6. gauge
(gāj)
(GAYJ)

(n.) a standard measure used to tell size, thickness, and so on; an instrument used to measure

A rain gauge measures rainfall.

(v.) to measure; to estimate

The cat seemed to gauge the distance before jumping onto the windowsill.

SYNONYMS: (n.) a scale, rule, yardstick; (v.) to judge, assess; to guess

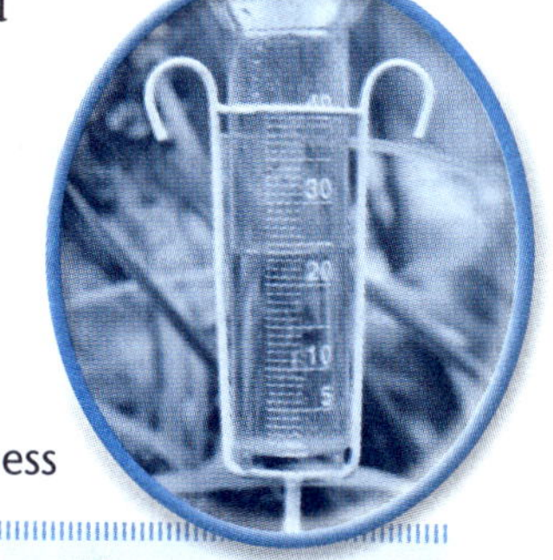

7. migrant
(mī′ grənt)
(MYE-gruhnt)

(n.) an animal or person that moves to a different region as the seasons change; a farmworker who moves seasonally to pick different crops

We passed a field full of migrants picking berries.

SYNONYMS: a traveler, nomad, drifter

8. neutral
(nü′ trəl)
(NOO-truhl)

(adj.) not taking any side in a disagreement or war; lacking distinction

Switzerland remained neutral in World Wars I and II.

SYNONYMS: uninvolved, uncommitted, impartial, open-minded; indefinite, vague
ANTONYMS: involved, committed, opinionated, heated; bold

9. pitiless
(pi′ ti ləs)
(PI-ti-luhss)

(adj.) showing no sorrow or regret for another's suffering or troubles

The audience booed the pitiless villain.

SYNONYMS: cold, merciless, heartless, unsparing, cruel
ANTONYMS: kindhearted, merciful, sympathetic

10. presentable
(pri zen′ tə bəl)
(pri-ZEN-tuh-buhl)

(adj.) fit to be seen or inspected

My parents insisted that I wear presentable clothing.

SYNONYMS: suitable, proper, respectable, passable
ANTONYMS: shabby, improper, unfit, unacceptable

11. rotate
(rō′ tāt)
(ROH-tate)

(v.) to turn around a central point; to alternate

Do you know how long it takes Earth to rotate once?

SYNONYMS: to circle, twirl, spin; to change, switch

Show your partner how to rotate in your chair.

12. shred
(shred)
(SHRED)

(n.) a thin strip; a tiny piece or amount

Not a shred of evidence was found.

(v.) to cut or tear into thin strips or small pieces; to rip up

The aide will shred the company's old files.

SYNONYMS: (n.) a scrap, tatter, bit, fragment
ANTONYMS: (n.) a whole; (v.) to fix, mend, repair

Synonyms

*Choose the word that is most nearly the **same** in meaning as the word or phrase in **boldface**. Then write your choice on the line provided.*

1. an electrical **device** for cleaning rugs
   a. shred   b. migrant   c. gauge   d. appliance   **appliance**

2. left behind by the **drifters**
   a. shreds   b. abuses   c. migrants   d. gauges   **migrants**

3. wore a **respectable** outfit for the class picture
   a. presentable   b. flimsy   c. neutral   d. pitiless   **presentable**

4. **numbed** by the terrible news
   a. gauged   b. dazed   c. rotated   d. confirmed   **dazed**

5. **assess** the value of the coin collection
   a. shred   b. gauge   c. abuse   d. rotate   **gauge**

6. **twirl** the plant to face the sun
   a. confirm   b. gauge   c. daze   d. rotate   **rotate**

Antonyms

*Choose the word that is most nearly **opposite** in meaning to the word or phrase in **boldface**. Then write your choice on the line provided.*

1. **mend** the old pillowcase
   a. shred   b. confirm   c. rotate   d. gauge   **shred**

2. **sturdy** shoes
   a. neutral   b. flimsy   c. presentable   d. pitiless   **flimsy**

3. reported their **kindhearted** treatment
   a. neutral   b. flimsy   c. presentable   d. pitiless   **pitiless**

4. refused to **deny** the rumor
   a. gauge   b. rotate   c. confirm   d. classify   **confirm**

5. painted in **bold** colors
   a. flimsy   b. neutral   c. presentable   d. pitiless   **neutral**

6. fans who **praise** the umpires
   a. rotate   b. gauge   c. abuse   d. daze   **abuse**

Completing the Sentence

Choose the word from the box that best completes each item. Then write the word on the line provided. (You may have to change the word's ending.)

abuse	appliance	confirm
daze	flimsy	gauge
migrant	neutral	pitiless
presentable	rotate	shred

A Toast to Toast

- One of the most common of household **appliances**, the electric toaster, was first introduced to American kitchens in 1910.

- Early models toasted only one side of the bread at a time. In order to toast both sides, you had to **rotate** the slice of bread yourself.

- These toasters did not have self-timers, either. If you didn't pay careful attention, your toast might not look very **presentable**.

Protecting Feathered Friends

- In the fall and spring months, many different kinds of birds make long journeys. These flying **migrants** are traveling between their winter and summer homes.

- Many of the birds face danger from objects we think of as harmless or **neutral**.

- In towns and cities, the birds collide with windows and are either killed or left injured and **dazed**.

- One clever solution offers more than a **shred** of hope for these long-distance flyers. Placing colored tape or decals on large picture windows makes them more visible to birds.

- A homeowner or building owner would have to be **pitiless** to refuse to take a simple step like this to save the lives of birds.

Running on Empty

- When our car came to a stop, I was afraid to look at the fuel **gauge**.

- But when I did, a quick glance was enough to **confirm** the worst: The car had run out of gas, just as I suspected.

- We had to walk two miles to a gas station, with nothing more to protect us from the rain than our **flimsy** jackets.

*Circle the letter next to the word or phrase that best completes the sentence or answers the question. Pay special attention to the word in **boldface**.*

1. If you **confirm** that something is true, you
   a. leave no doubt about it.
   b. take a hard look at it.
   c. consider other possibilities.
   d. remain puzzled about it.

2. Which might put you in a **daze**?
   a. a new friend
   b. simple instructions
   c. shocking news
   d. a happy pet

3. Something you might **gauge** is
   a. a favorite lunch.
   b. an old shirt.
   c. thought.
   d. snowfall.

4. Which could you **shred**?
   a. water
   b. paper
   c. coins
   d. scissors

Words with Latin Roots

The unit word *migrant*, meaning "an animal or person that moves to a different region as the seasons change," comes from the Latin *migr*. *Migr* is a Latin root meaning "to move." The root is used in the following words:

- migrate (v.): to travel to a different place (*to move to a new region*)
- migration (n.): the act or process of traveling (*movement, as on a journey*)
- migratory (adj.): tending to travel to a different place (*related to moving to a region*)
- emigrate (v.): to move out of one country to another (*to move out of*)
- immigrate (v.): to move into a new country (*to move into*)

Choose two of the words from the list. Write a sentence for each word to show you understand its meaning.

1. Accept answers that show an understanding of the vocabulary.

2. _______________________________________

 *Read the passage. Then answer each question.*

Orson Welles's War of the Worlds

1   In 1939, on an October night, an invasion was reported on the radio. The report put listeners in a **daze** as it described an attack on New Jersey by aliens from planet Mars.

2   The news bulletins were updated by **rotating** broadcasters describing various scenes. The **pitiless** Martians **crushed** the human army. They **shredded** property with their heat rays. The **neutral**, authentic-sounding radio broadcast brought fear to listeners who believed the events were true. The **gauge** of anxiety increased as the show described the invasion of New York City.

3   In reality, the broadcast was a drama based on the science-fiction novel *The War of the Worlds*. An actor named Orson Welles had directed and performed in it and co-authored the script as well.

4   The next day, Mr. Welles found his name on the front pages of newspapers across the country. Critics accused him of **abuse** of trust, because he knew the show would cause panic. Initially, Welles defended himself. However, he later admitted to poor judgement, saying, "If I'd planned to wreck my career, I couldn't have gone about it better."

1. What is the meaning of the word **daze** as it is used in paragraph 1?
   - (a) state of happiness
   - (b) state of shock
   - (c) confuse
   - (d) surprise

2. Pick the word that best defines **pitiless** as it is used in paragraph 2.
   - (a) heartless
   - (b) merciful
   - (c) powerful
   - (d) strange

3. What does the word **shredded** mean as it is used in paragraph 2?
   - (a) mended
   - (b) occupied
   - (c) destroyed
   - (d) stole

4. The Latin word *abusus* means "misuse." The word **abuse** in paragraph 4 means
   - (a) mistreatment
   - (b) respect
   - (c) creation
   - (d) withdrawal

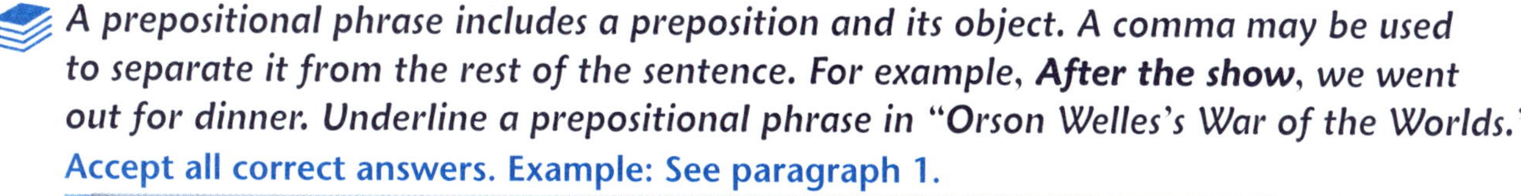

*A prepositional phrase includes a preposition and its object. A comma may be used to separate it from the rest of the sentence. For example, **After the show**, we went out for dinner. Underline a prepositional phrase in "Orson Welles's War of the Worlds."*
Accept all correct answers. Example: See paragraph 1.

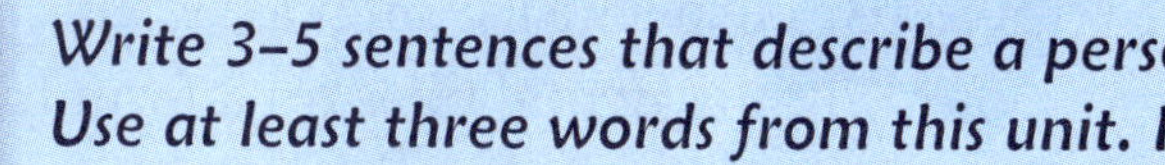

Write Your Own

Write 3–5 sentences that describe a person, place, or thing without naming it. Use at least three words from this unit. Have a partner read your sentences and guess what you have described.

For more practice with prepositional phrases, see Grammar Workshop, Level Blue, Lesson 39.

Vocabulary for Comprehension

*Read this passage in which some of the words you have studied in Units 7–12 appear in **boldface**. Then answer the questions.*

Free-tailed bats emerging from caves to hunt

Census Taking

1   The United States Census Bureau takes official surveys to gather data on our population. The formal count is called a census. Business leaders, educators, and politicians use the data to get an accurate picture of the people they serve. The census data is one their **primary** tools to understand the needs of the community. Some leaders criticize the census. They believe the survey can be **abused** by those who want to manipulate the data.

2   Scientists also use census data as an **alternate** source to support their studies. Scientists might track animal populations. They learn how animals and humans can live together safely. They might study a **migrant** butterfly population. They find out if the same number of butterflies returns to the same area each year. Or scientists might count the members of an endangered species in order to **appeal** for ongoing protection and ask for help. A decreased population number could be the **shred** of evidence needed to keep the species from going extinct.

3   Government census workers gather data in person and by mail. But scientists must find unique ways to count the plants and animals in a given area. For example, to estimate the population of free-tailed bats in Carlsbad Cavern, the largest cave in New Mexico, scientists made use of technology. They set up video cameras outside the entrance of the cave, which houses a large number of bats. The scientists filmed the bats flying out of the cave. Later, the scientists counted the bats in each frame of the video.

4   Scientists can sometimes just use their eyes to take a census, such as when counting the maple trees on a farm in Vermont. However, a more complex method would be needed to **gauge** the number of small animals, such as field mice, in the same vicinity.

Fill in the circle next to the choice that best completes the sentence or answers the question.

1. What is the main idea of this passage?
   - **(a)** Census takers and scientists use similar methods to gather data.
   - (b) Leaders abuse census data.
   - (c) Scientists work to protect endangered species.
   - (d) Scientists study free-tailed bats.

2. The Latin word *prīmus* means "first." The word **primary** in paragraph 1 means
   - (a) most important
   - **(b)** main
   - (c) election
   - (d) highest

3. What does the use of the word **abused** in paragraph 1 suggest?
   - (a) The census is incorrect.
   - (b) The census is always correct.
   - **(c)** The census can be misleading.
   - (d) Leaders do not like the census.

4. What does the word **alternate** mean as it is used in paragraph 2?
   - (a) replacement
   - (b) rotating
   - (c) varying
   - **(d)** another

5. As it is used in paragraph 2, what does the word **migrant** show about butterfly populations?
   - (a) They stay in one area.
   - **(b)** They move from one place to another.
   - (c) Their habitat is in trees.
   - (d) They move at high altitudes.

6. What does the author mean by the word **appeal** in paragraph 2?
   - **(a)** plead
   - (b) charm
   - (c) attract
   - (d) grab

7. Which phrase from the passage best shows the idea of **appeal**?
   - (a) "number of butterflies"
   - **(b)** "ask for help"
   - (c) "decreased population"
   - (d) "from going extinct"

8. What is the meaning of the word **gauge** as it is used in paragraph 4?
   - (a) scale
   - (b) meter
   - **(c)** judge
   - (d) referee

Write Your Own

Every evening at Carlsbad Caverns in southeastern New Mexico, nearly 400,000 free-tailed bats fly out of caves in search of food. Imagine watching this stunning display of bats. On a separate sheet of paper, describe how you might feel as you watch this scene unfold. Use at least three words from Units 7–12.

Classifying

Choose the word from the box that goes best with each group of words. Write the word in the space provided. Then explain what the words have in common. The first one has been done for you.

compose	famine	identical
pitiless	plea	presentable
primary	rotate	senseless
soothe	tart	verdict

1. comfort, _______ soothe _______, pacify, reassure

The words are synonyms.

2. sense, _______ senseless _______, sensible, sensitive

The words belong to the same family.

3. brainstorm, outline, draft, _______ compose _______

The words name steps in the writing process.

4. plague, earthquake, _______ famine _______

The words name types of disasters.

5. judge, jury, _______ verdict _______

The words relate to a court case.

6. _______ identical _______, similar, unlike, opposite

The words are comparisons of objects, in order from most similar to most different.

7. pity, pitiful, _______ pitiless _______

The words belong to the same family.

8. cookie, muffin, cake, _______ tart _______

The words name baked goods.

9. spin, twirl, twist, _______ rotate _______

The words are synonyms.

10. glee, flea, _______ plea _______, ski

The words rhyme.

11. considerable, dependable, reasonable, _______ presentable _______

The words have the same suffix.

12. _______ primary _______, middle, secondary

The words describe levels of school.

Completing the Idea

*Complete each sentence so that it makes sense. Pay attention to
the word in **boldface**.* Accept answers that show an understanding of the vocabulary.

1. I always **rejoice** when I ____.

2. An **observant** person will likely notice ________________________.

3. Our class took a **poll** to see ________________________________.

4. Some animal predators catch their **prey** by ____________________.

5. The **security** at the museum always __________________________.

6. To answer the **avalanche** of questions, the speaker ____________.

7. A flower may **shrivel** if ____________________________________.

8. When I feel **energetic**, I like to ____________________________.

9. The **downfall** of the king was caused by ______________________.

10. Someone who is **thrifty** will ______________________________.

11. When I am tired, I like to **nestle** __________________________.

12. It is best to stay **neutral** when __________________________.

13. In order to **enforce** the law, police officers ________________.

14. The thing I **cherish** most is ______________________________.

15. The town council voted to **abolish** ________________________.

16. Because I want to **expand** my vocabulary, I __________________.

17. The toy was so **flimsy** that ______________________________.

Writing Challenge   Check that vocabulary is used correctly and that each sentence is written correctly.

*Write two sentences using the word **loot**. In the first sentence, use **loot** as
a verb. In the second sentence, use **loot** as a noun.*

1. ____

2. ____

Introducing the Words

Read the following passage about an early hero in the fight for American independence. Notice how the highlighted words are used. These are the words you will be learning in this unit.
A differentiated version of this passage is available at **SadlierConnect.com**.

Crispus Attucks Changes History

(Historical Nonfiction)

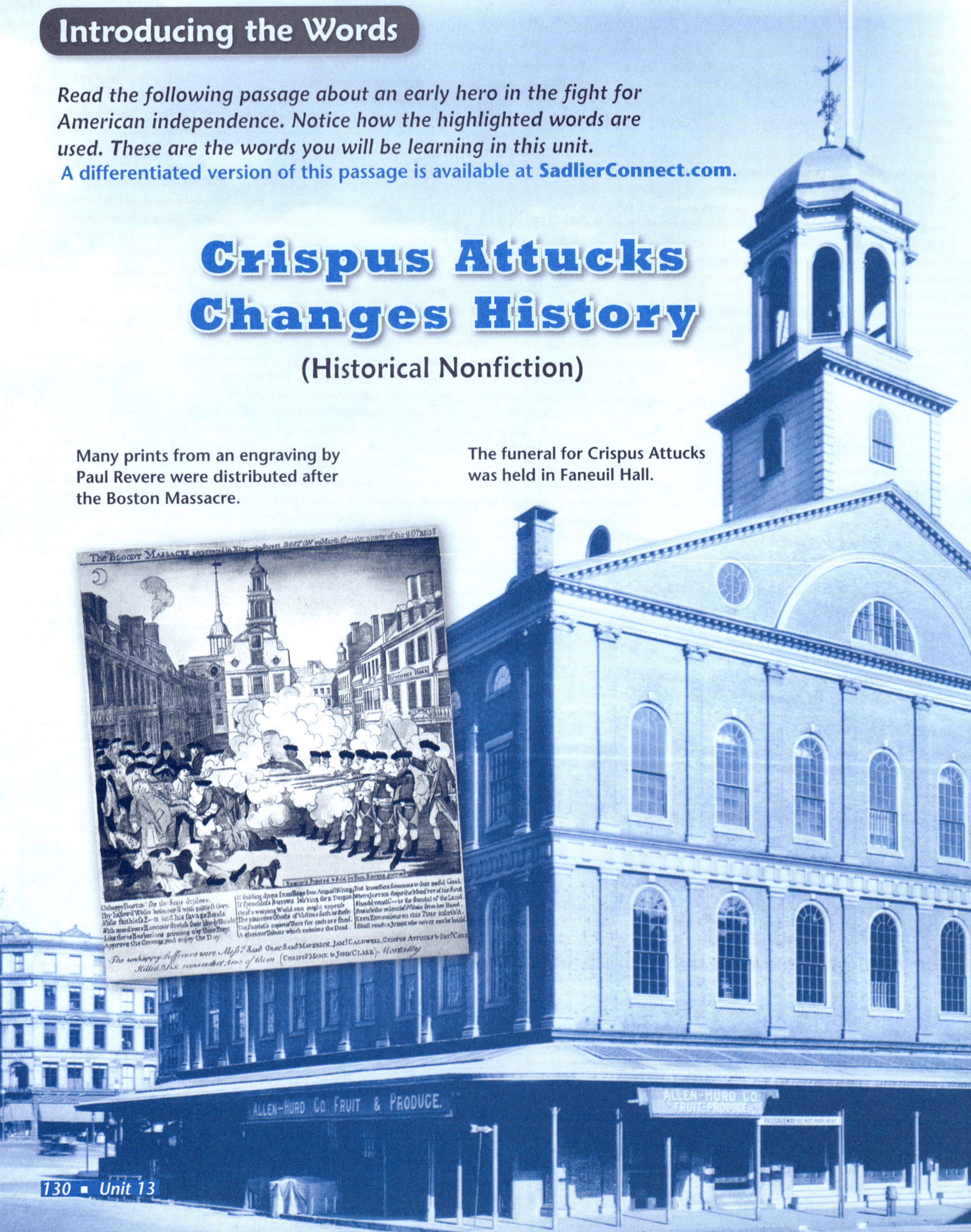

Many prints from an engraving by Paul Revere were distributed after the Boston Massacre.

The funeral for Crispus Attucks was held in Faneuil Hall.

A cold wind swept in from Boston Harbor on the night of March 5, 1770, and fresh snow lay on the streets. On Boston Common, the British soldiers, who later became known as redcoats, sat inside their tents. They had been camped there for months in conditions neither comfortable nor sanitary. At a time of rising tension in the colonies, the redcoats were there to preserve the peace and enforce the new trade laws.

For the soldiers, it was a monotonous assignment; they had little to do. Sometimes, they debated political issues with the colonists. More often, the colonists hurled insults at the redcoats, whom many regarded as foes. This night, some colonists were throwing snowballs from the darkness. Accounts vary about exactly what happened next. A scuffle seems to have broken out, and a nearby church bell rang an alarm. Citizens, angry and tense about the redcoats, gathered at Boston Common.

Some citizens carried sticks and clubs. As the crowd grew larger, the redcoats forced the colonists back.

According to several accounts, a small group of colonists suddenly charged the redcoats. Urged on by their leader, a tall black man named Crispus Attucks, the men waved their simple weapons and shouted insults at the British. Attucks may have taunted the soldiers by saying, "Shoot if you dare." Then, as the crowd began to throw things at the soldiers, Attucks is said to have clubbed one of the redcoats and grabbed for his bayonet—the blade at the end of his rifle.

Crispus Attucks

This latter move by Attucks proved too much for the soldiers. Fearing for their safety, the redcoats fired, and Attucks fell dead. When the smoke cleared, a number of colonists lay sprawled on Boston Common. In all, five died from their wounds, and six recovered. Although Crispus Attucks was probably the first victim in the cause that became the American Revolution, little is known about him. Said to be the son of an African father and a Native American mother, he grew up a slave in Massachusetts. In 1750, when Attucks was about 27, he ran away from his owner and may have gone to sea on a whaling ship. Nothing else was heard from him until the night of what became known as the Boston Massacre.

That's what the patriot leaders called it—a massacre—to build support for the cause of freedom. "On that night, the foundations of American independence were laid," President John Adams later wrote. Thousands of angry colonists attended a public funeral for Attucks and the other victims in Boston's Faneuil Hall. Speakers praised the bravery that Attucks had exhibited, and newspaper accounts retold the story. Attucks and the others acquired even more fame with Paul Revere's widely known engraving of the massacre. Prints made from the engraving were distributed around the colonies, building support for Boston and hatred for the redcoats.

For five years, the memory of the Boston Massacre fanned the flames of revolution. In the end, the reckless bravery of Crispus Attucks had widespread consequences. His achievement was nothing less than changing the course of American history.

You were introduced to these words in the passage. Study the pronunciation, part of speech, definition, and example sentence for each word. Then read the synonyms and antonyms.

1. achievement (ə chēv′ mənt) (uh-CHEEV-muhnt) (n.) something done successfully; something gained by working or trying hard

A perfect report card is quite an achievement.

SYNONYMS: an accomplishment, feat, triumph
ANTONYMS: a defeat, failure, setback

Tell your partner one major **achievement** that makes you proud.

2. acquire (ə kwīr′) (uh-KWIRE) (v.) to get as one's own

When did you acquire the ability to speak French so well?

SYNONYMS: to obtain, gain, earn; ANTONYMS: to lose, give up, surrender

3. debate (di bāt′) (di-BATE) (n.) a discussion of reasons for and against something

The town council held a debate on building a new library.

(v.) to discuss reasons for and against something; to think about carefully before deciding

What issue would you like to debate?

SYNONYMS: (n.) an argument, dispute; (v.) to discuss, consider
ANTONYMS: (n.) an agreement; (v.) to agree (with)

Have a **debate** with your partner. One of you will argue for starting school one hour earlier; the other will argue against it.

4. exhibit (ig zi′ bət) (ig-ZI-buht) (v.) to show clearly; to put on display

You exhibit great talent in gymnastics.

(n.) something shown to the public

We went to the diamond exhibit at the science museum.

SYNONYMS: (v.) to present, reveal; (n.) a display, exhibition
ANTONYMS: (v.) to hide, conceal, cover up

Describe to your partner one way stores **exhibit** their goods.

5. foe (fō) (FOH) (n.) one who hates or tries to harm another; an enemy

Identify yourself: Are you friend or foe?

SYNONYMS: an opponent, rival; ANTONYMS: a friend, ally, comrade, buddy

As time allows, have partners complete graphic organizers for select words, available at **SadlierConnect.com**.

6. latter
(la′ tər)
(LA-tur)

(adj.) closer to the end; relating to the second of two things discussed

The first part of the book is better than the latter part.

SYNONYMS: last, later, end, final; ANTONYMS: former, first, earlier, beginning

7. massacre
(ma′ si kər)
(MA-si-kur)

(n.) the cruel killing of many people or animals

The village was the site of a bloody massacre.

(v.) to kill many people or animals in a cruel way

The barbarians planned to massacre their rivals.

SYNONYMS: (n.) a slaughter; (v.) to butcher, slaughter

8. monotonous
(mə nä′ tən əs)
(muh-NAH-tuhn-uhss)

(adj.) dull as a result of not changing in any way

Shelling peas is a monotonous chore.

SYNONYMS: boring, uninteresting, tiresome; ANTONYMS: varied, lively, exciting

 **Which of your household chores feels monotonous?**

9. preserve
(pri zûrv′)
(pri-ZURV)

(v.) to keep safe from injury or ruin; to keep food from spoiling

I signed a petition to preserve the wetlands.

(n.) an area set aside for the protection of wildlife

Wild animals roam freely in the nature preserve.

SYNONYMS: (v.) to save, protect, conserve; (n.) a refuge, sanctuary
ANTONYMS: (v.) to waste, destroy, misuse

 **Use each definition of preserve in a sentence.**

10. sanitary
(sa′ nə ter ē)
(SA-nuh-ter-ee)

(adj.) having to do with health; free of dirt and germs

In a factory, the areas that produce computer parts must remain completely sanitary.

SYNONYMS: clean, pure, sterile, hygienic
ANTONYMS: dirty, filthy, contaminated, unhealthy

11. sprawl
(sprôl)
(SPRAWL)

(v.) to lie or sit with arms and legs spread out; to spread out in a disorderly way

Some nights I sprawl in front of the TV set.

SYNONYMS: to lounge, slouch, relax, stretch, extend

12. widespread
(wīd′ spred′)
(WIDE-SPRED)

(adj.) happening in many places or to many people; fully open

Interest in the lives of movie stars is widespread.

SYNONYMS: far-reaching, vast, common
ANTONYMS: limited, rare, unusual, uncommon

Synonyms

*Choose the word that is most nearly the **same** in meaning
as the word or phrase in **boldface**. Then write your choice
on the line provided.*

1. a worthy **opponent**
   a. preserve   b. exhibit   c. foe   d. debate   **foe**

2. **slaughter** the newborn harp seals
   a. preserve   b. exhibit   c. acquire   d. massacre   **massacre**

3. the **boring** refrain of "tra-la-la"
   a. latter   b. sanitary   c. widespread   d. monotonous   **monotonous**

4. **consider** going by train or by car
   a. sprawl   b. debate   c. acquire   d. massacre   **debate**

5. my proudest **accomplishment**
   a. preserve   b. exhibit   c. foe   d. achievement   **achievement**

6. **lounge** on the couch
   a. exhibit   b. preserve   c. sprawl   d. massacre   **sprawl**

Antonyms

*Choose the word that is most nearly **opposite** in meaning
to the word or phrase in **boldface**. Then write your choice
on the line provided.*

1. **conceal** your surprise
   a. exhibit   b. sprawl   c. massacre   d. preserve   **exhibit**

2. the **first** part of our vacation
   a. widespread b. latter   c. monotonous d. sanitary   **latter**

3. **lose** millions of dollars
   a. debate   b. sprawl   c. massacre   d. acquire   **acquire**

4. **limited** appeal among children
   a. sanitary   b. monotonous c. latter   d. widespread   **widespread**

5. **destroy** the town records
   a. massacre   b. exhibit   c. preserve   d. sprawl   **preserve**

6. found **unhealthy** living conditions
   a. latter   b. sanitary   c. widespread   d. monotonous   **sanitary**

Completing the Sentence

Choose the word from the box that best completes each item. Then write the word on the line provided. (You may have to change the word's ending.)

achievement	acquire	debate
exhibit	foe	latter
massacre	monotonous	preserve
sanitary	sprawl	widespread

You Can't Win Them All

■ The current events club had to decide whether to __________**debate**__________ hunters' rights or the child helmet law.

■ We chose the child helmet law, the __________**latter**__________ issue, because it was more relevant to students our age.

■ The members of our team gave such __________**monotonous**__________ speeches in favor of the law that the other team won, although their arguments were more emotional than fact-filled.

What Happened in Rwanda

■ In 1994 a brutal __________**massacre**__________ took place in Rwanda, a country in Central Africa. Hundreds of thousands of people were injured or killed.

■ The major __________**foes**__________ were the Hutu and Tutsi peoples.

■ In overcrowded refugee camps, __________**sanitary**__________ conditions were dangerously poor. Clean water, food, and medicines were in short supply.

■ Rescue workers found entire families __________**sprawled**__________ on the ground.

"Four score and seven years ago . . ."

■ Many historians consider Abraham Lincoln's Gettysburg Address to be the greatest __________**achievement**__________ in public speaking this nation has produced.

■ The fame of this brief speech is so __________**widespread**__________ that most Americans—and even many from other nations—know the opening of it by heart.

■ The Library of Congress __________**acquired**__________ a copy of the speech, written in Lincoln's own hand. Only four other copies in his handwriting are still in existence.

■ At the library the manuscript is carefully __________**preserved**__________ as a national treasure.

■ Sometimes the document travels to Pennsylvania for __________**exhibit**__________ in connection with special events at the actual site of the battle. The battlefield became a national park in 1895.

*Circle the letter next to the word or phrase that best completes the sentence or answers the question. Pay special attention to the word in **boldface**.*

1. A cafeteria that is **sanitary** has
a. good main dishes.
b. overflowing trash bins.
c. a clean kitchen.
d. high-priced lunches.

2. The **latter** part of December includes
a. the first day of the month.
b. the last week of the month.
c. four Sundays.
d. New Year's Day.

3. One way to **acquire** a rare stamp is to
a. mail a letter.
b. research stamp collecting.
c. buy one.
d. sell one.

4. I might **sprawl** on the couch to
a. relax.
b. wake up.
c. move furniture.
d. exercise.

Words with Greek Roots

The unit word *monotonous*, meaning "unchanging and therefore dull," comes from the Greek *mono*. *Mono* is a Greek root meaning "one" or "single." The root is also used in the following words:

- monotone (n.): a single, unchanging tone or pitch (*one tone or sound*)
- monotony (n.): dullness due to lack of change (*one activity repeated many times*)
- monologue (n.): a long speech by a single person (*one speaker*)
- monorail (n.) a single-track railroad (*one rail*)
- monopoly (n.): complete control of a certain business or industry (*the one and only owner or operator*)

Choose two of the words from the list. Write a sentence for each word to show you understand its meaning.

1. Accept answers that show an understanding of the vocabulary.

2. ____

Read the passage. Then answer each question.

Sons of Liberty

1 The Sons of Liberty was a group of American colonists who opposed British rule in North America. A famous patriot named Samuel Adams was one of its members. Like other members, he never kept a written record of his participation to help **preserve** the secrecy of the group.

2 In public, however, Adams would **debate** supporters of the British government. He expressed his disapproval of taxation without representation. He called for the British government to repeal the Stamp Act of 1765. This act required all printed materials, such as newspapers, to **exhibit** a stamp showing that a tax had been paid for the paper. The Sons of Liberty added to **widespread** opposition to the Stamp Act by publishing attacks against it. It was a stunning **achievement** when the act was repealed in 1766.

3 In 1770, members of the Sons of Liberty rallied colonists against the British after a **massacre** had occurred in Boston. Five colonists were killed in a confrontation with British soldiers. Perhaps the soldiers had become tired of their **monotonous** duties. The tension of keeping an angry mob in order had unnerved them.

1. What is the meaning of the word **preserve** as it is used in paragraph 1?
(a) sanctuary   (b) waste   (c) misuse   (d) protect

2. What does the word **debate** mean as it is used in paragraph 2?
(a) agree with   (b) dispute   (c) shame   (d) ignore

3. The Latin word *exhibere* means "to hold forth." The word **exhibit** in paragraph 2 means
(a) show   (b) uncover   (c) conceal   (d) manufacture

4. Pick the word that best defines **monotonous** as it is used in paragraph 3.
(a) boring   (b) lively   (c) various   (d) cautious

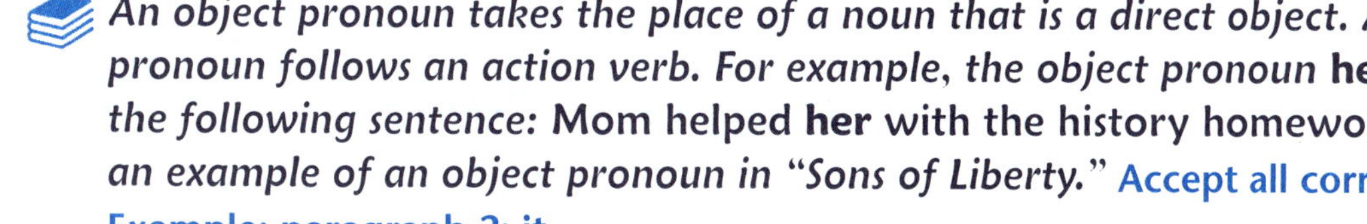 *An object pronoun takes the place of a noun that is a direct object. An object pronoun follows an action verb. For example, the object pronoun **her** is used in the following sentence:* Mom helped **her** with the history homework. *Underline an example of an object pronoun in "Sons of Liberty."* **Accept all correct answers. Example: paragraph 2: it.**

 ## Write Your Own

 *Imagine that, as an experiment, students in another grade have proposed a new rule for your grade: The students must pay five cents every time they enter and leave the classroom. Write 3–5 sentences with a partner explaining why this rule should be repealed. Use three words from this unit in your explanation.*

 **For more practice with object pronouns, see Grammar Workshop, Level Blue, Lesson 41.**

For teaching suggestions, see page T42.

Word Study — Suffixes -ion, -tion, -sion, -ous, -ic

You have learned that a **suffix** is a word part that is added to the end of a **base word** to make a new word. You can add the suffix *-ion* to *exhibit* (page 132) to make a new word.

> The suffixes **-ion**, **-tion**, and **-sion** mean "the act, state, or result of."
> exhibit + **ion** = exhibit**ion** → means "a display"
> compete + **tion** = competi**tion** → means "a contest"
> decide + **sion** = deci**sion** → means "something decided upon"
>
> The suffix **-ous** means "like" or "full of." The suffix **-ic** means "relating to."
> poison + **ous** = poison**ous** → means "full of poison"
> base + **ic** = bas**ic** → means "related to the main point"

PRACTICE *Write the missing base word, suffix, or new word. Then write the meaning of the new word. Use a dictionary to check your answers.*

Base Word	Suffix	New Word	Meaning
1. _prevent_	+ ion	= prevention	→ stopping something from happening
2. expand	+ _sion_	= expansion	→ an increase
3. hazard	+ ous	= _hazardous_	→ dangerous
4. _hero_	+ ic	= heroic	→ brave

APPLY *Complete each sentence with a word that contains the suffix **-ion**, **-tion**, **-sion**, **-ous**, or **-ic**. Choose from the words above.*

5. The park board made a ___decision___ to develop an ___expansion___ of the gardening program.

6. Before the ___competition___ began, the judges reviewed the ___basic___ rules of the game with the players.

7. The ___poisonous___ snakes were the main attraction at the ___exhibition___.

8. A ___heroic___ lifeguard rescued a swimmer from the ___hazardous___ waters and jagged rocks.

9. Daily exercise and a healthy diet are essential to the ___prevention___ of heart disease.

*Continue the chart in Practice. Work with a partner to list other words with the suffixes **-ion**, **-tion**, **-sion**, **-ous**, and **-ic**. Then list the base word, suffix, and meaning for each new word.*

Shades of Meaning   Word Choice
acquire, receive, purchase, borrow

In the passage "Crispus Attucks Changes History" on pages 130–131, you read the sentence: *Attucks and the others **acquired** even more fame with Paul Revere's widely known engraving of the massacre.* Here the word *acquired* means "got" or "gained."

You have learned that words may have similar meanings, but that no two words have exactly the same meaning. Look at the words in the chart. All the words involve getting or obtaining something. Notice how the meanings of the words differ.

acquire	When you **acquire** something, you get or obtain it for yourself.
receive	When you **receive** something, you get something from another person.
purchase	When you **purchase** something, you pay money to get it.
borrow	When you **borrow** something that belongs to someone else, you use it for a period of time with the person's permission.

PRACTICE   *Write the word from the chart that best replaces the word* **get** *in each sentence.*

1. We were able to **get** one of our neighbor's puppies. _______acquire_______

2. I can **get** my brother's ruler, but he needs it after school. _______borrow_______

3. What did you **get** for your birthday? _______receive_______

4. Mom asked me to **get** milk and eggs at the store. _______purchase_______

APPLY   *Respond to each situation below. Answer in a complete sentence.*
Accept answers that students can justify.

5. You want to try riding a skateboard. Should you **purchase** or **borrow** a skateboard? Why?

____

6. You need a graduation gift for your friend. Will you **purchase** a gift or **receive** one? Explain.

____

7. You practice dribbling and kicking a soccer ball each day. Are you **acquiring** skills or **borrowing** them?

____

UNIT 14

Read the following nonfiction narrative about a tourist attraction with an odd history. Notice how the highlighted words are used. These are the words you will be learning in this unit.

A Giant Hoax

(Nonfiction Narrative)

A differentiated version of this passage is available at **SadlierConnect.com**.

The well diggers on William Newell's farm in Cardiff, New York, got quite a shock one October morning in 1869. A few feet down, their shovels uncovered a ten-foot long man. The body appeared to be petrified—that is, over a very long time, it had turned to stone.

News of this singular discovery traveled fast. Was this proof that giants had once walked the earth? People from all over swarmed to see the giant fossil. Newell's relative, George Hull, spotted a money-making opportunity and charged each visitor ten cents a peek. As the crowds increased, Hull raised the price to fifty cents, the equivalent of about six dollars today.

Soon, a group of businessmen began to pursue Hull, begging him to sell them "the Cardiff Giant." Hull finally agreed to a price of

The Cardiff Giant

Crowds formed to see the Giant.

$37,000, and the stone creature was moved to Syracuse, New York. Now even more people lined up to see it.

Among the visitors were several paleontologists—scientists who study ancient remains. Their negative opinions of the Cardiff Giant revealed they were not impressed. Convinced it was not real, they labeled it a fraud. In support of these conclusions, they pointed out the rough chisel marks on the giant's body. They also noted that acids had been used to make the "fossil" look old. In short, William Newell and George Hull had some explaining to do.

When George Hull was questioned, he offered no cover story, no alibi. On the contrary, he was surprisingly frank. With the help of a confederate, an Iowa man who was a sculptor, he had carved the statue and modified its appearance with acid. The statue was shipped east by rail and then discharged with other cargo at a station near Cardiff. From there, Hull carted it to the farm of William Newell. He then buried the "giant" on the farm and waited a year before hiring workers to dig in the same spot.

Why would George Hull do such a thing? At the time of the hoax, many people believed that real-life giants had once walked the earth. Hull disagreed. Apparently, he just wanted to poke fun at this belief. When he saw how much money he could make, however, he decided to let people think the Cardiff Giant was real. A practical joke had turned into a money-making swindle.

The story should have ended there, but it didn't. At this time, P.T. Barnum reigned over the world of popular entertainment, and the great showman wanted the Cardiff Giant in his traveling circus. The owners, however, refused to rent it to Barnum, not even for $30,000 a month. In response, Barnum came up with a more economical approach. He had an exact replica made, put it in his show, and claimed it was the original one. This fraud should have led to a boycott or mutiny by Barnum's customers, but it didn't. Even more people lined up to see the counterfeit giant.

Like most sensations, the Cardiff Giant gradually faded from memory. For decades, it lay undisturbed in a barn near Syracuse. Eventually, however, it was put on exhibit at the Farmers' Museum in Cooperstown, New York. Today, visitors there still line up and pay to see the giant hoax.

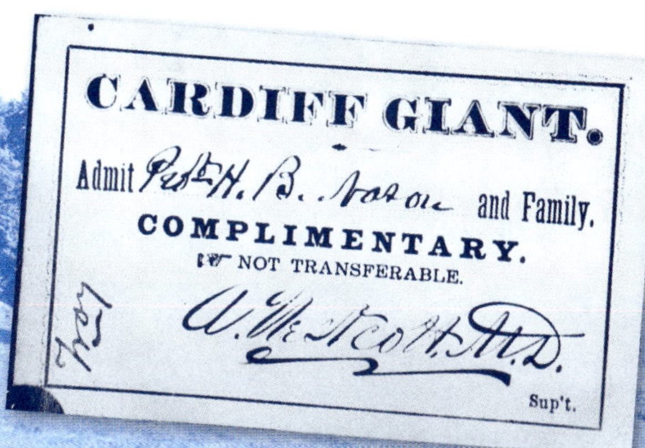

Admission ticket

Remember

A **noun** (*n.*) is a word that names a person, place, or thing.

A **verb** (*v.*) is a word or words that express action or a state of being.

An **adjective** (*adj.*) is a word that describes a noun or pronoun.

Definitions

You were introduced to these words in the passage. Study the pronunciation, part of speech, definition, and example sentence for each word. Then read the synonyms and antonyms.

1. alibi
(a′ lə bī)
(A-luh-bye)

(n.) a claim of having been elsewhere when a crime was committed; a reason given to explain something

> *Can anyone confirm your alibi?*

SYNONYMS: an excuse, explanation, story, defense

2. confederate
(kən fe′ də rət)
(kuhn-FE-duh-ruht)

(n.) a person, state, or country that joins with another for a common purpose; a partner in crime

> *Great Britain was a confederate of the U.S. in World War II.*

SYNONYMS: an ally, accomplice; ANTONYMS: a foe, enemy

3. discharge
(v., dis chärj′)
(diss-CHARJ)
(n., dis′ chärj)
(DISS-charj)

(v.) to let go; to unload cargo or passengers; to fire off; to give off

> *The cruise ship stopped in port to discharge the tourists.*

(n.) a release or letting go; a firing off; a giving off; something given off

> *The army gave the soldier an honorable discharge.*

SYNONYMS: (v.) to release, dismiss, shoot; (n.) a dismissal
ANTONYMS: (v.) to detain, imprison; to hire, appoint; to load; to absorb

Talk about what you do after you are **discharged** from school.

4. economical
(e kə nä′ mi kəl)
(e-kuh-NAH-mi-kuhl)

(adj.) careful about spending money or using resources

> *An economical shopper always looks for a bargain.*

SYNONYMS: thrifty, frugal, saving; ANTONYMS: extravagant, wasteful

5. frank
(fraŋk)
(FRANGK)

(adj.) honest in expressing thoughts and feelings

> *Don't be offended if I am frank with you.*

SYNONYMS: direct, blunt, straightforward, truthful
ANTONYMS: secretive, insincere, dishonest

6. modify
(mä′ də fī)
(MAH-duh-fye)

(v.) to change somewhat

> *You can modify a recipe to suit your taste.*

SYNONYMS: to adjust, alter, adapt, vary, revise

Talk about a time when you **modified** an answer on your homework.

7. mutiny
(myü′ tən ē)
(MYOO-tuhn-ee)

(n.) an open rebellion against authority

The Boston Tea Party was an act of mutiny.

(v.) to rebel against those in charge

The captain's cruelty led the crew to mutiny.

SYNONYMS: (n.) a revolt, uprising, riot; (v.) to revolt, rise up
ANTONYMS: (v.) to support, obey

8. negative
(ne′ gə tiv)
(NE-guh-tiv)

(adj.) saying "no"; not positive or helpful; less than zero

The reply to my question was negative.

(n.) a "no" expression; a photo image that reverses light and dark areas

"I can't" is an example of a negative.

SYNONYMS: (adj.) bad, unfavorable; ANTONYMS: (adj.) positive, helpful, good, favorable

Use each definition of **negative** in a sentence.

9. pursue
(pər sü′)
(pur-SOO)

(v.) to chase in order to catch; to strive to achieve; to carry out

During a hunt, the dogs pursue a hare.

SYNONYMS: to follow, hunt, run after, aim for, work for
ANTONYMS: to run away, take off, flee, bolt

What career do you want to **pursue** when you get older?

10. reign
(rān)
(RAYN)

(n.) the power or rule of a monarch; a monarch's period of rule

England prospered under the reign of Queen Anne.

(v.) to rule as a monarch; to be widespread

During the 1920s, prosperity reigned.

SYNONYMS: (n.) the regime, control; (v.) to govern, command

11. singular
(siŋ′ gyə lər)
(SING-gyuh-lur)

(adj.) referring to only one person or thing; out of the ordinary

The show was a singular success.

SYNONYMS: exceptional, unusual; ANTONYM: plural

12. swindle
(swin′ dəl)
(SWIN-duhl)

(v.) to cheat out of money or property

A dishonest shopkeeper tried to swindle me.

(n.) a scheme for cheating someone

The fraud squad uncovered the swindle.

SYNONYMS: (v.) to deceive, trick, gyp, con; (n.) a scam, fraud, hoax, racket

As time allows, have partners complete graphic organizers for select words, available at **SadlierConnect.com**.

Synonyms

*Choose the word that is most nearly the **same** in meaning as the word or phrase in **boldface**. Then write your choice on the line provided.*

1. a **blunt** answer to your question
   a. frank   b. negative   c. singular   d. economical   _____frank_____

2. **revise** the schedule
   a. discharge   b. pursue   c. modify   d. swindle   _____modify_____

3. **aim for** a career in medicine
   a. modify   b. discharge   c. swindle   d. pursue   _____pursue_____

4. an ironclad **excuse**
   a. confederate   b. reign   c. alibi   d. mutiny   _____alibi_____

5. a **regime** of terror
   a. swindle   b. discharge   c. mutiny   d. reign   _____reign_____

6. **cheated** by a con artist
   a. pursued   b. swindled   c. modified   d. discharged   _____swindled_____

Antonyms

*Choose the word that is most nearly **opposite** in meaning to the word or phrase in **boldface**. Then write your choice on the line provided.*

1. **positive** numbers
   a. negative   b. singular   c. economical   d. frank   _____negative_____

2. the **wasteful** use of natural resources
   a. frank   b. economical   c. singular   d. negative   _____economical_____

3. soldiers who **obey**
   a. discharge   b. mutiny   c. reign   d. swindle   _____mutiny_____

4. **load** a cannon
   a. modify   b. pursue   c. swindle   d. discharge   _____discharge_____

5. **plural** nouns
   a. negative   b. economical   c. singular   d. frank   _____singular_____

6. **enemies** of the tribe
   a. reigns   b. alibis   c. mutinies   d. confederates   _____confederates_____

Completing the Sentence

Choose the word from the box that best completes each item. Then write the word on the line provided. (You may have to change the word's ending.)

alibi	confederate	discharge
economical	frank	modify
mutiny	negative	pursue
reign	singular	swindle

Editing an Essay

- When I write an essay, I review what I have written to see how I can improve it. One way that I may __________ **modify** __________ the essay is to get rid of any repetitions.

- Because I want to keep the reader's attention, I try to keep my sentences clear and brief. Therefore, I look for more __________ **economical** __________ ways to make my points.

- For example, if I am writing about two people, I may want to use the plural pronoun *they* instead of __________ **singular** __________ pronouns such as *he* and *she*.

Trouble on the High Seas

- Captain William Bligh, an English admiral, __________ **reigned** __________ over his ship, the *Bounty*, as if he were its king.

- His harsh treatment and mean-spirited rules aroused __________ **negative** __________ feelings among crew members. Few viewed the captain in a favorable light.

- In a secret but __________ **frank** __________ discussion, the sailors plotted to take over the ship.

- A ship's officer named Fletcher Christian seized control of the *Bounty* on April 28, 1789. This daring __________ **mutiny** __________ has been the subject of several movies.

Crime at the Cash Machine

- Soon after my uncle opened a checking account at a new bank, he was the victim of a bank machine __________ **swindle** __________.

- A woman posing as a banker and her __________ **confederate** __________ advised my uncle to get $200 from the ATM to test his bank card. The crooks then ran off with the money.

- Using the descriptions given by my uncle and a witness, the police __________ **pursued** __________ the two thieves on foot, catching up to them a few blocks away.

- They soon arrested the suspects without having to __________ **discharge** __________ their weapons.

- At their trial, the two thieves claimed that they were innocent. But the jury did not believe their __________ **alibis** __________. It took only fifteen minutes to find them guilty.

*Circle the letter next to the word or phrase that best completes the sentence or answers the question. Pay special attention to the word in **boldface.***

1. A **frank** comment is
a. always complimentary.
b. never hurtful.
c. always appreciated.
d. never dishonest.

2. A **negative** person is likely to
a. take great vacation pictures.
b. be good at math.
c. find fault with any plan.
d. see the best in everyone.

3. If I **swindle** my little brother, I
a. cheat him.
b. read to him.
c. protect him.
d. draw a picture of him.

4. I would expect my **confederates** to
a. work together with me.
b. make fun of me.
c. refuse to help me.
d. plan family trips and activities.

Words with Greek Roots

The unit word *economical*, meaning "careful about spending," comes from the Greek *eco*. *Eco* is a Greek root meaning "home or settlement." The root is also used in the following words:

- economy (n.): management of resources, such as money (*managing resources in a home*)
- economist (n.): someone who studies the economy (*a person who specializes in the finances of a settlement or area*)
- ecocide (n.): destruction of the natural world (*destruction of the natural home*)
- ecology (n.): the study of a habitat or other natural community (*the relationships among things in a natural home or settlement*)
- ecosystem (n.): a community of plants and animals (*things living in a natural home*)

Choose two of the words from the list. Write a sentence for each word to show you understand its meaning.

1. Accept answers that show an understanding of the vocabulary.

2.

Read the passage. Then answer each question.

What Are Hoaxes?

1   Hoaxes have been around for a long time. They can be harmless practical jokes or pranks. They also can be more serious. Sometimes they are used to **swindle** unsuspecting victims out of their money. Those who **pursue** this type of hoax show a **singular** interest in deceiving innocent people. When this happens, authorities do their best to **discharge** their duties and punish the lawbreakers.

2   Art forgery is a type of hoax that has occurred throughout history. For example, in the late 1400s, during the **reign** of Pope Alexander VI, artist Michelangelo tried to pass off a sculpture he had just finished as an antique. He was young and unknown at the time, and antique artwork brought in very high prices. Michelangelo's forgery was discovered, but the outcome was far from **negative**. The buyer recognized the young artist's talent and invited him to Rome.

3   These days, online hoaxes spread fast. This is especially true during natural disasters. Con artists spread false rumors to scare the most vulnerable. Some hoaxes are so cruel they lead victims to **mutiny** against the offenders and demand justice.

1. Pick the word that best defines **swindle** as it is used in paragraph 1.
   (a) soothe   **(b) trick**   (c) reward   (d) condemn

2. The Latin word *singulus* means "only one." The word **singular** in paragraph 1 means
   (a) exceptional   (b) simple   (c) everyday   (d) mild

3. What does the word **reign** mean as it is used in paragraph 2?
   (a) govern   (b) spread wide   (c) date of birth   **(d) period of rule**

4. Pick the word that best defines **mutiny** as it is used in paragraph 3.
   (a) support   (b) blame   **(c) rise**   (d) report

A possessive pronoun takes the place of a possessive noun. It shows who or what has or owns something. The demonstrative pronouns this, that, these, *and* those *point out specific people, places, or things. Underline examples of both a possessive pronoun and a demonstrative pronoun in "What Are Hoaxes?"* Accept all correct answers. Examples: See paragraph 1.

Write Your Own

Write a 3–5 sentence story about an imaginary hoax, using at least three vocabulary words from this unit. Share your story with a partner and take turns discussing whether or not people would be fooled by either of these hoaxes. Give good reasons for your conclusions.

For more practice with possessive and demonstrative pronouns, see Grammar Workshop, Level Blue, Lesson 43.

Word Study Dictionary: Multiple-Meaning Words 2

You have learned that **multiple-meaning words** have more than one meaning. One example is *negative* (page 143). If you look up *negative* in a dictionary, you will find an entry with numbers showing the different meanings.

Read this sentence: *Someone who has a* **negative** *attitude may not be willing to try new things.* You can tell from the definitions that the sentence illustrates meaning 2 of *negative*.

Look at the chart to find other examples of multiple-meaning words.

barge	**1.** *(n.)* a flat-bottom boat used for moving things **2.** *(v.)* to enter or interrupt rudely
harvest	**1.** *(n.)* the crops picked from a field **2.** *(v.)* to gather crops, such as wheat, from a field
murmur	**1.** *(n.)* a low continuous sound **2.** *(v.)* to speak in a low voice

PRACTICE *Write the multiple-meaning word from the chart above that completes each sentence. Using the part of speech can help you choose the word. Then write the number of the meaning.*

__2__ **1.** Why did you ______ barge ______ into the room without knocking?

__1__ **2.** The ______ murmur ______ of the air conditioner put me to sleep.

__1__ **3.** The poor fruit ______ harvest ______ was due to the cold weather.

__2__ **4.** The shy student seemed to ______ murmur ______ the answer.

APPLY *Complete each sentence so that it makes sense. Use the multiple-meaning word in* **boldface**. *You may have to change the word's ending.*
Accept reasonable answers that demonstrate the correct meaning.

5. murmur If you need to talk in the library, ________________.

6. barge Along wide rivers, ________________.

7. harvest When the beans were ripe, we ________________.

8. negative People won't want you on their team ________________.

Search through newspapers, magazines, or books to find a sentence with one of the multiple-meaning words above. Write the sentence. Then write the meaning that is illustrated.

Shades of Meaning Adages and Proverbs 2

In the passage "A Giant Hoax" on pages 140–141, many people who saw the Cardiff Giant believed it was real and paid money to see it. You might use this proverb or adage to describe the Cardiff Giant: ***All that glitters is not gold.***

A **proverb** or **adage** is a short, well-known expression or saying that states an obvious truth or gives advice. *All that glitters is not gold* is a proverb. It cautions us that some things, such as the Cardiff Giant, are not always what they seem.

PRACTICE   *Read each sentence. Decide which proverb best expresses a truth about the situation described. Write the number of the sentence next to the proverb.*

1. Instead of sitting and waiting for my friend to call, I kept busy by cleaning my room.

2. Each night, Dad put loose change in a jar. At the end of the month, he had twenty dollars.

3. I learned my routine well, but I just didn't want to perform it.

4. The batter was skinny and small for his age, so we were all surprised when he hit a home run.

____4____ Don't judge a book by its cover.

____1____ A watched pot never boils.

____3____ You can lead a horse to water, but you can't make it drink.

____2____ A penny saved is a penny earned.

APPLY   *Write what someone might say to make you respond with each proverb below. The first one has been done for you.* Accept reasonable answers. Possible answers are given.

5. Appearances can be deceiving.

   The restaurant looks run-down, but it has the best food in town.

6. Beggars can't be choosers.

   There was no more juice, so I had to drink water.

7. Half a loaf is better than none.

   I wish my ice skates were not hand-me-downs.

8. Fool me once, shame on you. Fool me twice, shame on me.

   My brother tricked me into doing his chores, but I won't let that happen again.

9. Bad news travels fast.

   I'm sorry to hear that your team didn't win the championship.

Introducing the Words

Read the following tall tale about a larger-than-life hero of the Old West. Notice how the highlighted words are used. These are the words you will be learning in this unit.

Pecos Bill Ends a Drought

(Tall Tale)

A differentiated version of this passage is available at **SadlierConnect.com**.

According to the tales that Texas cowboys used to tell, Pecos Bill was raised along the Pecos River by coyotes. That upbringing might have been a bit unusual, but it gave Bill superhuman powers.

Just about everything Pecos Bill did was a **spectacle**. He had a lariat as long as Texas, so he could rope a herd of cattle with just one throw. To keep those cattle safe, he decided to use New Mexico as his pasture. Fencing in that pasture would have **complicated** anyone else's life, but not Bill's. He just persuaded the prairie dogs to dig the postholes for him.

These stunts that Bill performed had **universal** appeal. Even the sun showed its curiosity, straining closer and closer to get a better look at whatever Bill was up to. That's what caused the great Texas drought. Never had the state been so dry before! The sun didn't mean any harm, but it got so close that it **scorched** the land. Every blade of grass dried up and turned brown because of the burning heat.

Talk about a hot summer! The heat was so **severe** that the chickens laid fried eggs. People wanted to cry and **grieve**, but there wasn't enough water for tears.

Pecos Bill felt the **discomfort**, too. After all, the **tragic** situation was partly his fault. A **moral** man, Bill always tried to do what was right. He was also a man of action, so he decided to end the drought.

Hopping onto his horse Widow-Maker, Bill galloped north across Oklahoma. Halfway up Tornado Alley, he spotted what he was looking for. A big, black twister had just torn up half of Kansas and was heading down toward Oklahoma for a repeat performance. Bill didn't hesitate for a second. Taking out his lariat, he roped the tornado and climbed onto its neck.

"Howdy, friend!" said Bill in his **courteous** way, looking directly into the eye of the storm. "I could use your help down in Texas."

"How dare this cowboy trifle with a tornado!" the twister snorted to itself. Bucking like a bronco, the big funnel-shaped cloud whirled, twirled, and zig-zagged south, hoping to throw Bill off. Bill held on, though, digging his spurs into the tornado's sides and riding it south. Past Galveston and out into the Gulf of Mexico, the twister spun, quickly filling with water.

That's just what Bill was planning. Full of water, the tornado slowed down a bit, allowing Bill to steer it west over Texas. There, with a few well-placed kicks, Bill turned the twister into a giant watering can.

Once the tornado had dropped all its water, it turned nasty again, so Bill rode it back to the Gulf for more. In all, Bill made six trips, bringing enough water to end the drought and eliminate the hardship he had caused.

Actually, only five trips would have been necessary. When Texans saw Bill coming back with his sixth load, they waved their hats and shouted, "No!" Any more water and they'd have a flood. In the end, Bill rode the twister over to Arizona and dumped all the water in one great swoosh, a washout that created the Grand Canyon.

Definitions

You were introduced to these words in the passage. Study the pronunciation, part of speech, definition, and example sentence for each word. Then read the synonyms and antonyms.

1. complicate
(käm′ plə kāt)
(KOM-pluh-kate)

(v.) to make hard to understand or do

A lot of unnecessary details can complicate directions.

SYNONYMS: to confuse, muddle, mix up; ANTONYMS: to simplify, clarify, smooth, ease

2. courteous
(kûr′ tē əs)
(KUR-tee-uhss)

(adj.) considerate toward others

A courteous host makes her guests feel welcomed.

SYNONYMS: polite, well-mannered, respectful, civil
ANTONYMS: rude, impolite, ill-mannered, discourteous

3. discomfort
(dis kum′ fərt)
(diss-KUHM-furt)

(n.) a lack of ease and well-being

A nasty case of chicken pox can cause a great deal of discomfort.

SYNONYMS: pain, distress, irritation, suffering
ANTONYMS: comfort, peace, calm

 When was the last time that you felt **discomfort**?

4. eliminate
(i li′ mə nāt)
(i-LI-muh-nate)

(v.) to get rid of or do away with

By working together, we can eliminate hunger and poverty.

SYNONYMS: to remove, omit, leave out, exclude, drop
ANTONYMS: to take in, admit, acquire, retain, preserve

 If you could **eliminate** one problem in the world, what would it be?

5. grieve
(grēv)
(GREEV)

(v.) to cause to feel great sadness; to feel very sad

Reports of the many deaths and the destruction caused by the earthquake grieve us all.

SYNONYMS: to sadden, mourn, regret; ANTONYMS: to rejoice, celebrate, gladden

6. moral
(môr′ əl)
(MOR-uhl)

(adj.) having to do with what is right and wrong; being good and just

A moral question is sometimes very difficult to answer.

(n.) the lesson taught by a story or experience

I think that the moral of the story is "never give up."

SYNONYMS: (adj.) honorable, upright, honest; (n.) a message, teaching
ANTONYMS: (adj.) immoral, wicked, bad, wrong

 What is the **moral** of your favorite story?

7. scorch
(skôrch)
(SKORCH)

(v.) to burn on the surface; to dry out with heat

Did you scorch my brand-new shirt with the iron?

(n.) a slight burn

I placed the napkin so it would cover a scorch in the tablecloth.

SYNONYMS: (v.) to singe, brown, blacken, shrivel

💬 **Use each definition of scorch in a sentence.**

8. severe
(sə vēr')
(suh-VEER)

(adj.) of a serious nature; very strict and harsh; causing pain or hardship

Most parents think lying is a severe offense.

SYNONYMS: grave, stern; tough, bitter; brutal, rough
ANTONYMS: unimportant; mild; merciful

9. spectacle
(spek' ti kəl)
(SPEK-ti-kuhl)

(n.) an unusual sight or public display

Millions of people visit New York every year to view the spectacle of the Manhattan skyline.

SYNONYMS: a scene, show, exhibition, marvel

10. tragic
(tra' jik)
(TRA-jik)

(adj.) having to do with a serious story with a sad ending; very unfortunate

Stories with tragic endings make me cry.

SYNONYMS: dreadful, awful, sad, disastrous, unhappy
ANTONYMS: amusing, funny, humorous, comical, happy

11. trifle
(trī' fəl)
(TRYE-fuhl)

(n.) something of little importance; a small amount

It is not worth arguing over such a trifle.

(v.) to treat carelessly or playfully

It is unkind to trifle with someone's feelings.

SYNONYMS: (n.) a bit, knickknack, trinket; (v.) to fiddle, play, toy
ANTONYMS: (n.) a lot, lots of

12. universal
(yü nə vûr' səl)
(yoo-nuh-VUR-suhl)

(adj.) being everywhere; of, for, or shared by all

Food and shelter are universal needs.

SYNONYMS: worldwide, broad, general, widespread
ANTONYMS: local, limited, narrow

💬 **What is a universal need that people have?**

💬 As time allows, have partners complete graphic organizers for select words, available at **SadlierConnect.com**.

Synonyms

*Choose the word that is most nearly the **same** in meaning as the word or phrase in **boldface**. Then write your choice on the line provided.*

1. caused great **distress**
   a. spectacle   b. trifle   c. discomfort   d. moral   _discomfort_

2. a grand **scene**
   a. moral   b. spectacle   c. trifle   d. discomfort   _spectacle_

3. the **message** of the fable
   a. trifle   b. scorch   c. spectacle   d. moral   _moral_

4. **burned** the grass
   a. scorched   b. eliminated   c. complicated   d. grieved for   _scorched_

5. **fiddle** with the rules
   a. complicate   b. scorch   c. eliminate   d. trifle   _trifle_

6. **leave out** the negative comments
   a. eliminate   b. complicate   c. trifle with   d. grieve for   _eliminate_

Antonyms

*Choose the word that is most nearly **opposite** in meaning to the word or phrase in **boldface**. Then write your choice on the line provided.*

1. **simplify** things
   a. scorch   b. complicate   c. eliminate   d. trifle with   _complicate_

2. a **mild** winter
   a. severe   b. moral   c. universal   d. courteous   _severe_

3. having **limited** appeal
   a. tragic   b. severe   c. moral   d. universal   _universal_

4. **amusing** love stories
   a. universal   b. courteous   c. tragic   d. moral   _tragic_

5. a **rude** customer
   a. severe   b. universal   c. courteous   d. tragic   _courteous_

6. **rejoice** with the family
   a. trifle   b. grieve   c. scorch   d. eliminate   _grieve_

Completing the Sentence

Choose the word from the box that best completes each item. Then write the word on the line provided. (You may have to change the word's ending.)

> complicate   courteous   discomfort
> eliminate   grieve   moral
> scorch   severe   spectacle
> tragic   trifle   universal

Death of a President

■ When President John F. Kennedy was killed by an assassin's bullet on November 22, 1963, the ___**tragic**___ event shocked the nation. The President was only forty-five years old.

■ Americans ___**grieved**___ openly as they watched his formal state funeral on television or listened to it on the radio.

■ People still recall the respectful and ___**courteous**___ behavior of the huge crowds that lined the funeral route.

Why Save the Rain Forests?

■ The magnificent variety of animals and plants in the tropical rain forests creates a ___**spectacle**___ unlike anything else in nature.

■ The effort to protect these forests is ___**complicated**___ by the need to use some of their valuable resources—for example, by using plants to make medicine.

■ When any plant or animal is forever ___**eliminated**___ from the earth, the balance of nature changes. The loss of a single species may result in harm to many more.

■ A change in the balance of nature can cause a ___**universal**___ shift in weather patterns. A change that at first has only local effects may in time affect the world.

■ Many people now regard destruction of the rain forests as a ___**moral**___ issue, not just a political or legal one, because it can ruin the future of the entire planet.

Sunburn Really Hurts

■ Many people do not realize how easily they can ___**scorch**___ their skin just by walking or playing outside on a sunny day.

■ Even on a cloudy day, it is possible to get a ___**severe**___ sunburn.

■ If you get a painful sunburn, ask your doctor what you should do to ease the ___**discomfort**___.

■ Always remember that a sunburn is nothing to ___**trifle**___ with. It can cause serious harm to your skin.

Word Associations

*Circle the letter next to the word or phrase that best completes the sentence or answers the question. Pay special attention to the word in **boldface.***

1. A **courteous** person might say
   a. can't and won't.
   b. yes and no.
   c. please and thank you.
   d. when and where.

2. Which would you try to **eliminate**?
   a. good health
   b. happiness
   c. the sky
   d. a problem

3. A **severe** decision could be described as
   a. temporary.
   b. very strict and harsh.
   c. open to debate.
   d. cowardly.

4. A story with **universal** appeal is
   a. liked by everyone.
   b. read by only a few people.
   c. extremely funny.
   d. hard to understand.

Words with Latin Roots

The unit word *spectacle*, meaning "an unusual sight," comes from the Latin *spec*. *Spec* is a Latin root meaning "to see, to look, or to watch." The root is used in the following words:

- inspect (v.): to examine carefully (*to look at in detail*)
- spectator (n.): someone who watches (*a person who looks or sees*)
- aspect (n.): a feature of a person or thing (*a detail relating to the way a person or thing looks or appears*)
- speculate (v.): to wonder or think about (*to look at in one's thoughts*)
- retrospective (adj.): reviewing or dealing with the past (*looking back*)

Choose two of the words from the list above. Write a sentence for each word to show you understand its meaning.

1. Accept answers that show an understanding of the vocabulary.

2.

Words in Context

Read the passage. Then answer each question.

The Legend of John Henry

1   The legend of John Henry reveals that he was a six-foot-tall African American man who was born enslaved and then freed. Henry was known for his steel-driving, where he used a sledge hammer and a chisel to drive spikes into mountains. The holes steel driving created aided in the construction of railroad tunnels.

2   According to the legend, Henry worked for the C & O Railroad. He drilled through rock under a blazing sun that **scorched** the earth and created **severe** conditions. Henry competed against the newly invented steam hammer to prove he could drive steel faster than the machine. Henry worked through **discomfort** and pain caused by such physical exertion. As the legend goes, Henry beat the steam-powered drilling machine, but died from the effort of his attempt. Many **grieved** his death. The machine later replaced human labor when railroad tunnels were built.

3   Whether or not the legend is factual, the story of John Henry is no **trifle**. The **moral** of this legend is that humans can be victorious over larger power structures. To this day he's a **universal** icon for people who've needed to feel hope in the face of overwhelming challenges.

1. What is the meaning of the word **scorched** as it is used in paragraph 2?
(a) burned   (b) used heat   (c) a slight burn   (d) a small wound

2. What does the word **severe** mean as it is used in paragraph 2?
(a) serious   (b) harsh   (c) unusual   (d) ideal

3. The Latin word *gravare* means "to burden." The word **grieved** in paragraph 2 means
(a) forgot about   (b) felt anger about   (c) caused   (d) mourned

4. Pick the word that best defines **moral** as it is used in paragraph 3.
(a) right   (b) ending   (c) lesson   (d) honest

A contraction is a shortened word made by combining two words. An apostrophe (') takes the place of any letters that are left out. Many contractions combine a pronoun and a verb. **They're** *(they are) and* **you're** *(you are) are contractions with pronouns. Underline a contraction with a pronoun in* "The Legend of John Henry." **See paragraph 3.**

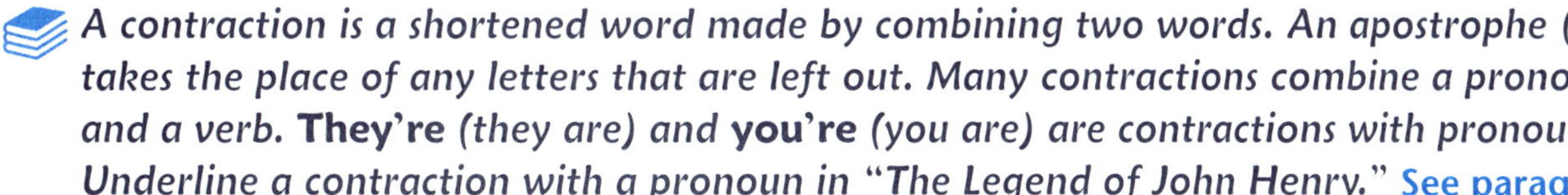

Write Your Own

Write a brief description of a legend or superhero, using at least three vocabulary words from this unit. Share your description with your partner, and have your partner replace the vocabulary words you used with synonyms.

For more practice with contractions with pronouns, see Grammar Workshop, Level Blue, Lesson 45.

*Read this passage in which some of the words you have studied in Units 13–15 appear in **boldface**. Then answer the questions.*

The Experience of a Lifetime

Ferris wheel on the grounds of the 1893 Chicago World's Fair

1   Carl, Anna, and their parents joined the crowd at the train station. They had prepared for this day since March: Carl earned money doing the morning milking, and Anna baked pies and biscuits and sold them. She brought along her diary so that she could **preserve** a record of the family's adventures. The family had been very **economical**, saving every penny for the train tickets and the admission fee. At last the children and their parents were ready for the celebration of the century— the 1893 Chicago World's Fair—and they joined travelers from all over the world to see the **spectacle** on Lake Michigan.

2   After an hour's rattling ride, the train was at the fair's main gate. Carl whistled, and Anna gasped in awe. Tens of thousands of visitors were strolling the walkways and inspecting the **exhibits**. Anna and Carl stopped to see a gigantic block of cheese from Canada that weighed in at 22,000 pounds!

3   "First, the wheel," said Carl with an enthusiasm that left no room for **debate**.

4   "The wheel?" Anna asked.

5   "You know, the one by George Ferris, the genius engineer from Pittsburgh," Carl answered. "Maybe we can ride twice!"

6   The family headed toward the wondrous wheel, which towered over everything else. It was huge! Its 36 wooden cars carried 2,160 people high above the ground for a thrilling 20-minute view of the fairgrounds. The ride had great popular appeal, and not a **negative** word was heard from the riders. People of all ages and nationalities waited in what seemed like an endless line. Carl and Anna joined the crowd and took their places in the line. "The **moral** was clear," Anna later wrote in her diary. "It was the ride of a lifetime!"

Fill in the circle next to the choice that best completes the sentence or answers the question.

1. Which statement best expresses a theme in this passage?
   a The Chicago World's Fair was a disappointment.
   b The Ferris wheel often broke down.
   c Some visitors had trouble getting to the fair.
   d The Chicago World's Fair was a thrilling experience.

2. The Latin word *servare* means "to guard." The word **preserve** in paragraph 1 means
   a save
   b refuge
   c misuse
   d certify

3. What does the word **economical** mean as it is used in paragraph 1?
   a wasteful
   b thrifty
   c urgent
   d selfish

4. Which phrase from the passage best shows the idea of **economical**?
   a "baked pies and biscuits"
   b "brought along her diary"
   c "saving every penny"
   d "the children and their parents"

5. What does the use of the word **spectacle** in paragraph 1 suggest?
   a a sad tragedy
   b a humorous skit
   c an unusual sight
   d a dangerous fire

6. As it is used in paragraph 3, what does the word **debate** show about Carl?
   a He was open to suggestion.
   b He was determined.
   c He was uncertain.
   d He wanted to talk about it.

7. What word has the opposite meaning of **negative** in paragraph 6?
   a depressed
   b impatient
   c positive
   d loud

8. What is the meaning of the word **moral** as it is used in paragraph 6?
   a upright
   b honest
   c message
   d summary

Write Your Own

Imagine that you are Carl or Anna. On a separate sheet of paper, write a journal entry about your day at the Chicago World's Fair. Include details that tell what you saw, heard, and did. Use at least three vocabulary words from Units 13–15.

Introducing the Words

Read the following journal article about huge animals that lived long ago. Notice how the highlighted words are used. These are the words you will be learning in this unit.

Why Did the Woolly Mammoths Disappear?

(Journal Article)

A differentiated version of this passage is available at **SadlierConnect.com**.

Before humans arrived in North America, giant-sized mammals walked the land. The best known were two elephant-like animals, the woolly **mammoth** and the mastodon. Less familiar is the short-faced bear, a rough and **rowdy** creature about thirty percent larger than today's grizzly. Sabre-toothed tigers, some weighing as much as 800 pounds, were a threat to any creature that **trespassed** in their territory. There were also giant wolves as well as camels, horses, and sloths. In terms of size, these creatures have no **peers** among the North American mammals of today.

The mega-mammals **fared** well on the continent for hundreds of thousands of years. At the beginning of the last ice age, about 130,000 years ago, the animals were still thriving. Even though ice covered much of the continent, the land was **fertile** enough to provide food.

Then, near the end of the ice age, something happened: The large mammals died off. It's impossible to give a **rigid** timetable for when these animals became extinct because these

extinctions happened too long ago. Yet at some point about 12,000 to 15,000 years ago, both the glaciers and many of the mammals seem to have disappeared rather suddenly, all at the same time.

For a long time, people assumed that the giant creatures had been hunted to extinction. The first human hunters had left Asia and wandered onto the North American continent about this time. Hunting with spears, the newcomers fanned out across the continent. As the colonies of humans expanded, the theory goes, they killed off many species.

Were there enough hunters to endanger so many species? Few archaeologists think so. Other facts also undercut this theory. For one thing, archeological sites are crammed with clues about what the early hunters killed and ate. Mammoths and mastodons were their favorites. Apparently, these people didn't hunt the other extremely large mammals. Yet these animals died off, too. Furthermore, the early people did hunt bison, but this species, of course, survived.

An exploding comet may have led to the extinction of the woolly mammoth.

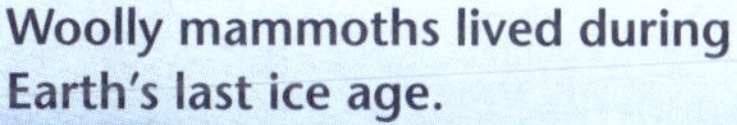

Woolly mammoths lived during Earth's last ice age.

Recently, scientists have furnished another explanation for the extinctions. A large comet, which is a traveling body of ice and dust, may have exploded on or just above Earth about 12,000 years ago. The clouds of dust from the disaster would have caused a long period of cooling on Earth. The cold temperatures would have led to the extinctions of dozens of species.

There is evidence for the comet theory. Arctic ice that formed about 12,000 years ago shows high levels of iridium, the element found in comets and meteorites. Also, tiny diamonds, called nanodiamonds, appear in soil samples dating from 12,000 years ago. The flash of the explosion could have formed them. This theory could explain why large mammal species would have died off so suddenly.

Many species, however, survived the disaster and cold climate. Among them are the wild animals that we're most familiar with today. Why were they safeguarded from the cooling while the larger species were not? By unraveling the history and mystery of ancient climate change, scientists hope one day to find the answer.

Definitions

You were introduced to these words in the passage. Study the pronunciation, part of speech, definition, and example sentence for each word. Then read the synonyms and antonyms.

1. assume
(ə süm′)
(uh-SOOM)

(v.) to take upon oneself; to pretend to have or be; to take for granted

My parents said I could have the puppy if I would assume the responsibility for it.

SYNONYMS: to accept, undertake, seize; to imagine, suppose, believe
ANTONYMS: to reject, refuse, give up

2. cram
(kram)
(KRAM)

(v.) to stuff tightly; to fill tightly; to study hard just before a test

Mom told me not to cram all my clothes into one drawer.

SYNONYMS: to pack, crowd, jam, load, squeeze
ANTONYMS: to empty, clean out, clear out

When was the last time you **crammed** for a test? What was the result?

3. endanger
(in dān′ jər)
(in-DAYN-jur)

(v.) to expose to injury or harm

Fire and drought will endanger the forest animals.

SYNONYMS: to risk, threaten; ANTONYMS: to protect, defend, preserve, save, secure

4. fare
(fâr)
(FAIR)

(v.) to get along

If you study hard, you should fare well in school.

(n.) the cost of travel on public transportation; food and drink

We can't afford the plane fare to the East Coast.

SYNONYMS: (v.) to manage, succeed; (n.) a charge, fee, price; a menu

Use each definition of **fare** in a sentence.

5. fertile
(fûr′ təl)
(FUR-tuhl)

(adj.) good for producing crops and plants; capable of growing

The Midwest's farms are located in one of the most fertile areas in the world.

SYNONYMS: fruitful, productive, rich; ANTONYMS: barren, unproductive

6. furnish
(fûr′ nish)
(FUR-nish)

(v.) to supply with furniture; to supply with what is needed

After the fire, neighbors helped to furnish the new house.

SYNONYMS: to equip, outfit, provide, give; ANTONYMS: to take, withhold

How is your classroom **furnished**? Explain your answer to your partner.

7. mammoth
(ma′ məth)
(MA-muhth)

(n.) a very large, long-tusked, shaggy-haired elephant, that is now extinct

No woolly mammoths are alive today.

(adj.) great in size

A skyscraper is a mammoth building.

SYNONYMS: (adj.) enormous, huge, immense, gigantic, colossal
ANTONYMS: (adj.) small, tiny, little, miniature

8. peer
(pēr)
(PIHR)

(n.) a person of the same age, rank, or ability; a British noble

As a gifted pianist, the child had no peer.

(v.) to look closely at

I tend to peer at people through my glasses.

SYNONYMS: (n.) an equal, colleague; (v.) to gaze, stare, scan

 **Peer** at an object in the room for 10 seconds.

9. rigid
(ri′ jəd)
(RI-juhd)

(adj.) not bending; very strict

Stand at attention, and keep your body rigid.

SYNONYMS: stiff, firm, inflexible; severe, stern; ANTONYMS: elastic, flexible, loose

10. rowdy
(raủ′ dē)
(ROU-dee)

(adj.) rough and disorderly

My teacher does not tolerate rowdy behavior.

SYNONYMS: wild, unruly, noisy; ANTONYMS: quiet, tame, gentle, mild

 **What does your teacher do if students in class become too rowdy?**

11. safeguard
(sāf′ gärd)
(SAYF-gard)

(n.) something that protects

A helmet is a safeguard against head injuries.

(v.) to protect against possible danger

Wear sunblock to safeguard your skin.

SYNONYMS: (n.) a protection, defense; (v.) to defend, guard, save
ANTONYMS: (v.) to endanger, threaten, risk

12. trespass
(n., tres′ pəs)
(TRESS-puhss)
(v., tres′ pas)
(TRESS-pass)

(n.) an action that is wrong; unlawful entry onto someone's property

The man was charged with criminal trespass.

(v.) to do wrong; to enter onto someone's property without right

I did not mean to trespass against you.

SYNONYMS: (n.) a sin, wrongdoing; an invasion; (v.) to sin, offend, intrude

 As time allows, have partners complete graphic organizers for select words, available at **SadlierConnect.com.**

Synonyms

*Choose the word that is most nearly the **same** in meaning as the word or phrase in **boldface**. Then write your choice on the line provided.*

1. **stare** through the window
   a. cram   b. trespass   c. peer   d. assume   **peer**

2. **rich** soil
   a. rigid   b. fertile   c. rowdy   d. mammoth   **fertile**

3. **defend** the planet
   a. furnish   b. endanger   c. cram   d. safeguard   **safeguard**

4. collect the **fee**
   a. mammoth   b. fare   c. safeguard   d. peer   **fare**

5. **equip** the lab
   a. furnish   b. endanger   c. cram   d. safeguard   **furnish**

6. **intrude** on private property
   a. peer   b. assume   c. trespass   d. cram   **trespass**

Antonyms

*Choose the word that is most nearly **opposite** in meaning to the word or phrase in **boldface**. Then write your choice on the line provided.*

1. **small** in size
   a. rigid   b. mammoth   c. rowdy   d. fertile   **mammoth**

2. a **quiet** activity
   a. rigid   b. fertile   c. mammoth   d. rowdy   **rowdy**

3. a **flexible** rule
   a. mammoth   b. rowdy   c. fertile   d. rigid   **rigid**

4. **empty** your locker
   a. furnish   b. safeguard   c. cram   d. endanger   **cram**

5. **protect** the spotted owl
   a. cram   b. endanger   c. furnish   d. safeguard   **endanger**

6. **give up** control
   a. furnish   b. safeguard   c. assume   d. endanger   **assume**

Completing the Sentence

Choose the word from the box that best completes each item. Then write the word on the line provided. (You may have to change the word's ending.)

assume	cram	endanger
fare	fertile	furnish
mammoth	peer	rigid
rowdy	safeguard	trespass

A Big Mistake

■ I made a big mistake when I ______**assumed**______ that I could wait until the night before the big test to start studying.

■ My ______**peers**______ teased me when I told them that I was worried about the test. They said I didn't need to study hard. I shouldn't have listened to them.

■ I had to stay up very late to ______**cram**______ my brain full of facts and figures. When I realized how much I needed to learn, I began to feel sick with panic.

■ To make matters worse, the people in the house next door had a ______**rowdy**______ party that lasted until one o'clock in the morning. I couldn't sleep because of the noise.

■ The next day I was so tired that I couldn't remember anything. So it was no surprise that I ______**fared**______ badly on the test.

Save the Wetlands

■ America's wetlands provide a rich and ______**fertile**______ environment for thousands of species of plants and animals.

■ But pollution and development more and more ______**endanger**______ these beautiful places. In some areas their very survival is at risk.

■ If we lose our wetlands, many of the creatures that live there will become as extinct as the woolly ______**mammoth**______.

■ Lots of concerned individuals and organizations are working to educate the public about how important it is to ______**safeguard**______ this precious natural resource.

Safety in a Dangerous Place

■ ______**Rigid**______ rules protect scientists who study deadly viruses.

■ All workers are ______**furnished**______ with special protective clothing that they must put on before going into the lab.

■ Only employees are allowed to enter the lab. Other people will be considered to be ______**trespassing**______. Security guards will escort intruders from the building.

Word Associations

*Circle the letter next to the word or phrase that best completes the sentence or answers the question. Pay special attention to the word in **boldface**.*

1. A **rowdy** greeting is likely to be
   a. stern.
   b. loud.
   c. gentle.
   d. whispered.

2. A **crammed** suitcase is probably
   a. well organized.
   b. half full.
   c. hard to close.
   d. locked.

3. If I **furnish** food for a picnic, I
   a. invite the ants.
   b. set up the lawn furniture.
   c. eat the lion's share.
   d. bring lots to eat.

4. An **endangered** species is
   a. threatened by extinction.
   b. dangerous to others.
   c. safe from harm.
   d. protected by the police.

Words with Latin Roots

The unit word *assume* comes from the Latin prefix *ad-* or *as-* meaning "to, toward," and the Latin root *sum,* which means "to take." Together, the word parts mean "to take upon oneself" or "to take for granted." The root *sum* is also used in the following words:

- resume (v.): to continue (*to take up again*)
- consume (v.): to use or use up (*to take for one's use*)
- presume (v.): to understand to be true without proof (*to take for granted*)
- consumption (n.): the act of using or using up something (*taking something for use*)
- assumption (n.): an idea accepted to be true or valid (*an idea taken to be true*)

Choose two of the words from the list. Write a sentence for each word to show you understand its meaning.

1. Accept answers that show an understanding of the vocabulary.

2.

 *Read the passage. Then answer each question.*

The La Brea Tar Pits

1   What was life like in southern California many thousands of years ago? In Los Angeles, the La Brea Tar Pits **furnish** an incredible window on prehistoric animal, bird, and plant life. Located in Hancock Park in downtown Los Angeles, the tar pits contain a **mammoth** trove of information. It is a site without **peer**.

2   Many of the largest mammal species trapped in the sticky tar puddles at La Brea are now extinct: saber-toothed cats, as well as mastodons, longhaired bison, and native horses. And most of the fossils belong to carnivores or scavengers. These flesh-eating species, experts assume, were trapped as they hastened to devour **fare** such as a bison or a horse. Unlike today, there were no **safeguards** such as **rigid** fences or railings around the pits! For the carnivores, a **trespass** turned into a death warrant. Scavengers that attempted to feed on trapped animals likely became trapped themselves.

3   Soon after 1901, scientists from the University of California at Berkeley began to work on the La Brea fossils. Today, many of these finds are displayed at the George C. Page Museum of La Brea Discoveries.

1. What is the meaning of the word **mammoth** as it is used in paragraph 1?
(a) elephant   **(b) immense**   (c) miniature   (d) intense

2. What does the word **peer** mean as it is used in paragraph 1?
(a) equal   (b) scan   (c) noble   (d) gaze

3. The Latin word *rigere* means "to be stiff." The word **rigid** in paragraph 2 means
(a) false.   (b) electric.   **(c) firm.**   (d) strict.

4. Pick the word that best defines **fare** as it is used in paragraph 2.
(a) charge   (b) manage   (c) fee   **(d) food**

 *A proper noun always starts with a capital letter. If the noun is more than one word long, capitalize all of the important words. For example, **New York City**. Underline an example of a proper noun in "The La Brea Tar Pits."* Accept all correct answers. Example: See paragraph 1.

Write Your Own

Imagine that you are writing an informational leaflet for the George C. Page Museum of La Brea Discoveries. Write a short paragraph about the museum using three vocabulary words from this unit. Then exchange leaflets with a partner and compare the information included.

 *For more practice with capitalizing proper nouns and adjectives, see Grammar Workshop, Level Blue, Lesson 47.*

Word Study Suffixes -ity, -ty, -ence, -al

Remember that a **suffix** is a word part that is added to the end of a **base word** to make a new word. When a suffix is added to a base word, the new word that is formed is often a different part of speech. You can add the suffix *-ity* to *rigid* (page 163) to make a new word.

> The suffixes **-ity**, **-ty**, and **-ence** mean "the act, quality, or state of." These suffixes form nouns.
>
> rigid *(adj.)*   + **ity** = rigid**ity** *(n.)* → means "the state of being stiff"
> frail *(adj.)*   + **ty** = frail**ty** *(n.)*   → means "weakness"
> violent *(adj.)* + **ence** = viol**ence** *(n.)* → means "the use of force to create harm"
>
> The suffix **-al** means "relating to." This suffix forms adjectives.
> accident *(n.)* + **al** = accident**al** *(adj.)* → means "happening by chance or mistake"

PRACTICE   *Write the missing base word, suffix, or new word. Then write the meaning of the new word. Use a dictionary to check your answers.*

Base Word	Suffix	New Word	Meaning
1. _absent_	+ ence	= absence	→ the state of being away
2. real	+ _ity_	= reality	→ the state of being real
3. topic	+ al	= _topical_	→ relating to a timely issue
4. _loyal_	+ ty	= loyalty	→ the quality of being loyal

APPLY   *Add a word for each missing part of speech. The word should be from the same word family. Use any suffix you know. The first one has been done for you.*

	Noun	Adjective
5. globe	_globalization_	_global_
6. prosper	_prosperity_	prosperous
7. person	personality	_personal_
8. music	musicality	_musical_

Work with a partner to list words with the suffixes -ity, -ty, -ence, and -al. Then take turns asking and answering questions that include those words.

Example: Q: What is the noun form of *differ*?
         A: difference

Shades of Meaning — Words that Describe Size

In the passage "Why Did the Woolly Mammoths Disappear?" on pages 160–161, you read about a large animal called the woolly **mammoth**. The word *mammoth* is also an adjective that describes size.

Look at the words in the chart. The words show a range of sizes, from very tiny to extremely large. When you describe the size of something, using the right word can help you communicate what you want to say.

mammoth	Something **mammoth** is huge and remarkable. It is almost unbelievable because of its size.
miniature	Something that is **miniature** is smaller than normal. The word is often used to describe a scale model.
microscopic	Something that is **microscopic** is so small that it can only be seen through a microscope.
vast	Something that is **vast** is very great in area, size, or amount.

PRACTICE *Write the word from the chart above that best completes each sentence.*

1. My parents set up the ______miniature______ train in the living room for my baby sister.

2. The scientist found ______microscopic______ rug fibers in one of the samples.

3. The first computers were ______mammoth______ compared to today's laptops.

4. In science class, we learned how ______vast______ the universe is.

5. The model of the White House on my desk is ______miniature______ in size.

6. The museum has a ______vast______ collection of antique pottery.

APPLY *List two items that can be described using each size word.*
Accept reasonable answers. Possible answers are given.

7. **mammoth** ______blue whale______, ______the Great Wall of China______

8. **miniature** ______toy truck______, ______doll clothes______

9. **microscopic** ______germs______, ______skin cells______

10. **vast** ______desert______, ______ocean______

UNIT 17

Read the following fable about a plan that backfires. Notice how the highlighted words are used. These are the words you will be learning in this unit.

The Hunger Strike

(an Aesop Fable)

A differentiated version of this passage is available at **SadlierConnect.com**.

Today, the parts of the body get along and work together surprisingly well, but that wasn't always true. Long ago, Head, Legs, and Arms had frequent squabbles with one another; there was a great deal of **friction** among them. One of the few things they had in common, in fact, was their dislike for Belly. Most of the time, they **disregarded** Belly completely and weren't even sure where he lived. When they did turn their attention to him, their main complaint was about his lack of purpose. They all agreed that Belly had never done an honest day's work and that he only cared about eating.

Thinking about Belly's laziness, Head eventually felt such **profound** anger that he called a meeting of the other body parts. "It's time to teach that lazy Belly a lesson!" he announced loudly. Legs and Arms couldn't agree more. They found the idea **irresistible** and immediately asked Head what he had in mind.

"Well, from now on," explained Head, "I'm not going to figure out any ways to find food." With his sharp eyes and quick brain, Head was the body part that found the **majority** of the body's food.

"Belly won't like that," remarked Legs with a smile. Then to show that he was in complete agreement with Head, he said, "And I promise not to walk over to any food, even if it's lying on the ground right in front of us."

"This is going to be good," giggled Arms, clapping his hands together for **emphasis**. "I won't pick up any food," he promised the others, "and I'm not doing any cooking either!"

All went according to plan, and after a few weeks of no food, Belly indeed was grumbling. "Please," he begged, "a crust of bread, anything."

The other body parts, however, could take no real joy in Belly's misery, for they were having problems themselves. Head, for example, experienced frequent dizziness. Then a new phenomenon—a splitting headache—made it impossible for him to think. Legs grew weaker and weaker, often stumbling into swamps and other desolate places. Even Arms, who was by now covered with sores from shoulders to fingertips, realized something was very wrong.

As the body's problems accumulated, Head had to intervene. He called the body parts to another meeting. "Even though Belly never seems to work," Head began, "he must have a purpose. Otherwise, starving him wouldn't have caused us so many problems. For our own sakes, therefore, I suggest we compromise and start feeding him again."

Legs and Arms agreed with Head. They were greatly relieved that the standoff had come to an end. Without wasting another minute, the whole crew went out to find some dinner. Once the meal had been eaten, Belly's loud grumbling subsided, and the other body parts started feeling much better, too!

Moral: *Each member of a group must do his or her part for the common good.*

Definitions

You were introduced to these words in the passage. Study the pronunciation, part of speech, definition, and example sentence for each word. Then read the synonyms and antonyms.

1. accumulate
(ə kyü′ myə lāt)
(uh-KYOO-myuh-late)

(v.) to gather together, often in an increasing number

I hope to accumulate a large collection of stamps.

SYNONYMS: to collect, hoard
ANTONYMS: to disperse, lessen, lose, spend

2. compromise
(käm′ prə mīz)
(KOM-pruh-mize)

(n.) an agreement in which each side gives up some demand

The battling senators reached a compromise and passed the bill.

(v.) to give up certain demands in order to settle an argument

I had to compromise and let my brother join our team.

SYNONYMS: (n.) concession; (v.) to cooperate, settle
ANTONYMS: (n.) confrontation; (v.) to confront

 When was the last time you had to **compromise**? Explain to your partner what made it a compromise.

3. desolate
(des′ ə lit)
(DESS-uh-lit)

(adj.) bleak and without any people; extremely unhappy

The abandoned gold rush town was desolate.

SYNONYMS: deserted, isolated, miserable
ANTONYMS: populous, happy

Draw a picture of a **desolate** area.

4. disregard
(dis ri gärd′)
(diss-ri-GARD)

(v.) to pay no attention to

I told my friend to disregard my earlier message.

(n.) the state of ignoring something

The driver who ran the red light showed disregard for the law.

SYNONYMS: (v.) to ignore, neglect; (n.) contempt, indifference
ANTONYMS: (v.) to heed, attend; (n.) concern, attention

What will happen if you **disregard** the classroom rules? Explain these consequences to your partner.

5. emphasis
(em′ fə sis)
(EM-fuh-siss)

(n.) the special importance or value given to something; stress given to a syllable or word in reading or speaking

Our school puts a strong emphasis on science.

SYNONYMS: prominence, weight; accent, stress

6. friction
(frik′ shən)
(FRIK-shuhn)

(n.) the rubbing of one object or surface against another; conflict

Tires wear down because of friction between the rubber and the road.

SYNONYMS: rubbing, grating; discord, trouble; ANTONYMS: agreement, peace

7. intervene
(in tûr vēn′)
(in-tur-VEEN)

(v.) to come between things, points, events in order to make changes

The referee had to intervene to settle the players' dispute.

SYNONYMS: to interfere, intrude, meddle; ANTONYMS: to avoid, ignore

💬 **How would you intervene in a disagreement between your friends?**

8. irresistible
(ir i zis′ tə bəl)
(ihr-i-ZISS-tuh-buhl)

(adj.) too attractive and tempting to be resisted

A swimming pool on a hot summer day is irresistible.

SYNONYMS: alluring, desirable, enticing; ANTONYMS: avoidable, undesirable

9. majority
(mə jôr′ i tē)
(muh-JOR-i-tee)

(n.) the greater number

The majority of the puppies were black.

(adj.) something made up of the greater number

The class president can be removed by a majority vote.

SYNONYMS: bulk, mass, more; ANTONYM: minority

💬 **Use each definition of majority in a sentence.**

10. phenomenon
(fə nom′ ə non)
(fuh-NOM uh-non)

(n.) something that can be taken in by the senses or mind; someone or something that is very unusual

Glaciers are a natural phenomenon.

SYNONYMS: occurrence, spectacle, wonder, sensation, exception
ANTONYMS: normality, regularity

11. profound
(prə faůnd′)
(pruh-FOUND)

(adj.) very great or intense; requiring deep thought or understanding

The family felt profound sadness at the loss of its pet.

SYNONYMS: insightful, heartfelt, overpowering
ANTONYMS: superficial, trivial, shallow

12. subside
(səb sīd′)
(suhb-SIDE)

(v.) to become less intense, violent, or severe

We waited for the rain to subside before going outside.

SYNONYMS: to fall, lower, settle, decline; ANTONYMS: to increase, grow, rise

💬 **As time allows, have partners complete graphic organizers for select words, available at SadlierConnect.com.**

Synonyms

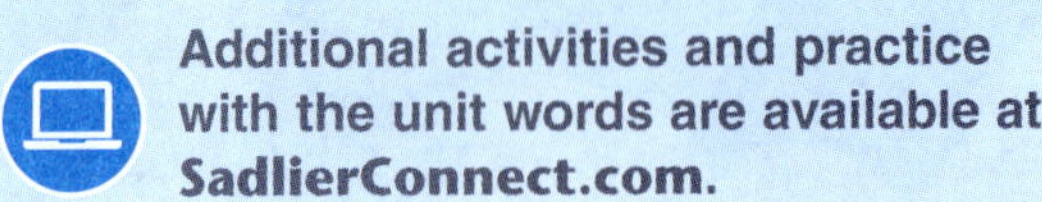

*Choose the word that is most nearly the **same** in meaning
as the word or phrase in **boldface**. Then write your choice
on the line provided.*

1. a **stress** on the syllable
   a. disregard   b. friction   c. emphasis   d. compromise   _______emphasis_______

2. reaching an acceptable **settlement**
   a. phenomenon b. emphasis   c. friction   d. compromise   _______compromise_______

3. **conflict** between classmates
   a. compromise   b. friction   c. emphasis   d. phenomenon   _______friction_______

4. **intrude** in the argument
   a. intervene   b. subside   c. accumulate d. disregard   _______intervene_______

5. once in a lifetime **spectacle**
   a. friction   b. phenomenon c. emphasis   d. compromise   _______phenomenon_______

6. **gather** a lot of money
   a. accumulate   b. compromise c. disregard   d. subside   _______accumulate_______

Antonyms

*Choose the word that is most nearly **opposite** in meaning
to the word or phrase in **boldface**. Then write your choice
on the line provided.*

1. a **happy** expression
   a. irresistible   b. desolate   c. majority   d. profound   _______desolate_______

2. **obey** the rules
   a. compromise   b. intervene   c. subside   d. disregard   _______disregard_______

3. an **undesirable** location
   a. majority   b. desolate   c. irresistible d. profound   _______irresistible_______

4. a **minority** group
   a. irresistible   b. profound   c. desolate   d. majority   _______majority_______

5. watching floodwaters **rise**
   a. accumulate   b. subside   c. intervene   d. disregard   _______subside_______

6. a **trivial** idea
   a. profound   b. desolate   c. majority   d. irresistible _______profound_______

Completing the Sentence

Choose the word from the box that best completes each item. Then write the word on the line provided. (You may have to change the word's ending.)

accumulate	compromise	desolate
disregard	emphasis	friction
intervene	irresistible	majority
phenomenon	profound	subside

The Sahara Desert

- The Sahara Desert is a natural __phenomenon__ that stretches across northern Africa in an area that is almost as big as the United States.

- The central area of the desert is incredibly dry, __desolate__, and famous for its seemingly endless sand dunes.

- With the exception of the Nile River, the __majority__ of the rivers and streams in the Sahara flow only seasonally.

- These sources of water rise in the rainy season and __subside__, or may even become completely dry the rest of the year.

- Even in the parts of the desert that receive the most rain, no more than five inches of rain __accumulates__ each year.

- In spite of the harsh conditions, some tourists find the adventure of the desert __irresistible__ and trek across the area on guided camel tours.

A Good Solution

- Our school puts an __emphasis__ on athletics, and we are encouraged to play sports at recess.

- Unfortunately, there was a great deal of __friction__ between the fourth and fifth graders about how to use the large ball field.

- The fifth graders always used the entire field for soccer, and they showed __disregard__ for the fourth graders who wanted to play kickball on the same field.

- Eventually, the principal had to __intervene__ because there was so much arguing at recess.

- The principal said that we would have to reach a __compromise__ that would allow both groups to enjoy the field.

- Finally, a fourth grader said, "I think we should each play a shorter game and share the time on the field." We all thought that was a __profound__ statement.

Word Associations

Circle the letter next to the word or phrase that best completes the sentence or answers the question. Pay special attention to the word in **boldface.**

1. A **profound** emotion can make you feel
   a. clumsy.
   b. overwhelmed.
   c. amused.
   d. prepared.

2. If you **disregard** a remark, you
   a. ignore it.
   b. respond to it.
   c. let it bother you.
   d. repeat it.

3. If the **majority** of students prefer math to science,
   a. more than half prefer science.
   b. more than half prefer math.
   c. science and math are liked equally.
   d. all the students prefer math.

4. To get a fever to **subside**, you might
   a. eat lunch.
   b. go for a run.
   c. sit in the sun.
   d. take medicine.

Words with Latin Roots

The unit word *intervene* comes from the Latin prefix *inter-*, meaning "between," and the Latin root *ven*, which means "come." Together the word parts mean "to come between things, points, or events." The root *ven* is used in the following words:

- advent (n.): a coming or arrival (*something that comes onto the scene*)
- convention (n.): a large and formal meeting (*a coming together*)
- prevent (v.): to ensure that something does not happen (*to keep from coming*)
- convenient (adj.): favorable, comfortable (*coming in handy*)
- venue (n.): a place or locale where something happens (*a place where people come*)

Choose two of the words from the list. Write a sentence for each word to show you understand its meaning.

1. Accept answers that show an understanding of the vocabulary.

2. ___________

Read the passage. Then answer each question.

Riddles in Oral Tradition

1   Oral tradition is the passing down of stories, proverbs, fables, and historical events by word of mouth. Among experts, **majority** opinion holds that writing was invented around 3000 BCE. Before then, humans depended on oral tradition for a wide range of needs.

2   Among these needs was entertainment. Epic poems telling of heroic deeds served this purpose. So did riddles. Riddles often consist of a question and an unexpected answer, with an **emphasis** on wordplay. Unlike epics, riddles are extremely brief. Unlike proverbs, they are intended to entertain rather than provoke serious thought.

3   Riddles usually hold the listener's age in **disregard**. However, they are a **phenomenon** that children in many cultures find especially appealing. It is easy to see, for example, how the riddling competitions held in some societies could have enlivened what otherwise might have been a dull, drab, or even **desolate** existence. Riddles offered at least a temporary **compromise** with hardship. The **friction** or tension produced by tests of knowledge and wit was generally creative and enjoyable.

1. What is the meaning of the word **majority** as it is used in paragraph 1?
 (a) mass
 (b) made up of the greater number
 (c) minority
 (d) made up of only a part

2. What does the word **disregard** most likely mean as it is used in paragraph 3?
 (a) state of ignoring
 (b) paying attention
 (c) pushing forward
 (d) making light of

3. The Latin word *compromittere* means "to make a promise and receive one in turn." The word **compromise** in paragraph 3 means
 (a) concession
 (b) confrontation
 (c) summary
 (d) relaxation

4. Pick the word that best defines **friction** as it is used in paragraph 3.
 (a) harmony
 (b) doubt
 (c) injury
 (d) conflict

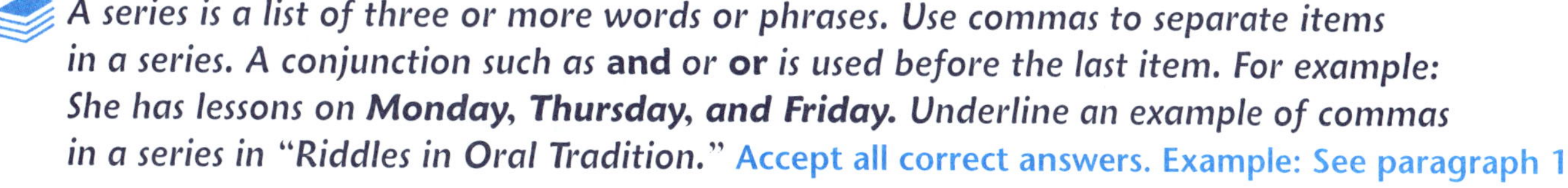 *A series is a list of three or more words or phrases. Use commas to separate items in a series. A conjunction such as **and** or **or** is used before the last item. For example: She has lessons on **Monday, Thursday, and Friday.** Underline an example of commas in a series in "Riddles in Oral Tradition."* Accept all correct answers. Example: See paragraph 1.

 ## Write Your Own

 *Write a riddle, the answer to which should be one of the vocabulary words from this unit. Then exchange entries with a partner and answer each other's riddles.*

 *For more practice with commas in a series, see Grammar Workshop, Level Blue, Lesson 50.*

Word Study Prefixes *de-, post-, trans-, sub-*

Remember that a **prefix** is a word part that is added to the beginning of a **base word** to make a new word. You can add the prefix *de-* to *emphasis* (page 172) to make a new word.

The prefix **de-** usually means "down."   **de** + emphasis = **de**-emphasis → means "the act of bringing down in importance"
The prefix **post-** means "after."   **post** + game = **post**game → means "after the game"
The prefix **trans-** means "across."   **trans** + plant = **trans**plant → means "to move from one place to another"
The prefix **sub-** means "under" or "less than."   **sub** + soil = **sub**soil → means "soil directly under the topsoil"

PRACTICE *Write the missing prefix, base word, or new word. Then write the meaning of the new word.*

Prefix	Base Word	New Word	Meaning
1. sub	+ zero	= subzero	→ below zero
2. de	+ value	= devalue	→ bring down in value
3. post	+ flight	= postflight	→ after the flight
4. trans	+ atlantic	= transatlantic	→ across the Atlantic Ocean

APPLY *Complete each sentence with a word that contains the prefix de-, post-, trans-, or sub-. Choose from the words above.*

5. Traveling from New York to London requires a _____transatlantic_____ flight.

6. I didn't want to _____devalue_____ my action figure by taking it out of the box.

7. During the _____postgame_____ show, the reporter will interview the winning team.

8. You must dress warmly to go out in _____subzero_____ temperatures.

9. I will _____transplant_____ the ivy from the smaller pot to the larger pot.

With a partner, list words with the prefixes de-, post-, trans-, and sub-. Take turns asking and answering questions that include those words.

Example: Q: How is a *submarine* different from a typical military ship?

   A: A submarine is a type of ship that can go underwater.

Shades of Meaning Idioms 2

In the passage "The Hunger Strike" on pages 170–171, the parts of the body are used as characters to tell the story. The parts of the body are used in some idioms, too.

Remember that an **idiom** is an expression with a meaning that is different from the meaning of the words that make up the idiom. Here is an example: *When I took two helpings of potatoes, my **eyes were bigger than my stomach***. Here the idiom *eyes were bigger than my stomach* has nothing to do with the size of one's eyes or stomach. Instead the expression means "wanting or taking more food than one can eat."

PRACTICE *Read each sentence. Figure out the meaning of each idiom in boldface. Write the number of the sentence next to the meaning of the idiom.*

1. My teacher said she **had her eye on** me after I whispered to my friend.

2. Yesterday, I told my friend about my problem. It felt good to **get it off my chest.**

3. Before it was my turn to sing, I had **butterflies in my stomach.**

4. At the end of the year, I was **up to my ears in** homework.

___3___ feel nervous

___1___ watching someone very carefully

___4___ to be very busy with something

___2___ tell something that has been bothering you

APPLY *Read each sentence. Figure out the meaning of each idiom in boldface. Write the meaning on the line provided.*

5. He **did not have a leg to stand on** because there was so much evidence against him.

   to be in a situation in which you cannot prove something

6. When the umpire made a bad call, I **lost my head** and threw my glove.

   to become very angry

7. My dad said our new car **cost an arm and a leg.**

   was very expensive

8. I really **put my foot in my mouth** when I told her what I really thought about her bad haircut.

   to say or do something embarrassing

Introducing the Words

Read the following biography about a leader who developed a writing system to help people communicate. Notice how the highlighted words are used. These are the words you will be learning in this unit.

Sequoyah, Advocate of His People

(Biography)

A differentiated version of this passage is available at **SadlierConnect.com**.

The Cherokee (cher′ ə kē) were an eastern woodland people whose original territory spread across a significant portion of the Southeastern United States. Many Cherokee villages had thirty to sixty homes built around a large meeting house known as a council house. At the center of each village was a town square where people gathered for dances, games, and ceremonies.

Sequoyah (si kwoi′ ə) was born in a Cherokee village in Tennessee around 1770. At that time, white colonists were moving onto Cherokee land, often signing treaties to do so. The Cherokee people, however, had no written language, only a spoken one, and they could not read English. This was a fundamental problem because the spoken promises of the white settlers often contradicted the legal terms of the treaties.

As a young man, Sequoyah moved to Georgia, perhaps to escape the white settlers.

Sequoyah

There he became a skilled silversmith. His ignorance of written English, however, prevented him from signing his craft items like other craftspeople.

During the War of 1812, Sequoyah, like many Cherokees, joined the American army. While on duty, Sequoyah often watched white soldiers reading battle orders as well as letters from their families.

Before the war, Sequoyah had begun his preliminary work on developing a Cherokee system of written communication. Now he turned his attention to this challenge. First, Sequoyah listened carefully to spoken Cherokee. Over time, he extracted 85 or 86 basic sound-syllables from his observations. Every Cherokee word is some combination of these syllables. Sequoyah next assigned one symbol to each sound-syllable. He borrowed some symbols, such as Roman numerals, and made up others. He also retained a few letters from English. By 1821, Sequoyah had completed his work. The Cherokees adopted his concept of representing sounds in the Cherokee language as written symbols.

An advocate of education, Sequoyah personally taught the written language to hundreds of Cherokees. He also publicly demonstrated the results of his efforts. No one could have anticipated the success of written Cherokee. In a short time, thousands of Cherokees learned to read and write.

In 1828, the Cherokee people began to publish their own newspaper. It was called the *Cherokee Phoenix*, and it is still printed today. The Cherokee also used their new language to write a constitution. This document helped them form their own government—the Cherokee Nation. The constitution described the internal workings of this government.

Sequoyah believed that reading and writing would help the Cherokee hold on to their land. Sadly, this premise proved to be untrue. According to the terms of the 1828 Indian Removal Act, all native Americans had to give up their land and move west of the Mississippi. Between 1838 and 1839, an estimated 17,000 Cherokees were forced to move to Oklahoma. About 4,000 people died on this terrible trip, causing the Cherokee to call it the Trail of Tears.

In Oklahoma, the Cherokee faced another challenge. They had to learn how to survive in a new and different place. To do this, they depended on their written constitution and laws. They published important information in their newspaper. Written communication helped the people adjust to a new way of life.

Sequoyah's Cherokee writing system

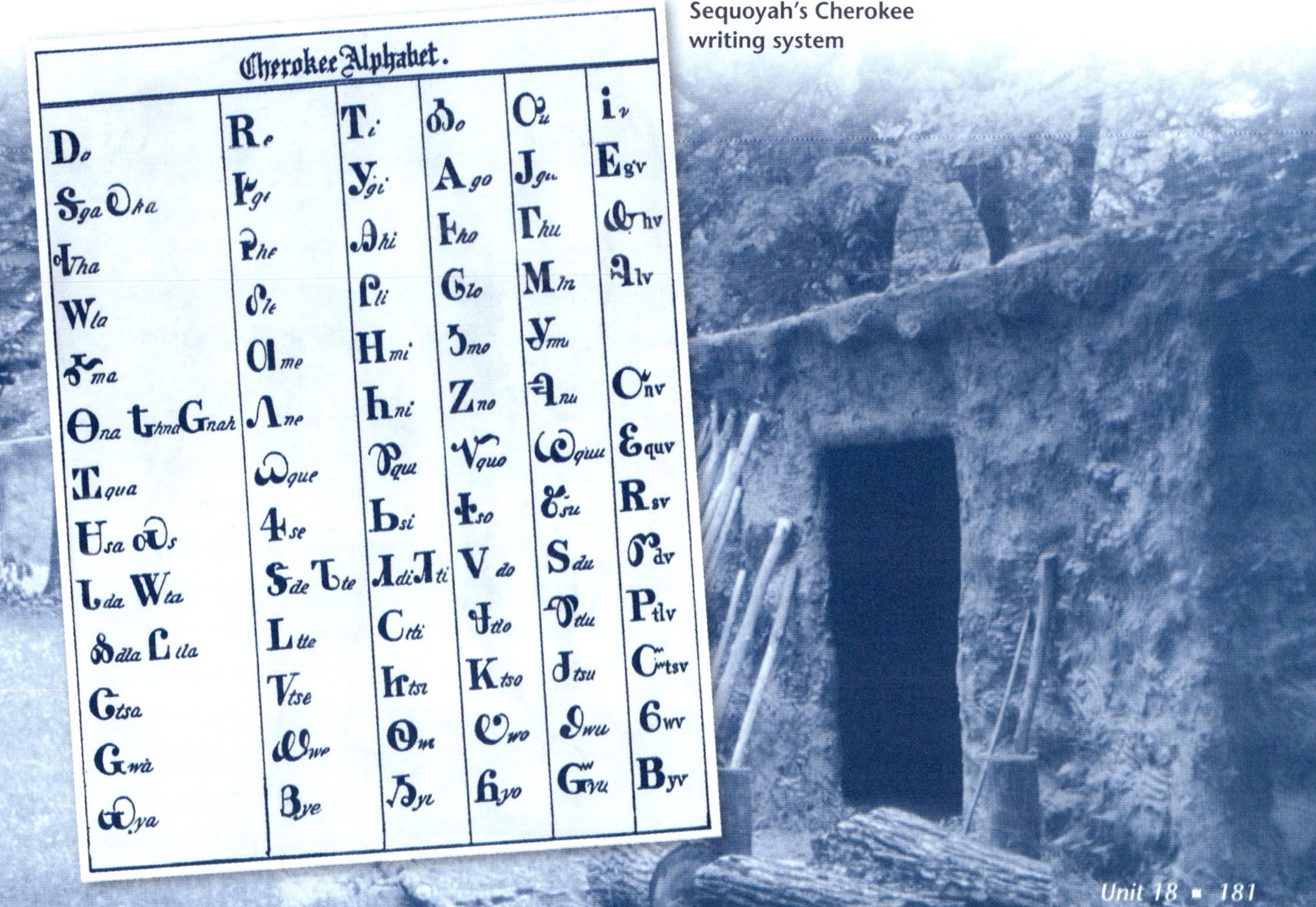

You were introduced to these words in the passage. Study the pronunciation, part of speech, definition, and example sentence for each word. Then read the synonyms and antonyms.

1. advocate
(n., ad′ və kit)
(AD-vuh-kit)
(v., ad′ və kāt)
(AD-vuh-kate)

(n.) a person who publicly supports a cause; a lawyer

I am an advocate of animal rights.

(v.) to be or speak in favor of

They advocate using computers in the classroom.

SYNONYMS: (n.) defender, supporter; (v.) to recommend, support
ANTONYMS: (n.) critic, enemy, opposition; (v.) to attack, criticize

Use each definition of **advocate** in a sentence.

2. anticipate
(an tis′ ə pāt)
(an-TISS-uh-pate)

(v.) to think of ahead of time

We anticipate there will be a large crowd at the book signing.

SYNONYMS: to expect, assume; ANTONYM: to doubt

What is one thing that you are **anticipating** this weekend? Explain to your partner why you are anticipating it.

3. concept
(kän′ sept)
(KON-sept)

(n.) a general idea

The concept of time travel interests me.

SYNONYMS: idea, notion

4. contradict
(kän trə dikt′)
(kon-truh-DIKT)

(v.) to say the opposite of; disagree with

The calls of the referees contradict each other.

SYNONYMS: to challenge, confront, deny, differ; ANTONYMS: to accept, agree, confirm

Share with your partner a few phrases you would use to **contradict** someone's statement.

5. extract
(v., ek strakt′)
(ek-STRAKT)
(n., ek′ strakt)
(EK-strakt)

(v.) to remove or take out

The dentist decided to extract my decayed tooth.

(n.) something drawn out of a natural substance, often used for flavoring

I like to add vanilla extract to cookie batter.

SYNONYMS: (v.) to detach, disconnect, remove; (n.) excerpt

As time allows, have partners complete graphic organizers for select words, available at **SadlierConnect.com**.

6. fundamental
(fun də men′ təl)
(fuhn-duh-MEN-tuhl)

(adj.) forming a foundation, basic

This country gives all its citizens fundamental rights.

(n.) a basic part, principle, fact, or skill

Knowing how to add is a fundamental of mathematics.

SYNONYMS: (adj.) basic, essential, important; (n.) basis, foundation, rule
ANTONYMS: (adj.) additional, extra, unnecessary; (n.) addition, extra

7. ignorance
(ig′ nər əns)
(IG-nur-uhnss)

(n.) a lack of knowledge or information

I felt embarrassed by my ignorance of American history.

SYNONYMS: dumbness, simplicity; ANTONYMS: intelligence, brilliance, knowledge

8. internal
(in tûrn′ əl)
(in-TURN-uhl)

(adj.) of or located within something

The internal parts of a kiwi look very different from its hairy outside.

SYNONYMS: inner, inside, interior
ANTONYMS: external, outer

Name two of your **internal** organs.

9. preliminary
(pri lim′ ə ner ē)
(pri-LIM-uh-ner-ee)

(adj.) coming before a main event or activity

I made preliminary notes before I wrote my speech.

SYNONYMS: introductory, initial, first
ANTONYMS: conclusion, final, closing

10. premise
(prem′ is)
(PREM-iss)

(n.) a statement upon which an argument or conclusion is based

The premise of my argument is that all students should take art class.

SYNONYMS: assumption, idea, foundation

11. retain
(ri tān′)
(ri-TAYN)

(v.) to continue to have; to hold or keep in

A cactus can retain water inside its thick stem.

SYNONYMS: to remember, contain, save
ANTONYMS: to lose, release

12. significant
(sig nif′ i kənt)
(sig-NIF-i-kuhnt)

(adj.) having importance; notable

There was significant damage after the storm.

SYNONYMS: important, considerable, noteworthy
ANTONYMS: insignificant, trivial, unimportant, minimal

Tell your partner about the most **significant** birthday that you have had. Explain why it was so significant.

Synonyms

*Choose the word that is most nearly the **same** in meaning as the word or phrase in **boldface**. Then write your choice on the line provided.*

1. **challenge** the evidence
   a. contradict   b. advocate   c. extract   d. anticipate   _____contradict_____

2. **basic** dance steps
   a. internal   b. fundamental   c. preliminary   d. significant   _____fundamental_____

3. **remove** unwanted pieces
   a. anticipate   b. advocate   c. contradict   d. extract   _____extract_____

4. a strange **notion**
   a. ignorance   b. concept   c. advocate   d. fundamental   _____concept_____

5. **save** the receipts
   a. extract   b. retain   c. anticipate   d. contradict   _____retain_____

6. a weak **assumption**
   a. premise   b. advocate   c. fundamental   d. ignorance   _____premise_____

Antonyms

*Choose the word that is most nearly **opposite** in meaning to the word or phrase in **boldface**. Then write your choice on the line provided.*

1. an **enemy** of the cause
   a. fundamental   b. advocate   c. premise   d. ignorance   _____advocate_____

2. **knowledge** about physics
   a. fundamental   b. premise   c. ignorance   d. advocate   _____ignorance_____

3. **minimal** amount of time
   a. significant   b. fundamental   c. internal   d. preliminary   _____significant_____

4. **closing** remarks
   a. fundamental   b. internal   c. preliminary   d. significant   _____preliminary_____

5. **doubt** it will rain
   a. contradict   b. advocate   c. extract   d. anticipate   _____anticipate_____

6. appealing **external** qualities
   a. fundamental   b. preliminary   c. internal   d. significant   _____internal_____

Choose the word from the box that best completes each item. Then write the word on the line provided. (You may have to change the word's ending.)

advocate	**anticipate**	**concept**
contradict	**extract**	**fundamental**
ignorance	**internal**	**preliminary**
premise	**retain**	**significant**

Olive Oil

■ Many nutritionists say that including olive oil in your diet can have **significant** health benefits.

■ This **premise** is based on findings that olive oil contains a special kind of fat that may help prevent heart disease.

■ The Greeks have been making olive oil for thousands of years, so using it in meals is not a new **concept**.

■ In fact, the process of obtaining an olive's **internal** oil has not changed much since ancient times.

■ The **preliminary** step in making olive oil is to grind the olives into paste.

■ Then the paste is placed in a press, where the oil is **extracted**.

The Right to Vote

■ Susan B. Anthony, who lived from 1820 to 1906, was an **advocate** for American women.

■ She challenged the **ignorance** of people who believed that women did not deserve the same rights as men.

■ Susan B. Anthony argued that women should be granted **fundamental** rights, such as the right to own property, to have a job, to earn equal pay, and to vote.

■ Susan B. Anthony voted in the 1872 presidential election. Her action **contradicted** the law that protected the voting rights of adult male citizens.

■ Despite her arrest and jailing two weeks later, Susan B. Anthony **retained** her belief in the cause of women's rights.

■ She **anticipated** that her trial would eventually result in granting women the right to vote. Unfortunately, the Nineteenth Amendment, which provides that right, was not passed until 1920.

*Circle the letter next to the word or phrase that best completes the sentence or answers the question. Pay special attention to the word in **boldface**.*

1. I might **advocate** a course of action that I
   a. oppose.
   b. don't understand.
   c. favor.
   d. want to discuss.

2. To **contradict** a statement, you might say
   a. "I disagree."
   b. "Let me explain"
   c. "That's the truth."
   d. "I'll say it again."

3. A leader who shows **ignorance** has
   a. a sense of humor.
   b. musical ability.
   c. lots of money.
   d. little knowledge.

4. A **significant** historical event might be
   a. soon forgotten.
   b. taught in history class.
   c. common.
   d. minor.

Words with Latin Roots

The unit word *extract* comes from the Latin prefix *ex-*, meaning "out of," and the Latin root *tract*, which means "to draw or drag." Together, the word parts mean "to remove or draw out of." The root *tract* is used in the following words:

- tractor (n.): a vehicle that pulls farm equipment (*a vehicle that drags things*)
- retract (v.): to withdraw (*to draw back*)
- detract (v.): to reduce the value of something (*to draw value away from*)
- protract (v.): to lengthen or stretch out (*to draw forward or ahead*)
- traction (n.): the act of pulling something (*drawing something over a surface*)
- distract (v.): to turn someone's attention away from (*to draw away attention*)

Choose two of the words from the list. Write a sentence for each word to show you understand its meaning.

1. Accept answers that show an understanding of the vocabulary.

2. ____

Words in Context

 *Read the passage. Then answer each question.*

The *Cherokee Phoenix*

1   On February 21, 1828, the *Cherokee Phoenix* became the first Native American and bilingual newspaper published in the United States. The day marked a **significant** accomplishment. The paper **advocated** for the preservation of Cherokee culture, history, and language. The newspaper was printed in New Echota, Georgia, which was then the capital of the Cherokee Nation.

2   Elias Boudinot was the first editor of the paper. He wanted to cover the topics and **concepts** that were **fundamental** to the interests of the Cherokee. Boudinot **anticipated** issues that would be important to readers. He once said, "We must have a newspaper that conveys the innate intelligence of our people."

3   The newspaper published articles about congressional debates and court cases. It also published articles about Cherokee rights and issues concerning Cherokee land. The newspaper printed **extracts** of Native American fiction writing. The *Phoenix* allowed members of the Cherokee nation to record important events and **retain** a connection with the Cherokee language.

4   The *Phoenix* is still in existence. Its print audience is 15,000 and its online edition receives 400,000 views per month.

1. What is the meaning of the word **advocated** as it is used in paragraph 1?
ⓐ spoke up   ⓑ substituted   ⓒ performed   ⓓ supplied

2. What does the word **fundamental** mean as it is used in paragraph 2?
ⓐ a basic skill   ⓑ important   ⓒ complicated   ⓓ a unique idea

3. Pick the word that best defines **extracts** as it is used in paragraph 3.
ⓐ removes   ⓑ observes   ⓒ finds   ⓓ excerpts

4. The Latin word *retinere* means "to hold." The word **retain** in paragraph 3 means
ⓐ to struggle   ⓑ to lose   ⓒ to continue having   ⓓ to keep in

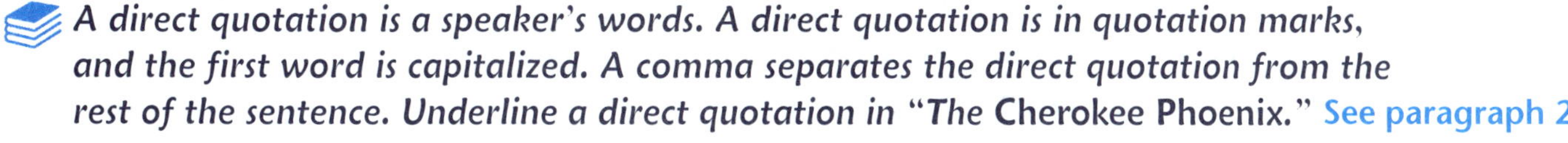

A direct quotation is a speaker's words. A direct quotation is in quotation marks, and the first word is capitalized. A comma separates the direct quotation from the rest of the sentence. Underline a direct quotation in "The **Cherokee Phoenix***."* See paragraph 2.

Write Your Own

Write 3–5 sentences that list ways you find out about current events. Use at least three vocabulary words in your list. Compare your list and vocabulary words with a partner. Then list the vocabulary words you each used and underline any words you both used.

 *For more practice with Quotations, see Grammar Workshop, Level Blue, Lesson 53.*

Vocabulary for Comprehension

Read this passage in which some of the words you have studied in Units 13–18 appear in **boldface.** *Then answer the questions.*

The Great Migration of the Dust Bowl

1   For many families in the American Great Plains, the 1930s was a time of great hardship. Even though the region had become known for its fertile soil, a severe drought created dangerous conditions. Certain farming practices had damaged layers of grass that held the soil in place. When the drought caused the earth to dry, the soil blew about easily. As the dried soil blew and collected, **mammoth** dust clouds formed and spread across large areas of land. The result was huge dust storms. This phenomenon and the region in which it occurred became known as the Dust Bowl.

2   The Dust Bowl had a significant impact on a large part of the country. Between 1930 and 1936, thousands of acres of land were affected by the dust storms. While states such as Texas, Oklahoma, and Kansas saw the worst damage, at times the dust rolled as far east as New York City. The poor conditions meant that many Americans did not **fare** well. The dust was so thick and the wind was so fierce that farms became useless and thousands of people were left without homes. The region was **desolate**.

3   Many people had no choice but to **extract** themselves from the area and move farther west. The trek was long and difficult. The **majority** of travelers struggled to find basic necessities such as food and water. Some people died from lung conditions brought on by the dust. Some died of starvation. This migration of people during the time of the Dust Bowl was the largest in American history. More than two million people had moved west by 1940. Many of them settled in California.

4   Eventually, the dust would **subside** and the land would recover, but only after people learned to **safeguard** the soil. New government programs were established, and farmers were taught farming practices that protected the land.

1. What is a main idea of this passage?
   - (a) The Dust Bowl caused great upheaval.
   - (b) The Dust Bowl could never happen again.
   - (c) The Dust Bowl only affected people on farms.
   - (d) The Dust Bowl built modern cities.

2. What does the use of the word **mammoth** in paragraph 1 suggest?
   - (a) The dust clouds settled on land.
   - (b) The dust clouds were enormous.
   - (c) The dust clouds became extinct.
   - (d) The dust clouds soon dispersed.

3. What does the word **fare** mean as it is used in paragraph 2?
   - (a) to get along
   - (b) a fee
   - (c) to do without
   - (d) a threat

4. The Latin word *desolare* means "to abandon." The word **desolate** in paragraph 2 means
   - (a) fortunate
   - (b) overcrowded
   - (c) deserted
   - (d) populous

5. As it is used in paragraph 3, what does the word **extract** show about the people?
   - (a) They were in limbo.
   - (b) They had to leave.
   - (c) They waited for help.
   - (d) They stood their ground.

6. What does the author mean by the word **majority** in paragraph 3?
   - (a) smallest sector
   - (b) largest difference
   - (c) weakest link
   - (d) greatest number

7. What is the meaning of **safeguard** as it is used in paragraph 4?
   - (a) progress
   - (b) save
   - (c) grow
   - (d) enrich

8. Which phrase from the passage best shows the idea of **safeguard**?
   - (a) "time of great hardship"
   - (b) "the region was desolate"
   - (c) "some died of starvation"
   - (d) "that protected the land"

Write Your Own

During a severe dust storm, the air often became so thick with dry soil that it could block out the sun. Imagine that you are living in Kansas during the Dust Bowl period. Write a letter to relatives, informing them about what life is like for you. Use at least three vocabulary words from Units 13–18.

Classifying

Choose the word from the box that goes best with each group of words. Write the word in the space provided. Then explain what the words have in common. The first one has been done for you.

achievement	contradict	desolate
extract	ignorance	latter
mammoth	monotonous	moral
reign	rigid	severe

1. honest, trustworthy, reliable, _____**moral**_____

The words are positive character traits.

2. saber-toothed tiger, _____**mammoth**_____, dinosaur

The words name extinct animals.

3. monotone, monotony, _____**monotonous**_____

The words belong to the same word family.

4. deserted, barren, bleak, _____**desolate**_____

The words are synonyms.

5. beginning, middle, _____**latter**_____

The words are terms related to order, arranged in time sequence.

6. ignore, _____**ignorance**_____, ignorant

The words belong to the same word family.

7. equipment, _____**achievement**_____, settlement, payment

The words have the same suffix.

8. spice, seasoning, _____**extract**_____

The words name items used for flavoring food.

9. mild, moderate, _____**severe**_____

The words describe measures of intensity, in order from least to most intense.

10. rain, rein, _____**reign**_____

The words are homophones.

11. predict, dictator, dictation, _____**contradict**_____

The words contain the same root.

12. stiff, firm, inflexible, _____**rigid**_____

The words are synonyms.

Completing the Idea

*Complete each sentence so that it makes sense. Pay attention to the word in **boldface**.* **Accept answers that show an understanding of the vocabulary.**

1. The doctor will **discharge** me from the hospital when ___________________.

2. To **modify** your diet, you can ___________________.

3. It is **courteous** to say "thank you" when ___________________.

4. If you **cram** too many things in a drawer, ___________________.

5. In order to reach a **compromise**, we ___________________.

6. One cause that I **advocate** is ___________________.

7. To **preserve** left over food, you should ___________________.

8. A **negative** person is more likely to ___________________.

9. I feel **discomfort** when I ___________________.

10. Rowdy fans at a sports game may ___________________.

11. One food that I find **irresistible** is ___________________.

12. A good coach will **intervene** when ___________________.

13. Sanitary conditions in a kitchen help prevent ___________________.

14. I would like to **pursue** a career in ___________________.

15. The **tragic** story ended with ___________________.

16. A **majority** of students in our school want ___________________.

17. After the **preliminary** round of competition, our team ___________________.

Writing Challenge

Check that vocabulary is used correctly and that each sentence is written correctly.

*Write two sentences using the word **fare**. In the first sentence, use **fare** as a verb. In the second sentence, use **fare** as a noun.*

1. ___________________

2. ___________________

The following is a list of all the words taught in the units of this book. The number after each entry indicates the page on which the word is defined.